Beat Up, Beat Down

&

STILL STANDING

The Rose Parker Story

Beat Up, Beat Down

&

STILL STANDING

The Rose Parker Story

Dr. Rose Parker

DEDICATION

To My Lord and Savior Christ Jesus

To the Loving Memory of My Natural and Spiritual Parents - Rev. Dr. Emanuel January and Bertha Lee January

For ALWAYS being there, teaching me about God, and for loving Him with obedience, truth, integrity, and faith.

My sons: Emzie IV (MZ4), Atujuan, and Darian: "I'm proud of the men you each have become, and for persevering & learning to trust God through the loss of your Mom for 15 years."

My brothers and sisters: David, Diane, Paul (deceased), Peter, Carol and Joseph (deceased)

Special thanks to my brother Peter and wife Anita For supporting me throughout my incarceration and taking care of my kids (your nephews) and our parents until the end of both their lives.

All my many nieces and nephews: David Michael, Michael Terrel, Donyel, Chastity, Darcel Dion, Leon, Patrick, James Dion, Chiquita, Peter II, Erik, Jonathan, Anthony, Paul Jr. (Deceased), Regina (Net), Jamal, Misty, Candace, Carol, Charles, Lakeeba, Joseph Jr., Brittany, Unique, Isaiah, Sammy, Donald, Justin, Carmel, Adriel, Kasheeba, Kenji, Darion, Autumn, and Darius (I hope that I didn't miss anyone!)

To Rose: On behalf of the entire January family, especially our parents, Momma and Dad (Rev. EM & Bertha January, who've gone to be with the Lord), We want you to know how proud we are of you and the great things God Is doing in and through you. Keep Standing and Stay Blessed—your Eldest brother,

Minister David E. January

SPECIAL ACKNOWLEDGEMENTS

Deborah Jenkins (my cousin), Elizabeth Dianne Ross, for always encouraging and staying on me, pushing me continuously with this project...thank you.

Pastors Grate and Lady Patty Shipp & the Carson Community Deliverance Center; Trinity Broadcasting Network; Bishop T.D. Jakes & the Potters House; Pastors Jim & Debra Cobrae & The Rock Church & World Outreach; Chaplain Ed & Providencia Mouton & on the Move Team Ministry; Pastor Ron & Lady LaVette Gibson & the Life Church Family; My Godmother Bernice Carrington – thank you MOM**; Candy Shaw-RIP, Joy Smith, and Karin Marrero; Dianna, Chaplain & Ministers: Dr. Lee Settgast, Frank Pica, Feliciano, Ted Johnson, Tommy Hawkins, Frank Chaney, Lydia Castillo; Debbie Lopez, Helen Trevizo, R. Siler, Lisha Bryant Wilcots – Norris, Debbie Sims, Herb Sanders, Barbara Jackson; Susan Poole; Richard Wright – a Godsend; The Jenkins Family: Antoine, Debra & Amber; Destiny & Tiffany; Debbie Shipply; Debra McCray; AD Watson; A Servants Heart, Paris Heard, Cheryl Jennings – ABC; Mary Parks – NBC; Felicia Cardona; The Word Network; Elizabeth Giles, DDS, Brenda & Genesis Hair Studio in Rialto; Prophetess Veronica Coffey & VCM; Westchester Legal Documents; Dreena, Andrea & Free Battered Women; All the Organizations and Coalitions to Stop Domestic Violence and aid in Healthy Families.

In Special Memory of: Benjamin Rheaves, Sr., my cousin; Rev. Dr. Donald Gardner & the Independent Faith Baptist Church and Chaplain Gerald Fortier and On the Way Team Ministry.

Additional Special Thanks to: Rose Bledsoe & Gayle Guest Brown; James & Candace Cole Kelly; Carstella, Carol and Cole Publishing; Pastor Dawn M. Harvey and Unlock Publishing House, Inc.; Chaplain Thomas Wimbush; Pastors Ray & Zella Washington, KOG – Claudia Marshall and last but not least Saving Our Women International an Outreach & Domestic Response Ministry. To all the people that made life hard for me...thank you. You kept me on my knees.

Visit the following websites:
www.roseparker.com
www.savingourwomen.org
www.savingourfamilies.com

If this book blessed you let us know at:

theroseparkerstory@yahoo.com or savingourwomen@gmail.com or call (951) 505-3698

FOREWORD

I consider it a privilege to have the opportunity to support the effort of Dr. Rose Parker as she shares her life story, one, which I am sure, will resonate with other women similarly situated. Her story is about moving from powerless to powerful, and about using her voice to shed light on a problem that is gravely affecting the lives of many people in our communities—DOMESTIC VIOLENCE.I first met Dr. Parker when she was an inmate at the California Institution for Women (CIW), where I was serving as the warden. She impressed me with her attitude and conviction to not just do her time, but to make it count for something. Her demeanor and involvement in positive activities during her imprisonment gained her the respect of many and the admiration of others. Though there were some that questioned her motivation and sincerity, Dr. Parker did not allow that to deter her from moving forward. After being released from prison, she has continued to use her voice to enlighten women and men about the choices they have when confronted with domestic violence and the consequences of making the wrong choice. Through her efforts, she hopes to reach many others who otherwise might have to suffer the same fate that she experienced—perhaps with a less positive outcome.

As a young woman growing up in a small town in South Carolina, I never imagined that I would have the opportunity to be involved in helping to positively impact the lives of incarcerated women. In fact, my childhood was, for the most part, idyllic. I had two loving parents, the benefit of a strong family, a good church, and community support, and I did not understand that this was not the norm for many women. Thinking back on it, I was pretty arrogant about women who "allowed themselves to be abused." As a result of my work in the prison system, I have come to know and understand the different paths that women have walked to arrive within the system. That knowledge has led me to support, nurture, and advocate programs and services that improve the quality of life for the women with whom I have come in contact. I am certain that there are many others, who, like me, do not understand the reality of many women and men who find themselves involved in abusive relationships. This book will serve as a means to enlighten some and enrich the lives of others.

It is towards that end that I am involved in acknowledging this effort. The job of a warden is a difficult one with the primary goal of overseeing the operation of a prison that safely confines convicted felons. In large part, we are confronted with our failures as we often see many inmates that return to the system, having re-offended. Less often, we get a chance to see the results of our efforts to make a difference. As I observe the work that Dr. Parker has embarked upon, and her mission to get the word out to practitioners and others about the impact of domestic violence, I have a sense that, like a pebble dropped in a pond ... the ripples will extend far beyond what can be measured.

Susan E. Poole CIW - Warden (Retired) California Department of Corrections

PREFACE

Everybody has a story. When I was 21 years old, I thought I should write my life story. Why? Because I believed that I had experienced so much as a young woman, and to me, I had seen it all. Being raised in a loving church, being on TV, attending the Grammy's and music award shows, etc., little did I know that I would end up using drugs and being involved with someone who would beat me as a sport until he was satisfied. And when that satisfaction needed more fuel, the beatings escalated to threats of death. This book has been hard to get out of me. Some things are absolutely too painful or shameful for me, but here I share in-depth; so that you, my readers, may know that you, too, can overcome your past and that you are not alone. I share a lot of my entire life, my family, and events that played major roles in my life.

The title, Beat Up, Beat Down and STILL STANDING, has a REAL meaning to me. I have literally been beat up, with black eyes, busted head, bumps and bruises to prove it. Beat down, well, that's a term I've used for the legal system that let me down beginning in 1986 through THE PRESENT—I'm STILL waiting on my pardon. At the time of my arrest, there was no law to protect me against someone who said he was going to kill me (now it's called a terrorist threat). From then till now, "I'm still standing," and having done all to stand, I STAND.

I write this book also for several additional reasons: 1) I desire inmates to be empowered through my story and gain hope for their lives life, contributing members of society. 3) I want society to know from the pages of this book and my personal experience that the legal system can fail, and if they have a loved one locked up, not to give up on them or the legal system—because all things are possible: 4) to wake up the effects of domestic violence and to bring awareness to this issue. 5)to literally show the process of "a life saved by grace" and how I "walked it out in".

Contents

Chapter 1: Your Life or Mine

March 27, 1986

"Everybody out of the house with your hands up!" the police yelled over the loudspeaker. I will never forget those words the night of March 27, 1986.

After pacing the floors, I finally exited the house first with my baby in my arms, blinded by the police headlights beaming in my face. I could barely see the officers standing between the cars with guns pointed in my direction.

"Put the baby down and lay down on the ground!" a male voice commanded. "I can't put my baby on the cold ground. The grass is wet!" I yelled back. After they kept hollering at me, I sat on the ground with my baby in my lap. I knew my mother would have killed me if I had done what the officer demanded.

Moments later, a white officer walked up to me very slowly that cold, damp night. "We received reports of shots fired from this house," he said. "Is there anyone in the house hurt? The paramedics are standing by.

"I'm not supposed to talk to you," I replied, recalling that my brother Joseph told me not to say anything before I walk out of the house.

But the officer kept talking to me and asking questions until I finally broke my silence.

"Come closer and I'll tell you what happened," I whispered. He came closer.

"Art tried to kill me and I shot him." "Where is he now? We need to help him."

"He's in the closet in the house," I whispered. The next thing I remember is that two other officers came over to read me my Miranda rights.

"I shot him; he tried to kill me," I said to them. They nodded at me as if they understood. From a distance, I saw my brother standing outside of the barricade trying to get to me, but the area was blocked off by the SWAT team.

"David, David," I yelled to him. "Officers, that's my brother, and this is his house. Please let him through." But they wouldn't let him come near me. "Ma'am, please get in the car," another officer said, reaching for my crying baby. "Why are you taking my baby?" "Don't worry, ma'am, we'll give you your baby back momentarily. We just need you to get in the car now." The other officer that was already in the backseat said, "There are only a few more questions that we need you to answer."

"Hurry, because my baby doesn't have anything on." I didn't want them to take my baby, all he had on was a diaper, but a few more minutes shouldn't hurt, I thought to myself. I was fading in and out emotionally, thinking about what happened in the house and what's happening right in front of me. The next words I heard were... "Do you understand these rights?" the officer asked.

"No, yea! I do. When do I get my baby?" "After you tell us what we need to hear, then you can have your baby back."

"Okay, officers, what else do you want to know?" "Tell us again, why did you shoot the man?" "I told you that he was trying to kill me. And, sir, my baby is sitting on top of the car!" "Did you act alone in this shooting?"

"Yes, it was just me. I want my baby!" "I know, ma'am. He'll be OK. Just answer the questions." "Art came to my house with a gun. He held me hostage for four days and wouldn't let me go anywhere or call anyone." I was crying now. "Did you shoot him, or did someone else shoot him?"

the officer asked. "I shot him—all by myself. You told me you were going to give me back my baby."

"Take it easy, ma'am. We're going to give you your baby, don't worry." "When?" I could feel myself getting angrier and scared. I saw one of the officers talking to my brother and pointing to my baby on the car. My brother went to get him and wrapped his coat around him. I kept thinking to myself, I can't believe they had my baby sitting on the top of their car.

Two hours later, they told me to get out of the car because I needed to sign papers. They also wanted to search the house and take gun residue off my fingers.

That was an odd request because they didn't even believe that I shot Art. They kept looking at my brother. So I cooperated and gave them my fingerprints to take the gun residue sample.

Next, the officers stepped out of the car to go talk to some other officers. I was growing more concerned about what was actually happening. Everything seemed to be a blur. At this point, I finally realized that they were not going to give me my baby. The tears rolled down my face like a faucet. What are they going to do? I wondered.

My thoughts were interrupted as my fingers ran across the large cocaine rock in my pocket. My heart skipped a beat, because I wanted another hit. I have to control myself, because I got to do something with this rock. In front of me was an ashtray on the back of the front seat. I put it there. Instantly I felt better and fell back into the seat.

"First, take her to the hospital," an officer said. They were behind me now and I could not see them clearly. I knew we only lived about ten minutes from Ontario Community Hospital. The two officers jumped in the car and began to drive off. "Where are we going?" I asked.
"To the Ontario Hospital."

"But what about my baby?" I knew inside myself that this question was pointless.

Ontario Hospital

The police scanner was loud. I heard someone say that Art was DOA. I could still hear the officers at my house talking in codes and descriptions. Then the first officer radioed in that they were taking me to the hospital.

"This is Officer Sloan reporting that Officer Peterson and I are taking Rose Parker to Ontario Hospital. Ten-four." As soon as I walked in the emergency room, the staff recognized me. They remembered me from the many times I had been there before.

The head nurse rushed over to me. "Rose, what happened this time, baby?" The rest of the staff stopped what they were doing and looked over at me.

"He tried to kill me." The police officers ignored our interactions and presented me to the nurse. "Somebody's been beating this child for a long time," the nurse said to the officer. "We're so glad the police are involved."

"This woman has been here many times and would not tell us who was hurting her because she was afraid for her life," another nurse volunteered. I'm so glad you said that, because I've been telling this officer that Art has been beating me," I said through tears.

After a doctor examined me, confirming my intoxication and the fact that I was pregnant, the officers returned with their pen and little pad in their hand for more questions. I was so tired of talking to them. I voluntarily told them about the cocaine rock that I put in the ashtray. One of the officers winked at me and said, "We have it; thank you for being so honest."

Leaving the Hospital

My stomach growled loudly as we were leaving the hospital. I was embarrassed and hungry. "Hey, Officer Peterson, can we stop and get something to eat?" "What do you want?" "Taco Bell. My baby likes Taco Bell." They took me directly to the West End Police Station to my surprise, where they handed me over to Detective Smith and Detective Black. For the first time, I was afraid because those two men were really mean looking. I timidly told them that I was hungry, and they promised that I could have a burger from Tommie's in a few minutes. Detective Smith and Detective Black followed Officers Peterson and Sloan as they escorted me to the interrogation room.

After answering questions and signing papers for about an hour, a clerk came to the door with a hamburger bag from Tommie's. The officers left me alone to eat. I devoured that hamburger and fries in record time. Then I began to think about Von, Art's cousin, who lived with him. I wondered if she knew yet that Art was dead. I needed to be the first to tell her to make her understand how it all went down.

The heavy interrogation door opened and in walked Officer Peterson, the nice one.

"I need to use the phone to call someone."

"OK, you only have one call to make, so make it worthwhile," he said with a smirk on his face.

My First Phone Call

I was so out of my mind that I wasted my first phone call. For some reason, I just had to call Von, Art's cousin, to make her understand what had happened. Why this was so important at that time, I'll never know.

I called Von and she answered the phone. "Von, it's Rose. I don't know if you know or if anybody has called you yet, but Art's dead." There was a heavy silence on the other end of the phone. "Rose, what happened?" she finally spoke.

"Art held me hostage for four days, threatening to kill me if I tried to leave. You know I'm pregnant, and I can't keep going through this emotional stuff.

"Do you remember on Monday when he called you and said to look in his closet in His black suit and get the money for Shawn's play because He was not going to be able to make it?"

"Yeah, Rose, I remember that."

"He also told you that he was with some white boys working on a business deal."

"That's right." Vons's voice sounded as if she had been suspicious of Art's behavior.

"Well, he wasn't with no white boys. We were at a hotel, and I couldn't leave. You know I'm pregnant, and I can't keep going through this emotional stuff."

"But, Rose, didn't you have a chance to call the police at some point?"

"Von, he was on me every second. You know how Art is trying to always control everything. Trying to keep me high and making me smoke with him. He didn't care about the baby inside of me."

"Yeah."

"Even this morning when he called you at 9, he called from a pay phone and I was outside the store with him, his arms wrapped around me because he would not let me out of his sight. He was telling y'all he was handling some business, but instead, he was taunting me with the threat of killing my baby and me. I couldn't let him kill my baby, Von."

"He wouldn't do that, Rose. You know he was probably just high and tripping."

"Von, he would have done it, I know he would have. I believe that it was just a matter of time before he killed us. Remember the damn jar in his house filled with pickled human ears? Who would have stuff like that? But he did. I'm sure someone said he wouldn't do that either, but his crazy ass did." "Okay, Rose, I have to go."

"I just wanted to call you and let you know straight from me what really happened. And I'm in jail right now."

"I got to go, Rose." She was rushing me off the phone. She hung up the phone without asking me how I was doing. I wondered if the phones were tapped here in the hallway. If so, at least they got an earful of how things really happened.

I dozed off while waiting for the officers to return. What seemed to be a few moments had to be an hour or so because it was midnight when they returned. "Rose, wake up! Rose!"

"I'm here. What's happening?" I was groggy with slumber.

"Can you re-enact the crime if you had to?"

"I don't know what you mean."

They told me that they wanted to take me back to the house so I could show them how everything happened and they would film me. They're gonna let me finally be on TV, acting out a real story, and I get to play the part to show them everything that really happened, I thought to myself.

Back Home

We drove back to the house and everyone was gone except for the local police, investigators, and neighbors peeking out of their windows. I recalled it was only a few hours earlier that this whole block was filled with people everywhere—from neighbors, ambulances, swat, and regular cops.

They told me to stay in the car until they were finished setting up the house. I couldn't believe it—they were setting up lights and cameras. Then they came to the car and escorted me into my own house.

"Rose, stand right here near this hallway."

I'm thinking to myself, Yes! This is my moment for real Hollywood. I wished I had my face made up and was able to change, but this would have to do. If I'm supposed to look like I've been suffering or beaten up, then I guess I look the part just fine. Several moments passed, and I'm still just standing there while they went through the house upstairs and downstairs. An officer that I never saw before came up to me.

"Rose, we need you to talk with Detective John Johnson and Detective Burger."

I snapped at him, "I thought we were going to re-enact the crime."

"We are going to film, but we're going to do it in a different way," another officer said.

"Oh, like Barbara Walters' interview format?" I asked.

"Yes," Detective Burger said.

When he agreed with that, I was truly disappointed because I wanted to do all the parts of everybody that were there tonight. They just didn't know who I was. They didn't know I had real acting credits to my background.

The videotape was running and while they were asking me more stupid-ass questions, it didn't even feel like a Barbara Walters' interview. It felt more like an interrogation! An hour, later my stomach began to hurt real badly and I needed to use the bathroom. They could see how tired and worn-out I was.

"Listen, we got enough. She's answering the same questions and giving the same answers," Detective Burger said to the other detective.

They let me go to the bathroom. I couldn't believe it. I felt tricked and manipulated. They didn't want to do a damn film or documentary about what happened. All they wanted was more evidence and information.

They were supposed to film this. That's what they said. They were liars. They told me I was getting my baby back—another lie. Thoughts of rage flooded my mind.

"We're going to take her to West Valley Jail to book her on a 187 first-degree murder charge. We have enough information," I heard them say when I re-entered the room.

My heart was pounding in my chest now. I was going to enter another jail, not knowing what was about to happen to me. I felt like I was sleepwalking through this process, but they just wouldn't let me go to sleep or rest.

West Valley Jail for Fingerprinting
After I was fingerprinted, stripped of my clothes, picture taken, and processed, I was finally able to collapse in a large dorm room that I didn't even remember entering. I believe they exhausted me with sleep deprivation all night long for their own purposes.

Chapter 2: An Uncommon Place

March 28, 1986
First Morning—Breakfast in Jail

The next morning when I woke up, a guard brought me a silver cup with hot coffee and a cardboard-type of tray wrapped in cellophane.

"Can I have some cream and sugar?"

The guard did not respond to me, and then I heard the skinny black lady across from me snickering. A Hispanic woman who never looked up was eating and reading a book. The more I looked at the food, the more I felt like vomiting, but I knew that my baby must eat. After a few minutes passed, I slowly chewed what appeared to be meat.

A worker passed by very quickly and again I yelled out, "Can I have some milk? I'm pregnant and it's for my baby." Still, nobody responded to me. Maybe they were on a time schedule to get the food out to everyone.

The Hispanic woman walked over to me and gave me her milk. "Thank you," I said. She didn't respond verbally, but tilted her head as to say, "It's cool."

"Hi, my name is Rose. What's yours?"

"Marci."

After I finished my breakfast, floor guards came to the area.

"Let's go, Parker," a tall, brown, skinny woman said.

"Where are we going now?"

"You're going to County Jail."

"I thought I was at County Jail."

"Well, you're not, but you're about to go there." She was very

Sarcastic.

"Can I call my mother?" The woman ignored my question.

Black-and-White Bus Ride
They walked me out the back way and there sat a large black and-white bus. I remembered seeing these buses as a young girl and feeling sorry for the people that were on them.

 Five other women were boarding the bus. I guess we were all going to County. A thin white man with black-rimmed glasses nodded "hello" as we boarded the bus. The other ladies boarded first. Then I boarded. Oddly enough, all the women were in cages in the front and the men were in the back. The section for them was much bigger. "Hello, gentlemen," I said. "How is everyone today?"

It was so sad to look at their faces. I was trying to spread some hope on that dreary, depressed array of faces I had to walk past. I ended up having to go all the way to the back, and as I did so, I noticed that there were an even amount of women and men on the bus.

As I got closer to the back, I heard my name. The voice had a familiar sound. I looked up and there were my brothers in the back. My heart raced. I walked faster, a smile plastered on my face. I was so happy to see them. They had white jumpsuits on. It felt so good that we were all together again.

"Rose, are you alright?" Peter, my brother, asked.

"Yeah, I'm much better now that I see y'all."

"Rose Ann, I told you not to say anything to the police," Joseph my youngest brother, whispered. It seemed like he couldn't wait to tell me those words. He didn't even say hi first.

"But I told them the truth, Joseph. The truth will set you free. Don't worry; they probably just have to check out everything." My brother shook his head; he knew something I didn't know about THE SYSTEM.

"Rose Ann, what have you done? What have you done?" Joseph kept saying. "Joseph, it's gonna be okay. God knows the real truth." The other men that were sitting nearby heard us and were shaking their heads, too, like my brother.

"Joseph, I bet you that we'll only be here for a couple of days. It's Friday now. We should be home by Tuesday. That's our arraignment."

Joseph was still shaking his head with tears rolling down his face. He was on parole, and he violated. Peter just remained quiet, but I could see the worry written all over him.

"Peter, did they do anything to you?" I asked. He just remained quiet, staring at me.

"Did they beat you up?"

Finally, he said, "I'm okay, sis."

The bus turned real sharp, jerking us as it drove slowly through a tunnel. When we came out, we were next to a large, grey cement building. The bus doors opened, and the jail deputies began to call names of inmates to exit the bus.

My brother stood up first. People started exiting the bus from the last rows first. When my brothers started walking, I noticed that they were shackled on their feet and handcuffed. My row was next. As I exited the bus, they told me to go right instead of left, like my brothers.

Booking Process in County, March–August 1986

A sign with the words "Booking" was printed on the door they were taking us through. "Everyone stands in this line for booking," an older, dark-skinned, motherly-looking woman barked.

"Ma'am, I've already been booked at the last place."

"Be quiet and keep looking straight ahead. They have to rebook you."

"Well, can I use the phone?" I kept remembering I had not called my parents yet. I should have called them first instead of Von. I know they had to be aware of what happened by now.

"You can't do anything until you're booked. Be quiet!" Her words were sharper than the crease in that beige uniform she wore.

I didn't want to make her even madder at me, but I really believed they were confused about me. I just wanted a chance to tell somebody in my family that Art tried to kill me and I had to defend myself. I wanted the officer to know, but she wouldn't let me speak. I didn't know why they were being so mean and treating me like some criminal.

"Rose, they don't care about you. They're just passing cattle along. That's their job," Marci said. She stood behind me.

"Listen, thank you, again, for giving me your milk." I learned that day that Marci was in for bank robbery and manslaughter charges. She and two of her friends got caught after holding up a Bank of America in Rancho Cucamonga. It got a little out of hand and someone was shot and killed.

Her partner forgot to take the license plates off the car before pulling up to the front of the bank to pick them up. Marci said the plan was tight except for that one little glitch. The police came right up to the doorstep of Marci's mother's house where she was staying and arrested them— with the car parked right in front of the house. Now I know what she was b--!-chin about all night before she went to sleep. By the time I fell asleep, she was still fussin' and cussin' about it. She continued even this morning when we rode to San Bernardino. I could see her as I was talking with my brothers in the back, throwing her hands up and other stuff. She kept punching the inside of her left hand. The other women that were riding with us kept teasing her about doing an amateur job.

Cavity Search

During the booking process, I went into an area called "Cavity Search— Inspection/Clothes." At first, I was puzzled. I wondered why we needed to see the dentist. I thought, they sure are really nosey about health conditions. Then, they made me strip buck naked.

"OK, it's time for the cavity search."

I immediately opened my mouth as wide as I could to show her I was cooperative and I had perfect teeth. I heard laughing from the staff and some of the women inmates. One of the women officers told me to bend over and spread my cheeks and cough.

"What do you mean, my 'cheeks'?"

"Spread your ass and cough."

I thought to myself, Oh my God, no—they are not! What are they looking for back there? What could anybody put back there and still want to use later?

There was a white woman next to me, crying out of control and screaming out her innocence. "I didn't do it! I didn't do it! I'm telling you, it wasn't me."

"I know, I know, they caught the wrong person, right, little precious?" a white, pot-bellied officer mocked her.

"Yes!" she screamed.

"Just bend over, baby. The cavity check don't take long. It'll be over within a minute."

I felt so stupid. That is what a cavity check was, and here I stood, my mouth opened wide. I also felt bad for that white woman who said she was innocent and didn't do it, whatever "it" was. In the corner of the room, officers seem to be whispering while looking my way. I could tell that they were whispering about me by the way they were cutting their eyes. I also noticed that the officers doing the searching were also talking to other inmates like they knew them personally. They were whispering to each other and, again, I thought they were talking about me. After they searched me, they sent me to the shower and gave me different clothes to put on.

"Where are we going next?" I asked.

The woman officer hit me on my a-ss and told me to keep walking. Next, I went to an area called "Hold for Housing."

Five women that rode the bus from the other facility and I were booked, processed, and searched together. There was no privacy at all in this process. I felt like I had no dignity or respect left when they finished with me. After having the most humiliating and embarrassing search an individual could have, they finally took us upstairs to our area. The noisy women's facility was filled with anger, cursing, and mocking laughter.

Dorm Assignments
"Inmate Parker," an older officer yelled out.

The room was big and had about ten beds spread in single file, one next to another, but spaced out pretty good. I watched the other woman put her stuff away very tidy under her bed. I put my stuff under there too. They gave me a toothbrush, soap bar, face towel, bath towel, and tooth powder.

When the guards left, all I wanted to do was to sleep. The inmates were somewhat sympathetic because I was pregnant. Although I was only five months, I looked much larger, so I noticed they let me sleep as long as I needed to. I was able to sleep most of the day, but at night, I tossed and turned. I recalled seeing Art in my dreams and woke up in a shivering sweat. So much for getting a good night's sleep! I was cold and wanted another blanket, but I knew asking for one was useless.

Late in the night, I couldn't sleep. Everyone else was snoring and dead to the world. I found myself not wanting to go back to sleep because I could see Art coming after me with this mean look on his face. Right before day broke, I finally was able to sleep. Just when the sleep got good, my "cellies" woke me up.

"Rose, you got dust under your bed."

I didn't know what they were talking about. I looked under the bed and saw some dust, but I didn't put it there. I'd been asleep. The three ladies in my cell were looking at me to see what I was going to do.

"If there's dust under my bed, you guys must have put it there." I rolled over, turning my back to them.

"Rose, it has to be cleaned up," the tough girl insisted.

"When do the cleaning people come in?"

I turned over to see who it was that kept calling my name. They were looking at me as if I was crazy. The one girl that was talking to me was a black girl on the floor in a tank top doing push-ups. She had muscular arms with a tattoo on her right arm inscribed "Hammer."

"What the hell you mean 'cleaning people'? Where do you think you are—the f--in Hilton Hotel? You are the cleaning woman, b--!ch. You better get up, mop up, and clean up on your side," Hammer said all that while doing push-ups. I guess the other girls standing nearby were her flunkies. I could hear them giving high fives to each other and laughing.

I was angry. I rose up in the bed, saying, "Hold up. I just got here. Y'all got me mixed up with somebody else."

"Yeah, we know what you in for—murderer!"

I rolled my eyes and said, "You want it cleaned up, do it yourself!" Then I lay back down and turned my back to them. I was told later by the cellies that you never turn your back on any inmate and go to sleep—especially Hammer. Later that evening before we went to chow, I kept seeing inmates on the phone outside of our cell. I wanted to talk with my parents so bad I could taste it. Hammer was the last one in the dorm, and I asked her about the process of using the phone.

"Do you like to be called Hammer, or is that your boyfriend's name?"

"That's my name! Ain't no boyfriend up in here."

"Alright, fine. Do you have to get permission from the guards to use the phone, Hammer?" I figured her boyfriend must catch hell from her.

"Yeah, you do have to get permission, but you can't use it for 48 hours after you arrive. Later, I got to go make my call to my girl." Well, that meant I could use it tomorrow. And I could tell this woman did not like me.

I couldn't wait to get up the next day to call home. My cellies knew I was running to the phone and Hammer said, "Wait, Rose, I'm waiting for a call." I backed up and waited for about 30 minutes, and then an hour, and then two hours. I asked the girl that was closest to me if she ever heard the phone ring.

Hammer followed me back in and hit me on my arm. She waited for me to hit her back. Instead, I said I was going to tell and she turned around and left. "I'm pregnant," I yelled out at her. "Rose, they playing you. Can't nobody call into a county correctional facility. The number is not listed or given out," someone told me. I felt so dumb. I never thought about it. Everybody within hearing distance started laughing at me. I was mad. I looked at Hammer and just shook my head at her and said, "I waited two days for the phone, then I waited a couple of hours more to use it because I thought a call was coming in for you." I stormed out to go and call my parents.

Call Home
I was a little hesitant to make this call, but I knew I had to contact my mother. I knew she'd been praying for me because she hadn't heard directly from me since the shooting. She had to be worried, and I needed to tell her what I did. I noticed my hands were shaking as I reached to press "O" for operator assistance. I stated my name and gave my mother's telephone number.

"I have a collect call from Rose. Would you like to accept?"

I heard my Momma's voice telling someone in the background that I was on the phone. It was probably my father.

"Hello?" Her voice was so sweet and accepting of me, I wanted to cry.

"Momma, I'm okay, and the baby's okay."

"Rose, are you eating? Do you have enough to cover you up and keep you warm?" Momma remembered I get cold easily, especially at night. I didn't want to tell her that I was cold and had not really gotten much sleep.

"Yes, I have enough." I didn't tell her I was scared to go to sleep for fear of having nightmares of Art haunting me.

"Rose, I've been praying for you. You need to get your hands on a Bible in there so you can read God's Word. He can keep you, baby."

"OK, Momma, I will and keep praying for me, please. Hey, Momma, I'll see you tomorrow at the arraignment, right? I should be home after that."

"Of course, baby." Momma had a familiar sounding smile in her voice that I ached to see.

"Momma, are you guys cooking?" It was Easter Sunday.

She said, "Baby, everything is not the same right now. We are simply remembering that Jesus was resurrected."

"Momma, I don't know how much time I have on this phone. It takes change, so I'll find some change so I don't call you collect all the time, but right now, they are calling for church over the loudspeaker and I really want to go—and I need to go."

When I got off the phone, I spotted a guard so I walked over and complained about Hammer hitting me earlier and lying about the phone.

The guard told me to grab my stuff, and they moved me. I protested that I wasn't the troublemaker and demanded to know why they were moving me out of the dorm.

Sunday, March 30, 1986—Church

One of my cellies told me how good the church services were and how they helped her. She was glad that I wanted to go with her that evening. I figured I should go because the Lord knew I needed Him. We entered the chapel to the sound of soft guitar strings playing gospel music. In the front of the chapel stood a total of six people, three young ladies, two young men, and one older gentleman playing the guitar. He was also the preacher for the evening. I went straight to the front row. After sitting for awhile, I started reminiscing about my childhood as I watched everyone intently. I could imagine my dad standing and preaching. This small group reminded me of the first choir at my daddy's church—me and my six siblings. My mother was the choir director and my daddy played the piano and did the preaching. I couldn't help but wonder if this ministry team was related to each other because they looked so much alike. They did a wonderful job. Where did my family get off-track? How I wished it was the other way around, that it was me and my family in front of all these inmates telling them about the light of Christ. But somewhere down the line, I lost my light and chose to go down a dark road that led me right here. I tried to look around without being so obvious sitting on the first row and I got a glimpse of Marci wiping a tear from her face. Hammer had her head down. I wondered what they were feeling. Many others were smiling and enjoying the music.

The ministry team had a joy about them that was so real you could feel it. They sang to a room filled with criminals of all types with real smiles and joy in their voices. The music sounded so good. I had not heard church music in a long time. I felt like a camel in the desert, thirsty for water. The songs watered my parched soul. The first song was Alive, alive, alive forevermore,

My Jesus is Alive, Alive forevermore, Alive, Alive ...

The second song they sang was called "Walk in the Light."

Some of the inmates were sitting in the back, talking away and being rude. I guess this was just a pass for them to be out. One thing I remembered about church when I grew up: if you talked in church, you got pinched. Then, the man laid down his guitar and told us to turn to the Book According to St. John. "Hello, my friends. My name is Pastor Michaels. We are glad to be here with you tonight to share the good news of Jesus Christ. For the newcomers, we are here every Sunday evening and hope you join us next week if you are still here. Tonight, I will be sharing from the topic 'The diamond light of darkness.'"

I was sitting there listening to this sandy-haired, small man who walked with a limp but had an abundance of energy and was excited. He was a fireball. His dark suit drooped on him, and he was very thin, but I could tell he was probably really cool in his younger years. His words were piercing and consoling at the same time. It seemed like he was talking directly to me. At the end of his dynamic sermon, he said, "If someone is here today and wants to publicly accept Jesus Christ as their Lord and Savior, please stand."

The man that was preaching told the women, "We have a total of one hour to be with you, and we have roughly 20 minutes left. We are willing to wait for more of you during this time to profess Christ. Jesus is patient."

My life with Art from 1982–1986 flashed before my eyes as I sat there listening. When I met him, I never would have dreamed even in my wildest imagination that I would be in jail because of him. Oh, God, why did this happen? Why am I in this place right now? Why, God? I stood up without even thinking about it. I knew I needed to accept Jesus in my life as a mature adult. I marched up front. One of the lady singers came to my side to ask me what my purpose was for coming to the altar.

"I have so many reasons." My body was shaking like a leaf. I had not had a hit now for three and a half days. I remembered putting that last piece of rock in the back of the police car.

"Ma'am, what's your name?" the freckle-faced lady asked. She had the sweetest angelic look on her face.

"My name is Rose." Before I knew it, I had grabbed her hand and pulled her a little closer to me as I leaned into her. "God knows I need deliverance from some bad habits and ways. I'm so sorry that I got caught up in a crazy life. God knows I'm sorry." I was crying hard. She put her other arm around me to hold me.

"My brothers and I will be arraigned on Tuesday. I'm praying for God's mercy on our lives and to let us go home."

I could feel her nodding yes. She pulled back and said, "You're pregnant, young lady. I also feel led to cover your unborn child in prayer, too, if that's alright." Her prayer gave me so much comfort and hope. I felt God would, and could, do anything for me.

Chapter 3: What God Has for You?

Tuesday, April 2, 1986 - Arraignment Morning 4 A.M. "Parker."

I heard my name over the loudspeaker, followed by a guard coming to my room. "Parker, you have court this morning, and you have to go to chow now." A dark-skinned, short, chubby woman with a tight-fitting deputy uniform on made the announcement. I jumped up and stepped outside of my cell to go shower first before chow as I hummed those songs from last night. Another song flowed from my lips, "I just got to be free." I smiled to myself. This will be over in a matter of hours, I kept telling myself. The chow room had about ten women in it who were all going to court. Marci, one of the nicest Hispanic ladies I had met, was one of them. But everyone at chow was kind of droopy and slow moving. Marci asked, "Why are you so damn happy, Rose?"

"Not an early riser, huh?" I joked.

Marci seemed really upset. "I'm still happy because I had a good time at church Sunday night, and I'm going home today after my arraignment probably."

Everyone at the table looked annoyed at me as if I were from another planet. I continued, "Once I get a chance to tell the judge what happened and give him the whole truth, he's gonna let me go." I popped the last piece of biscuit in my mouth. "Mmmmmmm, good. My last biscuit in County." They led us through the underground level where the buses were waiting. This time when I got on, I saw my brothers again and they were in different colored jumpsuits from before. Orange ones. I don't mean to be the jail fashion police, but that is not a color for a man. Surely somebody must have protested that color. This morning the bus was packed with about 20 inmates, men and women. Some had tired looks on their faces; others seemed very worried. Only a few wore smiles and winked. I spoke to them.

"God can do it!" I yelled out to everyone.

"Can He marry you and me?" this cute little guy answered back to me.

Guys will be guys. I looked back at him and laughed it off.

"Watch out, man. You heard what happened to her last ole man, didn't cha?" a brown-skinned dude yelled out. That comment took me by surprise, so I just remained quiet. I was glad my brothers didn't hear him, otherwise, we may not have made it to the court. We all arrived together and the police put us in the Jury Box. A straight-creased uniformed officer passed each of us some papers which stated the charges that were against us. The room was so quiet you could hear a mouse sneeze. I looked at the paper they gave me and in shock, could not believe what I was reading. Before I could even think, I blurted out, "FIRST-DEGREE MURDER? MALICE? PREMEDITATION? I didn't do any of this!"

A few moments went by, then someone came to get me and my brothers and instructed us to sit together at a table inside the courtroom. Peter was visibly nervous. "It's going to work out just fine, Peter." I wondered about what his paper said. After all, I was the one who shot Art in self-defense and accidentally shot Peter, too.

Court Outburst
After rereading the paper, I stood up and proclaimed, "I didn't do this; this is not what happened. I told the police everything that happened that night."

The judge banged the gavel loudly. "Ma'am, sit down and be quiet."

"I apologize, Your Honor, but they made a mistake on my paper. I'm supposed to go home today."

The judge looked at me sternly over his bifocals, and I slowly sat down, staring at the paper in my shaking hands. "People of the State of California versus Rose Parker, PC187." A medium-built man resembling Matlock made the announcement.

The judge clarified what was going on by saying, "Ms. Parker, these are the charges that are brought against you. How do you plead?"

"I plead not guilty. The only reason I shot him is because he was trying to kill me, Your Honor. How come no one understands that? Why are they trying to make me out to be a cold-blooded killer?"

Out of my peripheral vision, I saw my brothers Peter and Joseph putting their heads in their hands, but I continued to talk. "I didn't premeditate anything; this is wrong. I don't have malice in my heart for nobody, sir. I was just trying to defend myself and save my family. After I said that, the judge declared, "Ms. Parker, please sit down. The court will appoint you an attorney and you can take it up at that time. Next!" The gavel sounded as if the last judgment had just taken place. I jumped. Sadly, I turned to see Momma and Dad. Momma sat with a half-smile on her face while tears were flowing down. I told myself, "OK, this is going to take a little longer because maybe they have not finished checking my story out."

The bus ride back to the dorm was quiet as well as embarrassing. All the inmates that I had breakfast with earlier that morning snickered at me except for Marci. Nobody went home that day.

Visit from My Attorney
The next day, I was summoned to the visiting area. "Rose Parker, hi, my name is David Negus. I'm an attorney. You are facing a life sentence in prison." He pulled out a chair and plopped down in front of me.

"Sir, you must have me mixed up with somebody else. A man came to my house with a gun, and I'm pregnant. He held me hostage for four days in my house. How can I be facing a life sentence?"

"Ms. Parker, the law doesn't work like that." He cleared his throat.

"Well, I thought I was innocent until I was proven guilty."

"Ms. Parker, we have a record of you talking to the officers and telling them that you shot Art." With those words, he handed me a copy of the police report. "We also have a video enactment of you telling the story again and again. My job is to try and get all of that thrown out and deemed inadmissible based on the tactics they used on you. Rose, I understand that when they read you your Miranda rights, the first thing you told them was that you didn't understand it when they finished. And they were supposed to stop talking to you once you said you didn't understand."

I interrupted him, "Then I told them I did understand because I wanted my baby back, but they wouldn't give me my baby." The picture of my baby sitting on top of that car with no clothes on was burned in my mind. Before Mr. Negus left, he explained what our strategy and approach would be. "Do you have any questions, Rose?"

"No, I'm still a little stunned."

"We have three weeks to prepare for your preliminary hearing, which should be around April 21. Ms. Parker, I'll be visiting you once a week, and I'll also be sending an investigator out, so don't be surprised if you get a visit from a Ms. Lori Paranti."

I felt really good after our meeting, but was very confused about why it was taking so long for me to be released to go home. In the meantime, I still had problems sleeping. I continued to have nightmares about Art either running after me or torturing me in front of his friends and laughing. It seemed like every night that following week, Art was getting closer and closer in my dreams to killing me. In fact, the dreams got so bad; I called my attorney and told him I needed to see him. When he asked why, I said, "I just need to know that Art is really dead and not faking his death." I insisted so much that he promised to bring me proof. Before the end of that week, he brought me pictures from the coroner's office showing Art's autopsy.

Call to Gretchen, My Cousin
About midweek, I called my cousin Gretchen to see how she and the family were doing. She was so concerned about me and how I was doing, her first question to me was, "Do you have an attorney, Rose?"

"Yeah, I do. I just got one a couple of days ago. I just had my attorney visit yesterday."

When I described what my attorney told me, she said, "Rose, that sounds like a public defender."

"Well, when does my attorney come?" I asked.

She replied, "I don't know, Rose, but you got to know the difference between a public defender and an attorney."
"What's the difference, Gretchen?"

"The difference is that an attorney is hired by you or your family and is paid big money to represent you. The public defender is paid by the courts, and sometimes, they aren't that good." I interrupted her. "Look, Gretchen, I must have been special to the judge because he told me in front of everyone that if I could not afford an attorney, one would be appointed for me. So now the judge is paying for it, and he has to know some good attorneys. He's a judge.

"I know, Rose, but that's a public defender; it's the cheap side of defense and representation."

"Gretchen, he's gone, isn't he?"

"Who, Rose?"

"Art. He's gone, isn't he?"

"Yeah, cuz."

"I just wanted him to stop beating on me. I just wanted to try and stay clean. I just wanted to try to be a mother to my sons and change my life."

"I know, Rose. He didn't want that for you."

"He wouldn't let me go. He or his boys followed me everywhere. I shouldn't have to end up in here to change my life, Gretchen. That's all I wanted to do." I started crying. I think it was the first time I verbally acknowledged that I really wanted to change from the lifestyle that I lived for the past three years. The money wasn't worth it; hanging out with movie stars didn't have any appeal any more. I just wanted to be free. My soul ached deep inside. I had to shoot a man just to be free from it all. Art was right. He told me a long time ago it would cost me my life to get away from him. I wondered if he knew what he was saying then.

"Well, all I know is that he's the best. I read his card, and it says he is the Chief Deputy Public Defender, so there—you don't know what you're talking about—cheap side of representation!"

After I hung up the phone, a feeling so strong came over me. I couldn't shake it. It was the urge for some cocaine. I wanted a hit. I wanted it bad, too. "Oh, God, please take it away. Please take it away." I saw a Bible in my dorm and began to read it. Quickly turning to Psalms, I read Psalms

23:1 "The Lord is my Shepherd, I shall not want." The urge subsided. I was so scared. That feeling came out of nowhere. It felt like my knees were buckling from under me, it hit so hard.

I wanted to talk to my parents, but didn't want to put a collect call on their phone again. I pulled out paper so I could write. Then something in me hesitated because I felt I had disappointed them so much. But I knew deep down inside, no matter how much I may have disobeyed their wishes throughout my life, they loved me unconditionally. I wanted a copy of my letters so I wrote them twice. The Lord knows I had time on my hands to do so.

Dear Daddy,

I have messed up my life, and God has given me another chance. I love you, and I'm sorry that I didn't understand what you and Momma tried to teach me. I know that God loves me and He will take care of my babies. It's hard in here, and being pregnant only gets you an extra glass of milk. You know how I love milk. I know that you probably don't like long letters so I'm going to go for now. This letter will not go out until tomorrow. They only do mail pickup at certain times.

Guess what? I read the New Testament. I will read it again and the whole Bible next.

Love,

Rose Ann

Dear Momma,

How are you feeling? How is Atujuan? Did Brenda pick him up, or is he there? Anyway, they have me scheduled to go see the doctor to make sure that the baby is OK. I guess they're waiting a few weeks 'cause the police said that I was seen at the hospital and the baby is out of immediate danger. I did tell them that I'm high risk, and I have to see the obstetrician.

GUESS WHAT? I have a special Mother's Day present for you. I'm trying to get it now. I'll tell you more on Mother's Day. Momma, I really love you. You are beautiful and really love us almost too much. There were a lot of things I didn't understand, and I am honestly really just learning. I can't believe you survived with your whole family dying all before I was born. I can't even relate, I mean, to your mother who was 44 years old and your sister who was only 19 years old both dying at the same time with food poisoning. Momma, I have to trust that God brought you through it. I mean, your little brother died and your other sister was beaten to death by her husband, all before the 1950s. They told you your dad died in Jamaica, and in 1955, your last brother died rescuing his wife in a fire in Fontana. Even when I hear those stories today, I just can't imagine it.

I know I'm sounding a little morbid, so I'll say, after all that, God blessed you with ME. I'm sorry, Momma, for being rebellious and not listening, I know that you only tried to tell me what was right. Momma, after all the years growing up, I want you to know that even when I was mad and fussin' back, I always knew you understood what was best for me. I just didn't want to hear it or do it. I don't know why, I just didn't.

Oh, Momma, I'm reading the Bible. First, I'm going to read certain books in it and then the whole thing. I'm going to read it just like God has it. He made it like that for a reason. So I'm going to find out why, plus, it helps me go to sleep when I have trouble sleeping because it makes me sleepy. I remember when you used to tell me to read the Bible when I couldn't fall asleep, but I couldn't. Well, what can I say? I bet God doesn't have to tell me fifty thousand times, huh? Just twenty thousand!

Well, I've been trying to eat this food and trying to follow these rules. I guess we have to mind somebody. Oh, Momma, the baby kicks good. I feel it at night and we talk. I let him know that I will protect him and when I say stuff really important, he kicks me like he's answering me. I thank God for saving us and sparing our lives. Even if I'm here, we are alive. I love you, Momma, Rose Ann

P.S. Give Daddy a big kiss from me and then you can give him a huge kiss from you.
"Thank you, Jesus, for my family. Please keep them safe. Help me, Lord. I will trust and wait on You to deliver me. Amen."

Just writing my folks made my heart lighter. It felt like a good confession and a new beginning. I only pray that it feels that way to Momma and Dad.

Visit from Private Investigator
After breakfast the next morning, April 3, 1986, I received a visit from Ms. Lori Paranti, like my attorney told me I would. I felt she was a warm, yet, no-nonsense woman from how she spoke and asked questions. "Rose, or Rose Ann, which would you like for me to call you?"

"Rose is fine; whichever one makes you comfortable."

She gave a halfway smile. "I need to gather some really important information that would help us with your case. Please take this time to try and remember everything and everyone involved on the night of the shooting and if there are any credible witnesses that could testify on your behalf about the violent behavior of Art toward you." She sounded as if we were putting together something that didn't exist. As far as I was concerned, the case was solid. Art abused me, and when they heard what he did to me, it would touch their hearts if they are any kind of human being. But I kept that to myself.

"OK," I responded. "I may not know the right spelling of names that I'm going to give you, but I'm sure you can find that out."

"Rose, I know you have been through this story a zillion times, but as your legal defense team, you will need to repeat some things for our benefit so we can help you as much as possible. I don't want to only rely on the previous reports that have been taken. We want to hear it straight from your mouth, okay?"

I felt myself getting frustrated because I didn't want to relive that night again. "Sure, let's go."

After she took the information and names, I was exhausted. She looked down at my stomach. "When are you due?"

Rubbing my stomach, I answered, "August."

"Well, this is not exactly the greatest environment to carry such a gift. I wish you the best, Rose."

"Thank you, Ms. Paranti."
"Now, if anything else comes to you, call me right away. If I'm not available, leave the information with my assistant.

"If I think of something else I need, you'll hear from me. Try to have a good day, Rose."

"Do you have children?"

Her face lit up. "I sure do. Three girls."

"I can tell you really love them. Your whole demeanor changed when I asked you that question."

"Have a good day, Rose."

After she left, I went back to the dorm area, laid on my bed, and thought about my two precious sons, Emzie and Atujuan. I wished they could feel me. I wished so badly to hold my baby and to tell my older son to be strong. I know Momma and Daddy are taking good care of them, but I wondered if they missed me and asked about me. Oh, how I wished I could hug them and tell them how much I loved them. I fell asleep longing for my children.

When I woke up from my nap, I decided to read the police report Ms. Paranti brought with her. I didn't know why, but I pulled it out of my things under my bed and was shocked to read and witness again the manner in which I was handled by the officers. Reading the report made me ache again for my baby and grow angry at how they treated him. It read:

POLICE DEPARTMENT
200 N. CHERRY AVENUE
ONTARIO, CALIFORNIA 91764
3/27/87
Rose Ann Parker (Suspect)
Arthur Boga (Deceased)
Officers Tejas, Tomski, Bordon, Leigh, and Jones.

INTERVIEW OF SUSPECT ROSE ANN PARKER:

Approximately 2015 hours, I, Officer Tejas, am going to read ROSE ANN PARKER her Miranda rights via OPD Miranda Card.

AT: Rosemary, you have the absolute right to remain silent.
RP: Rose Ann.
AT: Rose Ann, I'm sorry ... you have the absolute right to remain silent. Anything you say can and will be used as evidence against you in court. You have the right to counsel with an attorney, to be represented by an attorney, and have an attorney present before any questions are asked. If

you cannot afford an attorney, one will be appointed by the court free of charge to represent you before any questioning if you desire. Do you understand these rights?

RP: I understand those rights.

AT: Keeping these rights in mind, do you want to talk to us about what happened here today?

RP: I really don't, but I feel that it's necessary.

AT: Okay, well ...?

RP: I have nothing to hide.

AT: Okay, you do want to talk to us then?

RP: The truth, it doesn't matter. I can talk and it's not going to change, you know? I don't understand, but ... I mean I understand the rights you've read me, okay?

AT: Uh-huh.

RP: And I don't know the law and as long as I know what I did and what was done to me, I have nothing to hide, okay?

AT: Okay, well ...?

RP: I could tell anybody, okay? He was going to find a reason to go off later on and have me killed. He wanted ... see, I was dressed, you know? You guys were watching, my nephew said the police were out there. So I went and changed clothes, you know? I put my shirt on and acted like he was going to take me out. But what he was going to do was take me away somewhere so he could have a reason to kill me. That's what he did to me this morning when we started to shoot and he pulled a gun on me this morning.

AT: Okay, but what happened today? You're still not telling me what happened today. Did you guys fight over a gun, or did he pull a gun on you, or did you pull a gun on him?

RP: We didn't fight over the gun. I told him to please put the gun over there, 'cause, you know, like my baby he was there. I said put it on the other side of the bed so my baby can't get to it. So, therefore, put it this way ... to be totally honest, because I have to be honest, I don't want to go to jail. I have my baby. I don't want to go to jail, but I have to say he didn't pull the gun on me, and I took it from him and shot him, okay?

AT: Uh-huh.

RP: That's not how it happened. So, therefore, I mean I guess ...

AT: Well, how did it happen?

RP: He told me he was going to shoot him if he found him.

AT: Okay, so what happened?

RP: He said "I'm gonna shoot you if—", so I'm scared. Where's my baby?

AT: He's okay; he's just a little cold. They're putting—

RP: I don't want my baby to suffer 'cause of me.

AT: He won't; he's okay.

RP: I don't want my baby to suffer. So then he was going to take me, so I knew what he was going to do, so I try ... In order for me to be able to shoot him ... the man is a gangster. He already knows the game 'cause he already told me if I was planning to do anything to him, he's got people watching and they're gonna get me, okay? So whatever happens to me, I don't know, 'cause I'm confused, okay? 'Cause I killed somebody, and it's against God, okay? And my baby's crying ...

AT: Okay, well, how did it happen?

RP: I told Peter while he was sitting there messing with the pipe or something, JoJo, that's my brother Joseph, was praying, and I said, "Something's wrong in here; what's going on in here?" He says, "It's not"—what's the word—he said "It's not pract—" He said, "It's not p—" It started with a "p"—practical—and I said "But it's not right." He had rent my mother—I didn't tell JoJo what he did to me. Peter knew. JoJo wasn't there. JoJo had come over and I didn't tell him that Art had tried to kill me or was going to kill me 'cause JoJo just got out of jail and would have shot him.

AT: Okay, did you shoot this guy, Art?

RP: I shot him.

AT: How many times?

RP: I shot him twice.

AT: Do you know where the bullets hit?

RP: I'm not 100-percent positive. I think one hit him at first in his back and I tried to shoot him between the eyes, but I'm—and I shot him behind the head.

AT: Okay, wait a minute.

RP: Please let me hold my baby.

GB: Now listen, okay?

RP: Okay.

GB: Okay, my partner and I are assigned to investigate this. We're both detectives, okay?

RP: Okay, I have nothing to hide.

GB: Okay, this is a "Consent to Search" form and this is for your signature here, saying that we can go in and take photographs and figure out what happened, okay?

RP: Okay, okay, but—

GB: Is that okay with you?

RP: I don't know. My baby is sitting on the car with nothing on.

GB: We'll take care of him. Why don't you—

RP: You're not taking care of him because he's sitting on the car with nothing on.

GB: Rose Ann, step on out here, okay?

RP: Okay.

GB: I just need you to sign the paper.

AT: Are you right-handed or left-handed?

RP: Right-handed. I did it, but to be honest, let me tell you one more other thing, okay? I shot him with my brother's gun first, okay? 'Cause my brother had his gun somewhere that I knew, okay? I shot him. I knew he was shot, and he ran down the stairs. I grabbed his gun and shot him with that. Does my brother know?

GB: Yeah, he's signing one also.

RP: Where's my brother David?

GB: He's in the house.

RP: I've gotta see him to know that it's okay, okay?

GB: He gave his permission to search, but he said that you rented the room upstairs.

RP: You know you guys want to play games, or whatever.

GB: We don't play games, we just—

RP: I mean, you already know I killed him, okay?

GB: Okay.

RP: What do you want to do?

GB: It's just consent to go in and investigate.

RP: I'll sign.

GB: You're just giving us permission to take photographs and things like that.

RP: Wait a minute. I mean, I killed the man. God has forgiven me, okay? I might suffer the consequences of the law, okay? Let me see what I'm doing first, so give me the piece of paper. "This officer and others who may assist him ... enter the premises and conduct any necessary investigation, including but not limited to ... for possible evidence." I understand. I want to sign this because I don't want to act like I'm hiding anything. GB: Okay, sure, that's fine with me. I understand.

RP: See, you can take anything you want out of the house. You know what's on my mind? I been on coke, okay? There's still some left, and I still want some, and I don't want you guys to find what little bit I tried to hide from you.

GB: But we've not concerned about that.

RP: But I'm concerned ... I'm just telling you because I want another hit. But one thing I'll have to make sure is that it's okay with my parents because it's his house, too.

GB: Okay, your brother signed it.

RP: Okay, I know his handwriting, okay? So you can use that, right?

JJ: Yes, ma'am.

RP: Can I take my baby?

JJ: Well, wait a second.

RP: Okay, I hope you guys aren't fooling with me.

JJ: No, okay?

RP: Is he dead?

JJ: Where are the guns?

GB: We just got here.

RP: I already told you where the body is.

AT: Rose Ann, where are the guns now?

RP: I don't know where the guns are. Joseph didn't want me to get in trouble.

JJ: So did JoJo hide the guns?

RP: Yeah, well, I'm not supposed to tell you. I don't want ... he didn't know, okay? He's.... Jo Jo's innocent. He's on probation, okay? Jo Jo gave the gun to my nephew.

JJ: Is he on probation or parole?

RP: I don't even know. But JoJo told my nephew to put the guns up and don't tell nobody where they at, okay? So I don't know.

JJ: Okay. How many guns did you use?

RP: I used two guns. What kind ... I don't know nothing about no guns. All I know is if you can get the things working ... Can you pull it out a little bit?

GB: It's a .38.

RP: No, his was a .44, something like this. Is this some kind of .44?

JJ: Why did you do it?

RP: He was going to kill me.

JJ: He was going to kill you?

RP: He was going to kill me. I've had bumps all over, he busted my head open, I'm pregnant, I got x-rays.

JJ: Did he hit you tonight?

RP: Yeah, he hit me tonight, but the only reason why he didn't do it harder is because my brother knew if we weren't back he'd come for us and he knew where we were going.

JJ: Okay.

RP: Okay, so he brought me back and said to kind of make me think everything was going to be—

JJ: Did you wash your hands or anything?

RP: No, my hands are—

JJ: Okay, are you right or left-handed?

AT: She's right-handed.

RP: I didn't know what I was doing, okay? I was so nervous and I was so scared and I knew if I didn't shoot him, he was going to kill me. I had to make sure he was dead. That man is 56 years old. He's got millions. He knows how to not get killed, okay?

—END OF POLICE REPORT

Tears rolled down my face as I finished reading the report. It once again made me understand the finality of my actions. Why was I crying? This is the man that beat me mercilessly in front of my kids, in front of his friends, or anybody else, at any time he wanted to. Part of me knew that he was crazy, but I wanted so badly to be the one to fix him. I guess I must have been crazy too.

After I finished reading the police report, I needed God to hold me. How I wished with all my heart that He could talk to me. So I decided to write to Him.

Dear Father,

I can't believe what I read today in the initial Police Report. No wonder I ended up here. I talked too much.

Now I understand when Proverbs says "speak when you are spoken to." They didn't have to ask me anything because I talked too much. Of course, I still feel justified in what I did. But it was stupid of me to tell the officer, "I don't know the law and as long as I know what I did and what was done to me, I have nothing to hide, okay?" Man, what a dummy! I should have shut my mouth and not said a word like my brothers kept telling me.

Lord, will You look at this? It's a wonder I didn't get my brothers charged with murder. Here I am telling the police about Jo Jo's criminal past and that I used Peter's gun to shoot the man! Boy, they must have had a good laugh when I told them that I was on coke, too, and that I had some more and wanted a hit right then. They say that You take care of fools and babies, and now I know it must be true.

April–July 1986

When I was in the County, I used to notice certain ladies up and walking in the middle of the night with blankets. I gave them what they asked for, like chocolate and cigarettes that I bought at canteen with money put on my books by my family. I found out those ladies were kicking heroin. I really them, one in particular. Eventually, those same women I helped grew to despise me.

On one occasion, we were housed in the infirmary. We ate there and while I was eating, I went to the restroom. When I came back, I continued eating. After a while, everyone started laughing. The girl I helped the most, the one I stayed up with and prayed for, had spit in my food and I'd eaten it. When I lay down in my bed, tears rolled down from my eyes. It was the most horrible feeling to have helped her from my heart, and then she repaid me by spitting in my food. And there was nothing I could do about it; it was already in me. That night I talked to God about it. "God, I don't understand how I am giving my heart and life to help some people and they can be so cruel." He reminded me of the Scripture that says, "Blessed are they that are persecuted for righteousness' sake, for theirs is the kingdom of heaven."

The next morning I wanted to speak with my son Emzie because his father had picked him up a week before all this happened at Easter. I had to find out what he knew. Nobody knew Boonie's telephone number but me.

The operator answered, "Hello, may I help you?"

"Yes, collect call from Rose Parker to Emzie Parker."

I could hear the telephone ringing and someone picked up. As soon as the operator said, "Collect call from Rose Parker," the person immediately hung up. I was devastated. I fell to my knees and prayed after I got back to my dorm.

"Lord, why wouldn't that person take my call? That has to be that silly girl Boonie is with. I just want to talk to my son. I wonder if Art's family got to Boonie. They have lots of money; they could have done that. Lord, please help me find my son."

PRELIMINARY HEARING DATE

April 21, 1986

I woke up with a smile on my face. I knew this was the day I was going home. Something in me just told me that over and over again.

"Everybody is here," someone announced. My brothers had their attorneys, too. The judge must have liked them as well, because I knew my brothers couldn't afford an attorney. I was seated at the very end of the table and was able to see everyone in the courtroom. So many familiar faces, my friends and my relatives—or shall I say, those that I thought were my friends. The investigator contacted everyone I gave her names of. My family was smiling and waving, and then I looked at my friends on Art's family's side who were showing no emotions. In fact, they were trying to avoid eye contact with me. I was dumbfounded, so after the first break, I tried to get their attention by waving until the bailiff told me that there was no waving in the courtroom.

Threat in the Courtroom

I looked at one of Art's friends, who we called Doc, and he motioned with his finger moving across his throat as if he were going to cut off my head or slit my throat. I nudged my attorney when I saw that and told him what Doc just did. At that time, the judge announced a recess for five minutes. All counselors and the bailiff were called to approach the bench. I wondered what was going on. Then everybody took their seats again and my attorney called the bailiff to the witness stand and asked him if he just witnessed an incident within the past ten minutes in the courtroom concerning Rose Parker and anyone else.

"Yes, I just happened to be looking where she was looking, and I saw the man in the back with the brown suit on give her the cut-throat gesture."

The bailiff was released from the witness stand and the district attorney called Doc Augustine to the witness stand.

"Did you just threaten Ms. Parker?"

"I don't know what you're talking about. I was fixing my tie."

So my attorney stood up and stated that he wanted on record my fear of this man. He then asked Doc, "Why were you fixing your tie, looking at Ms. Parker? We have the bailiff on record stating that he saw the same thing that Ms. Parker saw."

"I said I was fixing my tie. That's my answer, and I'm sticking to it."

I heard what he said, but I couldn't help but remember what I saw him do. My heart began to beat rapidly. I knew I wasn't seeing things. I was so grateful for that bailiff who saw it too. Thank you, God.

Sad Testimonies
The testimonies started one by one. Mistakes were made by Officer Tejas, a Hispanic. He had talked to me for three hours and was the same one who testified on the witness stand about the night of my arrest. The judge asked him where his notes were. He didn't have them. I went to court four days in a row and saw and heard the most horrible liars on the stand. I couldn't believe they put their hands on the Holy Bible, too.
One of the worst lies on the witness stand came from Maya, Art's sister. She painted a picture of Art that I didn't even recognize. She claimed he was an upstanding citizen, never in trouble, always helping people. She also said he never used cocaine, and she never saw him hit me or was aware of any abuse. "She killed my brother!" she screamed from the witness stand. I could have fallen out of my seat.

The last testimony was the hardest. It came from Art's cousin, Von. I really liked Von and thought she was a sweet person, but I guess people change on you. I called her the night of my arrest and used my one dime to call her instead of my family because I was so worried about her. While riding back to the jail, all I thought about was Von's testimony against me and the officer who interrogated me for three hours, but lost his notes.

Before court ended, my attorney tried to get the case thrown out because of the inappropriate use of the Miranda rights, along with the video re-enactment of the shooting. He said it was done through entrapment means, but the judged denied the motion and said it stayed in. The final business they took care of that day was to sever the cases between my brothers and me and bound me over to Superior Court to answer charges of manslaughter.

Chapter 4: Settling In

The Dorm Is Not Too Bad After All

The two weeks of court felt like a lifetime of judgments being pronounced upon me. I felt so beat down every time I left there. It just didn't make any sense to me. How could I be at fault, and how could Art be the victim? I asked myself over and over again.

Life has a way of introducing new appreciations. In a strange way, I was thankful that the courts were closed on Fridays. I was glad to get back to my dorm area. I needed the break; I wanted to go back to rest and think. Never thought I'd say that! But truly, at this time, it was the better of two evils.

Later, at chow, Marci sat next to me. She rubbed my back for a quick second in a consoling way. "How's it going, Rose?"

"It's stupid, Marci. I don't understand the system. Now I think I know why my brothers kept telling me to shut my mouth. It seems like everything I say only makes things worse for me."

"Yeah, the system is hard, baby girl. If I was a judge, I would say you don't belong here."

"But, Marci, I feel I do because I shot Art. I've learned there are no good excuses for breaking the law."

"That's right, it can be a matter of life and death and you end up with the sentence."

I asked her what she meant by that.

"My dad is poor, and we live in a very poor part of town. He has cancer and needs surgery bad or else he will die, the doctors told my Momma. She don't have no money, I don't have no money. My family barely makes rent every month. The hospital don't have no special programs for sick people that don't have insurance or money. They don't care. They're cold-blooded. Either you pay or you lay ... lay in a grave, you know what I'm sayin'?"

"Yeah," I replied. I could tell Marci was growing angrier and angrier as she talked about her dad. I rubbed her back.

"You're in an f--in Catch-22, like they say. So I got my homies together and we robbed a damn bank. It was the best solution we could come up with—and it would have worked if Pablo would have taken the damn license plates off the car like we told him to."

"I saw you crying at the church service they had the other night. Is that what was on your mind, Marci?"

"Yeah, I was thinking how stupid I was because now I can't help him at all; and if he dies while I'm in here—"
Marci couldn't finish her sentence. She broke down and left, walking fast. She didn't want me to see her cry too much, I could tell.

That night I added her and her family in my prayers to God. I prayed that somehow God would send them help and let Marci know that her dad would be alright.

Lori Paranti
The next morning, I had an early visit from the investigator.

"I've researched everything that you told me and found everything to be accurate.

"I need you to find my son, Emzie. I have not seen him since a week before my arrest."

She encouraged me that they would do their best to find him, but she wanted to know if my family was looking for him too. I was relieved that someone was going to help me find him. The investigator needed to question him. "Well, just remember that he is young and only nine years old. I don't want my son being traumatized because of this stuff."

She got up and told me not to worry; they would find him. The following day, the public defender came to see me and tried to tell me that I've been bound over for manslaughter and that I should take the offer and plead guilty, but I said, "Why should I go to prison for saving my life?" And then I told him I didn't want to talk about it. "That's crazy—a man comes over to my house with a gun and you want me to plead guilty? That doesn't even make any sense. I'm pregnant and about to have a baby in a few months. I don't want to talk about it. I don't want to talk no more." He left but I knew he was disappointed.

Another Visit
Then I got another visit, back to back. What was happening? I knew the attorneys come whenever they want, but I couldn't get any rest. My name was called again. "Rose Parker, you have a visitor."

I was walking toward the visiting room, complaining. "Can't a person get some sleep around here? You know I'm six months pregnant."

I walked into the visiting area and to my surprise, my Momma and dad stood there. I couldn't wait to tell them that my attorney wanted me to plead guilty. It made no sense. My dad wanted me to settle down and tried to tell me that I needed to think about it carefully. I looked at him. "What do you mean? God knows. You're a preacher; you know I'm not a killer, Dad. I only shot Art because he was going to kill me. That means

I'm innocent. It was self-defense. Why would I even think about saying I was guilty?"

Momma said, "Calm down, Rose Ann, so you don't upset the baby. Did you eat anything?"

I could tell Momma was trying to change the subject so I could calm down. We were quiet for a while and nobody said anything. Momma said they needed to get back before it got too late. I cried again as I watched them walk out of my sight.

Brenda Visits
"What's going on, Rose?"

"I hope you have time for me to tell you, girl, because I am hot!"

"Well, that's why I came to visit you, to see how you were doing," she encouraged me. She had such a warm smile about her that's why I named her Atujuan's Godmother. But I was so upset I had to let off steam.

"Brenda, my public defender wants me to plead guilty. It doesn't even make any sense, Brenda!"

"Who's he?" she asked.

"Mr. Negus, my court-appointed attorney."

"Did he tell you why he wanted you to plead guilty?"

"Because he's scared!" I replied. "Even Dad wanted me to consider it, but I kept telling him that it just didn't make any sense. I was defending my life. Why am I being penalized for surviving and saving my own life?"

By the time I finished fussing and walking up and down that visiting room, I knew Brenda was really upset. She kept trying to talk, but I couldn't shut my mouth one second to let her speak. I needed her to understand that my side made much more sense. Brenda was not able to add or take away from the conversation and so she patiently sat there and listened attentively. I felt better after I was able to get all that off my chest.

The next two days, more visitors came, including my brother David and sister Carol. I didn't spare them either. This system of justice was not making sense to me, and I couldn't understand, for the life of me, why others couldn't see what I was saying. Instead of saying anything, David and Carol politely listened too.

Investigator
At the end of the week, the investigator came by. It was about 9 A.M. when I got another visit. I automatically thought it was Mr. Negus, but to my surprise when I walked in the visiting room, it was the investigator, Lori Paranti.

"We found your son, Rose."

Tears welled up in my eyes. "Thank you, Jesus," I whispered under my breath. "Thank you, Jesus."

"I want to share the interview with you that I had with your son. I think you will find it quite interesting, and it will make you a proud Momma," she said.

I listened and couldn't believe what I was hearing. My son actually told them that when Art busted my head on Christmas and made me go back in the room to lie down, that he was trying to get the gun from Art. My heart started pounding because that man could have killed my son. My baby risked his life trying to save his mother. He even described the type of gun that Art had and gave her a description of other guns that he saw Art with.

"Is my son OK?" I asked.
"Yes, he looks really good. Rose, thank God you had full legal custody and that you had your papers in order; otherwise, I would not have been able to interview him legally."

That was my good news for that day, but I still needed to hear from my baby to tell him how much I loved him.

That whole day I thanked God that my son was found and he was alright. I knew God was able to lead Lori to him.

April Showers Bring May Flowers, 1986
My public defender told me that there were not going to be as many court dates now. On one hand, I was so thankful because I was burned out with all the interrogations and the lies and disappointment of not going home and not being able to be with my kids like I needed to be.

Walking in Favor
When we had dorm check, the guards would always deal nicely with me, I guess because I was a big, talkative, and silly pregnant girl that made everyone laugh. In fact, I was the only pregnant lady in the unit at that time. They were kind of tough on the other inmates, but I noticed a difference when they told me to do things or informed me about something. I don't know, but I was grateful.

I remember waiting for them to come put the chains on my ankles, but they never did. I knew murderers were supposed to be locked down and wear chains on their ankles. They would let my ankles go unchained because they would swell and the guards were sympathetic toward me. But they would cuff my hands. I knew it was the work of God, nobody else but God. I didn't know why He showed me so much mercy through these people, but He did. I shot a man and God still loved me and didn't kill me because of it. I know God wasn't pleased with Art's life or mine, but it's so amazing to think that I survived at all.

I got to know most of the guard staff by name and made sure I spoke to each one when they would pass by or come to do dorm checks. The bigger I grew, the more they seemed to really look out for me. Deputy Jennie Massarotti was a middle-aged white woman who would ask me how my baby was doing on a daily basis. I could always depend on her to say good morning and then ask about the baby. I eventually found out that she was married and was unable to have children, but she wanted them so badly.

Church Time, Sunday Night, May 1986
The pastor from Living Waters Worship Center, along with several of her workers, came to give us a personal introduction to Love. She said, "Good evening, precious daughters of God. My name is Pastor Liz. I'm on assignment here at County for the next six months, and the Lord has told me to do a series on Love.

"Now, you need to know that we give the Holy Spirit the freedom to detour at any time, so be flexible in your expectation. Just expect the Lord to show up and show out in your life from now on." Pastor Liz started questioning us after her brief introduction. I liked her questions; they were interesting.

They took care of your children that you had by other men as if they were their own. Today, in your bible turn with me, if you will, to Hosea. In your own devotional time, please read chapters 1 and 2 in their entirety.

But remember, He says that "Today if you hear my voice, harden not your heart." He says that tomorrow is not promised. You need to know that one day, it will be too late. Today, Love is holding out His hands to you, saying, "Will you come? Will you come?"

The minister was waiting at the altar, and I practically ran down. It felt like she was talking about me personally. I had children out of wedlock. I took money and provisions from someone that loved me very much (even though I was not married to him) and slept with Art among others. I felt dirty.

I received Love that day, and I will never let Him go again. Jesus has cleaned me up and set me free. The pastor promised to continue on this topic the following week and I could hardly wait. Never had the Lord spoken so clearly to me before in a service. I was so excited. Thank you, Lord!

Another Bible Study with Living Water

"Ladies, ladies, let's get started now." Pastor Liz had to call us to order because everybody was talking and laughing loudly. She continued, "Last week, we were introduced to Love via the book of Hosea. I hope you read up on it a little more. This week, we will add to last week's Scripture with I Corinthians 13:4–7. Can I get a volunteer to read?"

I raised my hand and stood up immediately. "I will, Pastor Liz." I flipped through the New Testament to find it quickly.

As soon as I finished reading, I sat down. I remembered when I was at Daddy's church, we would always stand when the Scripture was being read. Daddy said that's respecting God's Word.
Then Pastor Liz said, "Thank you, Rose. Ladies, I want you to make that your devotion for this week. Study it daily and get it in your heart." I felt as if she were speaking only to me. I loved to hear her teach. She continued.

Through Hosea, we can easily see that Love is unconditional. Love is patient, and Love is kind. Love is long-suffering. Could you see all of that in Hosea as he dealt with his adulterous wife? He put no conditions on his forgiveness of her. He simply said, "I forgive you, and I take you back." He was patient as he waited for her to get tired of running the streets and come to her senses. He was kind to her. How many men do you know that would do that? When he came to take her home with him again, she probably cried, recognizing her backslidden state.

I needed to discuss this with my friend Sadie tomorrow. I wouldn't talk in church. I knew that was rude. Maybe we could begin the discussion on the way to our dorm. I wondered if she really understood this love thing. I don't see how God can love us that way. I can't see how He expects me to love others that way. I know that pastor said that I'm to allow God to love through me, but the people in here are pretty tough to love. They do stupid stuff all the time.

I dreamed about my daddy, he was in the park with my children, and they were playing and running. It was so beautiful. I think that was God's way of showing me that my boys were going to be alright. After I showered, and I waited for the phone to be free. I really hated having to call home collect. I never wanted to feel like a burden to anyone, especially my parents.

"Hi, Daddy, thanks for accepting the call."

"Rose, how are you doing?"

"I'm doing better each day. Dad, I've been studying I Corinthians Chapter 13 and I can't wait to go to Bible study tonight."

"That sounds wonderful, daddy." "Everybody sends their love to you, Rose. The kids are doing fine."

"Give my love to everyone, too, Dad, and hug the kids tight for me." As soon as I said those words, I felt sad and lonely for them. How I wished I could hold them myself.

Later that evening, Sadie and I were sitting around, just laughing in the dining hall when all of a sudden—bam, bang, dang. Two girls started throwing down.

"Fight in the dining hall! Fight in the dining hall!" the guards
yelled. "All inmates return to your cells immediately. Lock Down!"

"Hurry, Rose!" Sadie yelled. "We probably won't be going anywhere tonight."

I sat on my bed waiting for the next announcement when I heard the intercom come on. "Attention, all inmates! We will remain on Lock Down for the rest of the evening. All activities have been canceled."

"Oh, no! That means no Bible study tonight! Ooooh! That makes me so mad. But that's alright, I guess. I'll just read some more." That night, I read to myself and completed all of Corinthians I and II. I wanted to know what came before chapter 13 and what made the Apostle Paul write such a hard thing. I wonder if he loved like that.

Dear Momma,

HAPPY MOTHER'S DAY - May 1986!
A lot has happened and I'm changing, thank you Jesus. I've learned that being locked up presents choices and decisions on a moment by moment basis. I must admit, Momma, I have needed these moments alone, but not alone. What I'm trying to say is that YOU have your daughter back. This is the "special" Mother's Day present that I was telling you about and that I said I was trying to get—ME—YOUR DAUGHTER—ROSE ANN. Momma, remember when I used to love to go to church? And when I was about nine or ten, Daddy let me go to the holiness church with the Magee's and I joined it so I could go all week and play my tambourine? Well, I go to church in here, and it's been so good. I feel like a sponge. Oh, yeah, Momma, remember I used to like Micah, and Peter liked Rachel, his

sister? We always wanted to go over to the Magee's house. Anyway, I was working on reading my Bible regularly and listening to God. I wanted to give you the best present ever. Thank you for the love that you give. I mean, I know that I'm loved and you would prefer that I knew God more than anything. That's real love. Tell Daddy about me, but this is special for YOU.

Momma, I'm going to go now. They're calling us to go to "hold for housing" to do our clothing exchange. That's jail language where we go to get our two sets of clothes for the week. I'll write more soon. Here's a Scripture for you, Momma.
PSALMS 27: The Lord is MY light and MY salvation, whom shall I fear?

Love,
Rose Ann

Friends in Unexpected Places
When Officer Massarotti completed her rounds, she stopped by to chat for a minute. Afterwards, she told me she was going to lunch. I asked her where she was going to eat and she said Taco Bell. "Oh my God, that's my favorite place," I told her.

"Is it now?" she said.

"It sure is. Can I give you some money to pick me and the baby up a couple of those soft chicken tacos with the mild sauce?" I laughed, but I was so serious inside, even though I knew I didn't have any money.

"Let's see what we can do." She winked and walked out of the dorm.

Officer Massarotti returned about thirty minutes later. "Rose, get up. You're wanted in search."

One of the new ladies looked over at me, shaking her head as if to say, "Leave the pregnant lady alone."

When I got to the office, two women were there. Officer Massarotti said, "Look to your left, Rose," as I stood in the middle of the doorway. On a desk in the corner were two bags from Taco Bell. Oh, this felt like Christmas to me! A black lady with long braids turned and said, "I gave Officer Massarotti the approval to pick you and your baby up two tacos, but you're going to have to keep this to yourself."

"No problem, thank you so much. My baby thanks y'all too." I ate those so fast I was wishing I would have asked for four of them, two for the baby and two for me. Before I went back to my area, I met the sergeant lady who gave the approval to Officer Massarotti. Her name was Mary Miller.

From that time on, I was ordered to come up front at least three to four times a week. Many times, my cellies didn't know where I was. I'd be up front eating with the staff at lunch or enjoying an early dinner. Some of my favorites were Kentucky Fried, Taco Bell, Carl's, Jr., and McDonalds. I didn't tell a soul. I started having so much fun with the staff every time I would go up front. They were always upbeat with me and keeping me laughing about life. I would have them laughing, too, about my crazy life. At times, they couldn't believe their ears, especially Sgt. Miller and Officer Massarotti. Over time, I noticed I was drawing closer to Sgt. Miller than Officer Massarotti. I wasn't used to a lot of female friends. I never even bonded with my own blood sisters. I wished now that we were closer.

June 3, 1986
I was thinking about my sisters and how I never really bonded with them. I miss them. It's my birthday and my whole family always made my birthdays special.

A couple of weeks later, I thought about Dad and wanted to send him a letter. I hadn't written him in a while and wanted him to know I hadn't forgotten about him.

Hi, Daddy,

First off, I love you. I know that you know that, but I love saying it. Happy early Father's Day and just know I believe you are THE GREATEST FATHER IN THE WORLD. Well, anyway, your baby is now 27 years old, and guess what, Daddy? The Lord loves me so much HE made me have a nice birthday, even here. Today I went to the hospital, and the officers, or deputies, which is what we call them, well, they were really nice to me. Remember the one that's named Dourough, the same pronunciation as Douroux? He looked after me. It was a special day because when I got back to the jail, the ladies had put a couple of matches in a cupcake and surprised me and sang happy birthday. God knows (and you, Momma, and everyone else)how special and excited I get about my birthday and for me to be here and feel this blesses me, and sometimes makes me mad that I have to be here to realize the kindness and goodness of God. Anyway, Daddy, I have been writing Momma, 'cause I know how much she needs us and I don't want her to worry about me. Oh, I read the Bible through. I wanted to finish before I turned 27 and I did. I'm gonna do it again.

I just wanted you to hear from me now that I'm older. I love you, and God will make a miracle. I read a Scripture in Proverbs 21. It said that the king's heart is in the hands of the Lord and as the rivers of water flow, He turns it whatsoever way HE chooses. That means to me that the judge's heart in my trial is in the hands of the Lord, so He is again telling me that no matter what it looks like or what they say, God will work a MIRACLE again. I'll see you Sunday. Daddy, if you are tired, just let Brenda or some of the others come. I'll be OK because I'm not forgetting that God is our Father.

Love,
Rose Ann

June 1986 Public Defender's Visit

"Inmate Parker, visiting room." It was 9 A.M. I jumped up and thought to myself, It's got to be my attorney because no one else is visiting me this early. Today was his visiting day. I hated these visits because I didn't understand why we have to keep going through this long process and going back and forth to court.

"I told them what happened; I don't understand why they just don't look at his record. Art had a gun, and he came to kill me. This is so irritating and confusing." I said at my public defender.

"Rose, I need to discuss our strategy," he pleaded.

"Look, I thought I was innocent until proven guilty. Apparently, I am guilty unless I prove I am innocent."

"Rose, you are absolutely right. There is no self defense law in the State of California. We have to establish your innocence with justifiable homicide. Do you understand that, Rose."

"Not really, plus I still have nightmares of Art coming to get me. My baby is being affected by this whole process that I'm going through."
"Listen, why don't you ask the judge to just give me an OR (Own Recognizance) like everybody else? I see girls come in here that intentionally rob, steal, and hurt people, and they ask for an OR and get one. I didn't even intentionally hurt anybody, so they have to give me one."

"Well, Rose, you're not even supposed to have—have—have a—a—a bail, let alone an OR." He was very nervous and started stuttering.

I could tell he was feeling pressured by me and even that made me mad. How come this man of the law can't even handle my frustration? If he crumbles under me, how can he properly represent me and fight for me in a court of law?

"Mr. Negus, just ask the judge for the OR, please. Let the record speak for itself. Those girls get OR and then don't show up for court and get rearrested and charged with a FTA (Failure To Appear)."

He looked shocked as I gave him the rundown.

"That's right, I'm learning this, Mr. Negus. See? I know you can get me out; use the OR word." With that, my counselor hurried up and got out of the visit as fast as he could.

Parent's Visit

My Momma and Daddy came today, and it was so good to see them. I love walking in that waiting room and seeing Dad's eyes light up and Momma's smile just brighten the place.

"Rose, how are you doing?" Momma asked.

"I'm doing fine, Momma, thanks. I'm so happy that the investigator found Emzie."

"Yeah," Dad smiled.

"He's in school and doing very well. He gave the investigator a good interview, and I learned he was being his own little hero, trying to save my life."

My Momma looked good. I didn't like the fact my parents were visiting me in this jail, but Lord knows I needed to see them as often as they could come.

"How is everyone else doing, Momma?"

"The family is doing alright."

We talked about church and Dad told me that God would be faithful. I told Dad that God was going to work a miracle for me, and I would be coming home soon. He responded with what he always said about miracles: in God's timing, in God's way.

The Next Day
At one o'clock, a deputy announced that I had a visitor. It had to be a family member. I bet Carol, my sister, had her baby. I walked swiftly down the hall to find out who was here to visit me.

"Hey, Diane." It was my big sister. I hadn't seen her in a long time.
"Carol had another girl. She named her little Carol."

"I can't believe she named the baby after herself. Have you seen the baby yet?" I asked.

"Yeah, we went up there last night."
"Well, hopefully, I'll see the baby soon," I replied. "Her baby is going to be a month older than mine. I figured out my due date.
"Why did you come here so late? Visiting hours are almost over."

"I wanted to make sure you knew as quickly as possible. Plus, I hadn't come to see you yet, and I wanted to know how you were doing."

"Well, I've been thinking about you and I miss you. Thanks for coming. Tell everybody I said hello and pleeease put some money on my books."

"I gotcha, baby girl." Diane winked as she was leaving.

I yelled out, "Put a lot on there. You know I don't understand the 'po' word." We both laughed.

August 1986

After my routine visit to the hospital, all I wanted to do was get back to my Oreo cookies that I loved.

To my surprise, I got back to my dorm area only to find that my canteen had been stolen. I just stood there for a few moments before reacting. I tried to get my thoughts together. How can I get robbed in jail? I couldn't believe it. I thought about Cathy the one I had help that turned on me, after all that I had done for her. She was the one who spit in my food and was now stealing my stuff.

"Officer Sabena, please check this infirmary and see who has my stuff. I have my slip, and it tells you how much I paid for it."

People started getting nervous. And before the day was over, some items were found. She stole my canteen, my lotion, candy, and toiletries, and the sad part about it is that I gave her that same stuff. Cathy had also stolen my stuff when I was at the hospital. Like the Lord instructed, I just turned the other cheek.

Chapter 5: A Mother's Aching Pain

August 1986 Public Defender

"Visiting Room, Rose Parker."

I was lying down in pain when my name began echoing over the intercom. I didn't want to move at all, but I knew it was my attorney and I had to see him. I knew we were getting close to the court date, and he had important information to share about my case. I pulled myself up.

"Rose, how are you doing?"

"Not good." I was in pain.

"What's wrong?"

"I'm ready to have my baby. I'm in pain."

"This won't take too much time. I just need to brief you on something about tomorrow," he said. I was in so much pain I almost didn't hear a word he spoke.

"Do you understand, Rose?"

"Yeah, ouch! The baby's kicking me hard! I believe he wants to come out right now."

"Rose, it's important that you understand all the possibilities," he stressed.

"Look, my baby is due soon. I need to see my doctor, and I'm not feeling good in this place. I just want to go home! I want to see my sons; I want to see my mother and father. I don't belong in here!"

"Rose, calm down. We're doing everything that we can so that the jury will see that you don't belong in here."

All I could do was nod my head up and down while the tears began to flow down my face. I wasn't planning on having a meltdown, but some things you just can't hold in, I guess.

"Can't you ask the judge to let me go home?" "Rose, we'll see, but it's complicated."

Phone Call to Atujuan
After I went back to my cell, I lay on my bunk wondering who I could call. I felt lonely and just wanted to hear from someone ... anyone that loved me. I couldn't call Emzie because he has been MIA (Missing In Action) since March. Though I hated running my parents' phone bill up, I had to call home. I wanted to hear Atujuan say, "Mommy!" I called and had them put the phone up to his ear.

"Hi, Loutie," I said, calling him my favorite nick name. "I love you and miss you."

He was just learning how to talk. "I love you Momma." He said. Oh, how it ached my heart to not be able to play with him face-to face and hold him. Just then, the pain in my belly intensified. I kept on talking to him though.

"This is Momma, Momma wants to see you. I want you to spend the night with Brenda this weekend so she can bring you to see Momma, OK? I love you."

Momma got back on the phone.

"Momma, I'm going to have Brenda pick up Atujuan to spend the weekend with her to give you and Daddy a break and that way, she can bring him to see me. I love you, and I'm going to go ahead and get off the phone. Thank you so much, Momma, for taking the call. Thank you, thank you."

I went back to my bed and began to talk to God. "Lord, I know You are going to do a miracle for me and let me out of this place." Next, I thanked Him that my parents were always there for me, even though I didn't feel deep down inside that I deserved it. Oh, how I loved them. They always prayed and encouraged me to keep holding on to God always. After talking to them, I had this urge to write them a letter, so I wrote Momma and talked to Dad in the letter, too. My stomach seemed to ache even more, but I still pressed on and wrote the letters.

Dear Momma and Dad,

Don't worry. God is the judge, and He will get me out of here. I know it. I have to breast-feed my baby, I told everybody. God knows that YOU said we all have to breast-feed our babies. Remember the song you taught us, "He may not come when you want Him, but He is always right on time"? I'm remembering everything slowly. The baby is not due until tomorrow, the 20th, at least that's what they said at first. Also, remember to ask Brenda to bring Atujuan on Sunday, and that way you can rest. I'm fine. I really have been trusting the Lord like you guys tell me to do.

I love you, Momma. I love Dad, too. I love each of you very much.

Your favorite daughter (smile),
Rose Ann

August 19, 1986
P.S. Proverbs 3:5–6: Trust in the Lord with all your heart, and lean not on your own understanding; in all your ways acknowledge HIM and HE will direct your paths. As soon as I finished writing the letter to Momma, Vincent popped into my mind. Looking back, it seems that he was the

best thing that had ever happened to me. He was always there for me, caring, loving, and providing as best he could. I decided not to call him that night 'cause I didn't think I could handle it. He was the one man that had really respected me and honored me like a lady. I thought that maybe a better idea was for me to go to sleep right then. I would call Vincent another time.

Court Hearing

The next morning I felt even worse. I was slumped over and barely able to walk straight. I was told by the jail doctors that my baby was due in two days, on August 20th. Everybody in the court could see I was having difficulties.

I reached over to my public defender again and asked him to ask for an OR. He conferred with the other side, and the DA said it was impossible and that I am not even supposed to have bail, let alone an OR. Within minutes, right in that courtroom, I saw God touched the Judge and he reduced my bail (which started at $150,000) to $10,000. I did not really try to make bail; I was trying to be released on my own word that I would be back.

My public defender told me to just calm down and listen to what was being said. He reminded me that the bail had been decreased by $140,000. I said, "I know, but I want to go home."

Disappointed and Back at Jail

I did not go home that day and people in the jail didn't let me live it down. People can be so cruel. They made fun of me all night throughout dinner until the next day, making cracks every time I waddled by someone.

"Oh, you know, Rose's God gonna get her out with a 'get out of jail free card,'" Hammer kept yelling out. I trusted that God was up to something. He was the ultimate judge, and He knew the truth.

Another Court Date in August

The next week I was scheduled to be back in court. I had the surprise of my little life when I arrived. An unfamiliar, tall, handsome man walked up to me and introduced himself to me as my attorney for the day. I didn't understand how they could simply give me another attorney who didn't know me, my case, or my history. I was furious when he introduced himself to me. I panicked inside and just started talking to God.

The new attorney was telling me that we were confirming my hearing and pretrial motions for the 27th. I looked at him and asked if he would request an OR for me.

"Rose, I'm not going to do that. That is not what this day is all about."
"Well, that's what this day, and every day, is all about to me. If you don't, I will by raising my hand and asking myself."

He knew I was serious when he heard my tone and saw the pain I was in. "Okay, I will, just calm down. What can we lose by asking?" he said.

"That's what I'm saying; we can't lose anything," I replied.

I sat in the Jury Box and listened to them confirm my August 27 hearing date. When they concluded, I noticed that the attorney did not request the OR like I asked him to do. I raised my hand and when they saw me raising and waving my hand, my newly assigned attorney said, "Your Honor, Ms. Parker would like to request an OR." A different judge that was hearing the cases that morning noticed that previously my bail had been reduced to only $10,000 and said, "I decline your motion to release Ms. Parker on her own recognizance."

I felt devastated for the first time—devastated and hopeless. A word came to my mind that I didn't understand—it was the word "morbid." I didn't really know what it meant, but it was what I felt.

After going back to the bus, I was glad I didn't have to wait long in the holding cell because it was the end of the day. Everybody was looking at me funny because I was so quiet. I just didn't have a thing to say.

I arrived back at the County and people began to ask me what happened. My heart fell. No words came out. I went to eat, but I didn't want to eat. I could hear my Momma say to take care of my baby, so I forced the food down and made sure I drank the milk. Afterwards, I went straight to bed and thanked God anyway. I didn't like the way I felt, and in my mind I heard the words floating in my memory: "Why is my soul cast down? Hope in the Lord." I smiled and told myself I was going to look up that Scripture tomorrow and read it.

August 27, 1986
Finally, the day arrived, and I was so glad I found that Scripture because it got me through those last days of waiting for my first day of pretrial hearing. I still felt like I was in a tunnel and detached from everyone. Everybody seemed to notice that I was not very talkative, and it appeared they felt sorry for me. After the morning hearing was over, it was my turn.

I sat at the table. I could hear the DA and my attorney talking about releasing me—or was I imaging it? I could just hear the Lord saying not to faint according to Psalms 27, so I just watched God move this same DA and judge that declined me being granted an OR previously now agreeing to let me out. My heart started beating rapidly, and joy welled up in me. "Thank you, Jesus, thank you, Jesus," I whispered under my breath over and over again.

Yes, I was being released. But, before I was released, the judge made me promise to appear for any subsequent court appointments and he made me promise not to contact any of Art's family. I agreed to honor his request. It was awesome, I didn't say anything on the bus ride back to the county, but I wanted to say "hey everyone, I'm out, I told you my father was the judge", I was released that night at 11:00 P.M.

I was never so happy to see my parents in all my life. I told them that they were the best parents in the world for picking me up in the middle of the night from jail. They told me that they had been parked outside, waiting since 8 P.M.

"Oh, Momma, I'm so sorry that you and Dad have been out here that long."

"It's okay, Rose," Dad said.

"They let me out this late so there wouldn't be an uproar in the jail because previously, no murderers have ever been released like me."

"It was a miracle," Momma said.

"Yes, Momma, exactly right. It was a miracle from God. Plus, I told them this time I would be going home and they didn't believe me. I just felt it in my spirit."

Dad pulled off and I looked back at that dark building that held me for the last five months of my life. I remembered that in just one more hour exactly, it would have been five months to the second that I arrived there. I leaned back into the cold leather seat of my father's Cadillac and wished that I could have heard the normal intercom announcement that said, "Inmate Parker, roll it up for release." They didn't say it, but I still heard it loud from heaven. God Himself said to me, "ROLL OUT!" I also thought about Ms. Santiago and how she tapped on the infirmary door indicating I could leave. That was the most bizarre thing that I had ever heard. But the even stranger thing about it was that I knew that the tap was for me.

My stomach started growling, so I asked my folks, "Where can we get something to eat at this time of night?"

"Rose, would you like Taco Bell or McDonald's?" Dad asked.
"My favorite — Taco Bell. I hope they're still open," I eagerly exclaimed.

Thank God, they were opened—just for me.

Dad said, "You can get a taco and a burrito."

"Rose, remember you are eating for two. I don't know why you're getting all that spicy stuff."

"Momma, the baby has eaten worse at the jail."

When we arrived home, I was amazed to see my parents had moved away from the senior citizens' place into a nice apartment. I looked around and walked in every room. I kept busy looking at everything until Brenda arrived with Atujuan. I wanted to surprise him. When I heard a noise at the door, it was Brenda. Dad answered the door, and they walked in. Momma said, "Come in here to see Grandma." When Atujuan came in to see his grandma, I was standing there next to her. He looked so happy. I picked my baby up and held him so tight, then I sat him on top of my belly and held him as I sat down. This was the first time I was able to have him in my arms. How my arms ached for him. I never wanted to let him go. He lay in my arms all night.

The next day was Monday, September 1. We concluded with pretrial motions and were going to start with jury selection. Tuesday, September 2, we continued on with jury selection. Wednesday, September 3, the judge was sick and court was cancelled and we convened on Thursday, selecting the jury. Thursday, September 4, I thought about how the jury selection was a complicated process because so often, when my public defender wanted one person, the prosecutor found a way to disqualify that person, and then they go back and forth. By the end of the day, my stomach was all cramped up and I was in great pain.

Went into Labor

On Friday, September 5, while sitting in court, my time came. I was not doing too well this particular morning, but still kept my word to the judge to make all scheduled appearances. Before the opening remarks were completed by the judge, I went into labor.

The ambulance sirens blared loudly. By the time I reached the hospital, I had dilated to about 4 cm. When they rolled me into the operating room, I was in distress and my baby was, too. I heard the doctors say they were going to do a Caesarian.

My family left the court when I did and were trailing close behind the ambulance I learned later. My son, Darian, came forth on September 5 with loud, healthy lungs. I was so happy to see my baby boy. He was so handsome.

I stayed in Doctor's Hospital in Montclair, California, until September 10, 1986. The nursing staff and doctors were nice. I was grateful to have good food as well.

Atujuan was so excited to see his baby brother when Dad and my brother, David, brought him to the hospital. I put Darian in Atujuan's arms. He was two years old and so proud. He acted like he was the dad. Daddy looked at his new grandson as if he were the very first, even though he had so many. He always made each one feel like he or she were the very first. Carol brought Momma to the hospital the next day. She was the typical, doting grandma.

After my hospital stay was over, the doctors gave me my aftercare instructions and stressed the fact that I probably would not be able to walk my normal pace for a while. I promised myself as soon as I got enough strength, I would find Emzie. The day I left the hospital, I made a decision that I was going to enjoy every day that I got to spend with my children. I wanted to hold them, love them, and train them in the way they should go. I didn't want them to be spoiled like I was, to think that the world owed them something. My parents were great to me when I was a child, but if I could change anything, I would ask for just a little more discipline. I wanted what I wanted and I believed I could do all things. I always thought that. I heard my father preach it. I forgot the part that says, "It's through Christ that I can do all things." I really want my boys to learn that.

I was barely able to move, but I played with the kids until, finally, I had enough strength to go find Emzie because the trial was going to begin soon. I wanted all of my children with me so we could make beautiful memories together—just in case.

Lori Paranti pulled up to my parents' house to pick me up. I got in. We rode all the way from Ontario to San Pedro. I knew that my son was somewhere in that area, and I was determined to go to every elementary school until I found him.

"Rose, do you have all your legal documents proving that you have full custody of your son? If you have all the papers that prove that you are his mother and have legal custody, then you should have no problem getting him."

I did. We had the yellow pages of all the elementary schools and took Emzie's IV picture and showed it to many kids. After five schools, we still had no luck. But something inside me told me to tell Lori to park her car on the side street where my ex-husband Boonie's new wife, Sharon, lived. That's exactly what we did.

We parked and we waited. Two hours went by. Kids came up and down the street, each getting out of school at different times. At 12:30, no Emzie; at 1:30, no Emzie; at 2:30—Emzie. Finally, I saw a group kids

walking down the street. One kid stood out as if he was holding and controlling the conversation. If any child was mine, I said it would be that one. I got out of the car and before I knew it, I was walking toward them. The closer I got, the harder my heart began to pound. That same kid looked at me as I looked at him—intensely. It was my son. He stopped dead in his tracks. Everybody said to him, "What's wrong, Emzie?"
I said, "I'm Emzie's Mom."

Emzie became afraid and said, "My dad's gonna get me."

I said, "Emzie, come with me; come with Momma. Honey, you prayed for this day. You prayed for your Momma to appear and you cried and told God to let your Momma come, and here I am. Come and get in the car with me."

I asked which kids lived with him, and he pointed to two boys and said they were his cousins. I told them to tell Emzie's dad, Boonie (Emzie III) that he was with his Momma and he was OK.

We got in the car. Emzie got in the back and was nervous and afraid. "Honey, it's your Momma; it's your Momma. It's your Momma, baby, and you are OK. Everything's OK."

All of a sudden, it was like he heard me. He brightened up and got excited and said, "Momma, Momma, I wrote a song."

"What's the song, baby?"

He said, "Break the pipe, you know it ain't right; break the pipe; it ain't nothing but a high; break the pipe, kibbles and bits."

"Baby, you wrote that?"
"I did." He sounded so proud as if he had written a platinum record.
"Momma, I knew you would find me. I knew you would."

"Are you okay, honey?"

"Yeah, but you know my dad's gonna be mad," he warned me.

"Your dad was supposed to bring you back, and he promised me that he would bring you when I had the baby." I looked over and Ms. Paranti was smiling and nodding yes. I could tell she was happy.

"Rose, I didn't believe that child was yours."

"I told you if any of those kids were mine, it woulda been that one, and it was."

As soon as we got to the house, little Emzie gave me the number to his dad's house. I called Boonie to let him know that I had Emzie.

"Rose, how you gonna just come up here and take that boy?"

"How you gonna not bring him like you promised me?"

"Boonie, are you forgetting that I have legal and full custody of him? The whole time I had your son, you didn't pay one dime of child support. Don't tell me what rights I have. You're wrong. You're wrong."

He sighed.
"And you need to tell him everything's okay. I'm gonna call him to the phone, and I want you to let him know that everything's okay, you hear me? Tell him it's okay so he won't be scared or confused.

"Boonie, how could you have kept Emzie away from my Momma and my dad and his little brother for six months? You didn't even bring him by for them to see him. That's cruel. Now hold on. I'm about to go get him.
"It's your father, Emzie," I told him.

"Hello ... uh-huh, okay, okay, I love you too." Emzie handed me the phone afterwards and ran back to the room to play with his baby brother. I got back on the phone and Boonie confirmed what he told our son.

"OK, Rose, I told him everything was OK."
"Thank you. That wasn't just for me, it was mainly for him. I'll talk to you later, and you can call here anytime. I'll give you this number, and, of course, I already have yours."

I fell back in my mother's comforter chair with tears streaming down my face. My three sons were home. My mother was so happy to see her baby with all three of her babies. God is good, I thought to myself.

After a couple of days, court began again. The night before, I couldn't rest. Anxiety hit me really hard. I needed something to calm me down. I hated where my mind wandered to. I thought about a hit. I cried unto God to help me and take away these evil thoughts as He had in the past. That night, I needed to write God.

September 16
Dear God,

I love you, Father. Darian was born in freedom and not a prison hospital, thank you. He was born on September 5th; I got out of the hospital on the 10th; and on the 15th, fear hit me hard! I went to the only friend I knew that would take my mind totally off my situation. I went to friend that I trusted to get me through any hard situation. I got some rock cocaine. I felt like crap and left the drug house crying. How could I have stooped so low? I thought. I've killed a man, and I just had a baby. I need You to move on my behalf, and I'm doing stupid crap like this? What's wrong with me? Maybe Art was right. Maybe I don't deserve to live. Help me, Jesus! I want to do better. I want to BE better!

September 17, 1986 - Trial
I could hear the sound of footsteps behind me and heavy panting ... Someone was after me! I began to run very fast and everything around me was bright red and hot. Oh, my God! I thought, Am I in hell? Are demons after me? Is it Art? As I continued to run, I looked for water because I was so thirsty. The thing behind me caught me by the arm and began wrestling with me and I screamed.
"Wake up, honey, you're dreaming," Momma said. "Time to get up and get ready for court."
I opened my eyes. The sun bathed my room with white light through the open curtains on the window. "Thank you, Lord," I whispered as I realized that the bright red heat all around me was only the sunshine. The hands shaking me were my Momma's. She left after seeing that I was fully awake. After about 15 minutes, she returned since she hadn't heard any noise in my room.

"Rose, Rose? Are you ready?" Momma asked.

"It's hard, Momma. I can barely move."

"Do you need your pain pills?" Dad asked, peeking his head through the door. My parents were waiting on me hand and foot as if I were still in the hospital.

"Yes, please, and bring some water too."

The pain killers didn't start working until I walked in the doors of the courtroom. Then the room started spinning and, boy, did I feel nauseated. I couldn't eat too much because I really didn't have an appetite. I just wanted to lay my head on the table and sleep as soon as they sat me down. I fought sleep as much as I could, but I felt myself falling asleep every few minutes. Then it was my turn to take the stand. I could only pray inside for God to please speak through me. I was still slightly light-headed from the medication. It seemed like such a long journey to the witness box. It felt like forever. My feet dragged.

The prosecutor gave me no slack at all. He kept drilling me as hard as he could. He didn't even care that I couldn't understand a thing he was saying.

Lord, please help me, I prayed. I don't understand what's being said and everybody that gets on the stand is lying through their teeth. Please fight for me, Lord. Let the jury see that I'm not a cold-blooded murderer. Let them see that I was only defending myself and fighting for my life. Please, God, tell them that. You can if You want to.

The day ended badly. The DA seemed convinced that I was a monster, and I felt the jury believed him. When court was over for the day, I practically ran out of there. I could hardly breathe. I wanted to get home to my babies as soon as I could. Sleep would be hard that night.
I got home, prepared dinner for my boys, and put them to bed. Then I found myself pacing the floors. Emzie tried to stay up.

"Momma, what's wrong?"

"I'm nervous, honey. Momma has to testify on the stand soon."

"Momma, I want to stay with you."

"No, Momma is going to be downstairs. Everything's going to be alright."

Emzie wanted to stay with me, but I knew I needed to get something to calm my nerves, and I didn't want my kids up when I left the house.
A little later, I got in my car and took off. My heart was racing. As I was driving, I remembered a familiar street where rock cocaine could be bought through an old associate of mine. I decided to go there. If they were still in the same spot, I'd do it, but if not, I'd go home and just go to

bed. Just my luck, the same people were hanging out on the same corner. I parked the car and noticed someone I didn't recognize before, a man.

"Hey, cutie pie, what you do'n over here? Ain't seen you before."

"Ah, man, I've been out of pocket."

"You look'n for something?"

"Just a little something, just enough for a couple of hits."
"Come on in, baby."

I started to get nervous because I wasn't sure if he was trying to hit on me and wanted sex, or just wanted me in off the streets. I just had a baby, and my stomach still had stitches.

When we walked in, I saw a guy that was toh' up from the flo' up. We walked towards the back room and he told me to have a seat next to the bed. Some rock sat on a plate with a pipe beside the bed. "You want to do something for me?"
"I got money, man."

"Baby, you don't need no money as fine as you are. Won't you just do a brother?"

"I got some money. I just want a couple of hits."

A few moments later, tears started coming to my eyes as my head was going down to hit it for a second time. My son's song entered my mind that he sang to me earlier in the week. "Break the pipe, break the pipe, you know it ain't right." I jumped up out of that chair and headed for the door, got into my car, and drove off as fast as I could. As I was driving home, shame and guilt flooded my heart and I began to cry even harder. Here I am on trial for my life and with a new baby. God delivered me from prison on my word, and all three of my sons were with me. What was I doing?

When I got in the house, Emzie was awake. "What are you doing up, Emzie?"

"Momma, I couldn't sleep. You know I ain't a baby. I know you've been through a rough time and it's hard on you. I've been praying for you real, real hard, and God said He was gonna bring you home, so I walked down the stairs to see—and you walked in the door. "Okay, baby, Momma's home for the night. Let's go upstairs and go to bed. You have to testify tomorrow in court."

"I know."

"Are you gonna be okay?"

"Momma, I told you I'm not a baby."

Chapter 6: Emzie's IV Testimony

Court Day Monday, September 29, 1986 9:43 A.M.

September 29, 1986, was not a day I was proud of. It was the day my baby would testify in court. Oh, how I wished I could save him from having to go through this process because of me. No child should have to relive all the terrible things that he has seen with his eyes and heard with his ears. It's bad enough that I have been away from him for six months, and now he has to spend precious time testifying for me. My public defender, Mr. Negus, would be questioning him, as well as Mr. Boyd, the district attorney.

"Good morning, ladies and gentlemen, and welcome back to the Courthouse Facility of San Bernardino County. We will continue with the Rose Ann Parker case at this time," the judge announced.

Mr. Negus stood up and called the witness to the stand. "Emzie Parker IV."

My child has never been called this by anyone. This was all so different and so uncomfortable for me as his mother. Emzie stood up, then walked towards the witness stand. All I could do was sit back and pray, watch and pray some more for him.

The judge told the witness to take the stand and said rather sarcastically, "How old is this lad?"

MR. NEGUS: Nine.
THE COURT: Nine? All right.
THE CLERK: Would you raise your right hand, please? Do you promise to tell the truth and the whole truth and nothing but the truth, so help you God?

THE WITNESS: Yeah.

THE CLERK: Thank you. Will you please be seated?

THE COURT: Just have a seat. What is your name, and will you spell your name, please?

THE WITNESS: My name is Emzie, E M Z I E.

BY MR. NEGUS:

Q: How do you pronounce your name?

A: Emzie.

Q:: And what is your last name?

A: Parker.

Q:: Are you Emzie Parker IV?

A: (Nods)

Q: You have to say "yes" or "no."

A: Yeah.

Q: Okay, now, Emzie, who is your mother?

A: Rose Ann Parker.

Q: And that's the lady that is seated over here in the multicolored dress?

A: Yeah.

Q: Okay. Did you ever meet a person by the name of Art Boga?

A: Yeah.

Q: Where did you meet him?

A: On the airplane.

Q: Where was that airplane?

A: In the air.

Q: Okay. Did you ever go over to Art's house?

A: Yeah.

Q: Did you live at Art's house for a while?

A: Yeah.

Q: Did Art ever come over to a house with you and your mother?

A: Yeah.

Q: Okay. The little boy that's just going outside over there, who is that?

A: My brother.

Q: What's his name?

A: Atujuan.

Q: How old is he?
A: Two.
Q: During the time that you were living at Art's house or he was coming over to your house, did your Momma take any drugs?
A: Yeah.
Q: You know what kind of drugs she took?
A: Yeah.
Q: What was it?
A: Rocks.
Q: Rocks? Okay. How did she take it?
A: With a pipe.
Q: Before your Momma met Art, did she use cocaine very much?
A: No.
Q: After she met Art, was she still as good a Momma as she was before?
A: No.
Q: What did she do wrong?
A: Drugs.
Q: And what—how did that—how did that—how was that bad for you? Well, let me ask you the question another way. Did she take care of you as much as she did before?
A: No.
Q: Did she take care of Atujuan as much as she did before?
A: No.
Q: Who had to take care of Atujuan?
A: Me.
Q: Who gave your Momma the rock?
A: When?
Q: What?
A: When?
Q: At Art's house.
A: He did.
Q: Did you try and get your Momma to stop using rock?
A: Yeah.
Q: How did you do that?

A: Kept telling her quit.

Q: Did you do anything else?

A: Yeah.

Q: What did you do?

A: I ... I tried to break the pipe.

Q: Okay. Did you write a little song about breaking the pipe?

A: Yeah.

Q: Now, when your Momma was with Art, did he ever beat her?

A: Yeah.

Q: How many times can you remember that happening?

A: What I saw, it was two.

Q: Okay, now, let me ask you about one of those times. Do you know where you were last Christmas?

A: Yeah.

Q: Where was that?

A: Over at my Momma's friend's house.

Q: And what is your Momma's friend's name?

A: Iris.

Q: Okay. Where is that house? You know, is it near Art's house? Near your grandmother's house? Where is it near?

A: It was near my cousin's house.

Q: Okay. Is that in Ontario?

A: Yeah.

Q: Now this particular time at Christmas, what did you see Art do to your Momma?

A: He hit her.

Q: With what?

A: A gun.

Q: What kind of gun was that?

A: An automatic pistol.

Q: And what did it look like?

A: It was gray and black.

Q: How many times did you see him hit her? Once? More than once?

A: More than once.
Q: Did she bleed?
A: Yeah.
Q: Where was she bleeding?
A: Right here on her face.
Q: On her face? Did the blood get anywhere besides on her face?
A: Yeah.
Q: Where else?
A: On the couch.
Q: And you saw that?
A: Yeah.
Q: Now, while this was happening, what were you doing?
A: Hollering.
Q: What? Hollering?
A: (Nods)
Q: And what was your Momma doing?
A: Hollering.
Q: You were trying to get Art to stop?
A: Yeah.
Q: Did he stop?
A: Yeah.
Q: What did he do when he stopped?
A: He put the gun in an orange bag.
Q: And then what did he do?
A: We went in the bedroom.
Q: Who is "we"?
A: Huh?
Q: You said, "We went in the bedroom." Who was it that went in the bedroom?
A: Me and my Momma, my brother, and him.
Q: Okay. Then what happened?
A: She got in the bed.
Q: Your Momma did?
A: (Nods)

Q: You have to say "yes" or "no."
A: Yes.
Q: Okay, then what happened?
A: Then he tried to hit her again.
Q: With what?
A: The gun. It was in the orange bag.
Q: Okay. He tried to hit her with the gun inside the orange bag. Is that right?
A: Yeah.
Q: Okay, then what happened?
A: Then he went to go to sleep.
Q: Then what happened?
A: Then I started taking pictures.
Q: What did you take pictures of?
A: Her head.
Q: And why did you take pictures?
A: So we could have some more witnesses.
Q: What do you mean, some more witnesses?
A: What?
Q: You mean so that you could prove that Art had beaten your Momma?
A: (Nods)

MR. BOYD: I object. That's leading the witness and suggesting the answer.
MR. NEGUS: He is nine years old, Your Honor. THE COURT: Overruled. He may answer. BY MR. NEGUS:

Q: You said "yes" to that?
A: (Nods)
Q:: You have to say "yes." Now please look at this Exhibit 65. Do you recognize that picture?
A: Yeah.
Q: What is it?
A: My Momma's head.

Q: And who took that picture?

A: Me.

Q: And there's some red stuff up at the top of your Momma's hair. What's that?

A: Blood.

Q: And was that particular picture taken after Art had pistol-whipped your Momma on that last Christmas?

A: Uh-huh.

MR. NEGUS: Thank you. I have nothing further, Your Honor. THE COURT: Okay, any cross-examination?

BY MR. BOYD:

Q: Emzie, when your Momma took you to live at Art's, where did you stay?

A: I slept downstairs.

Q: Do you know how long that you used to stay at Art's house?

A: Probably about two weeks.

Q: Two weeks? Okay, did your mother use the rock when she was over there?

A: Yeah.

Q: Did you know that that was cocaine?

A: Yeah.

Q: How do you know that?

A: She told me.

Q: Who told you?

A: My Momma.

Q: Your mother did? When did she tell you that?

A: She told me when she was doing it.

Q: She told you when she was doing it like, a long time ago?

A: Uh-huh.

While all this was going on, I was squirming in my seat, thinking, I hate what I did. I can't believe that I really told my son the truth back then, and he remembered everything. Thank you, Lord, for keeping my son safe.

Q: When you were with Art and your Momma, did your mother like Art?
A: Yeah, for a friend.
Q: Okay, did she stay over at Art's house?
A: Yeah.
Q: And did Art come stay with you and your Momma at your house?
A: No.
Q: He never did? He never did that?
A: Uh-uh.
Q: When your Momma and Art were using the pipe, what were you doing?
A: I was downstairs watching TV and getting something to eat.
Q: And you saw them?
A: Yeah.
Q: How many times have you seen them use the pipe?
A: Lots of times.
Q: Lots of times? More than once?
A: Yeah.
Q: More than ten times?
A: Yeah.
Q: Okay. Have they been using the pipe for a long time?
A: Yeah.
Q: Now, did your Momma have other boyfriends other than Art?
A: One.
Q: And what was that person's name?
A: Don Juan.
Q: What?
A: Don Juan.
Q: Okay. Did he come over and stay with your mother?
A: No, because he worked far away.
Q: Far away? Did he come over to your house?
A: Yeah.
Q: Okay. Did they ever use the pipe then?
A: No, he didn't use it.

Q: He didn't use any type of things like that?
A: Uh-uh.
Q: Okay. Now, how about your uncle Peter? Did your uncle Peter come to your house?
A: Yeah.
Q: Did you ever see your mother and Uncle Peter or Uncle Joseph use the pipe?
A: Yeah.
Q: How many times did they use the pipe that you saw?
A: They didn't use it a lot.
Q: Not very much?
A: No.
Q: More than ten times or less than ten times?
A: It was like ten times.
Q: About ten times? Okay. When you saw Uncle Peter and your Momma using the pipe, was Art always there?
A: No.
Q: Okay, so they used the pipe at times when Art wasn't there; is that right?
A: Yeah.
Q: Was that before your Momma knew Art or after your Momma knew Art?
A: After.
Q: I want to ask you questions about the day or the night that Art hit your Momma, okay? Was there an argument? Were they yelling and screaming at each other?
A: No. He was just hitting her.
Q: Okay. Did you see it at the beginning, or were you in another room when you heard some noise?
A: I was in another room sleeping, then I came in.
Q: What woke you up? Do you remember?
A: Momma was hollering.
Q: Do you remember what he was hollering?
A: Who?

Q: Art.

A: No, my Momma was hollering.

Q: Do you remember what she was hollering?

A: She was going "a-a-a-u-h," like she was hurting.

Q: Did you hear any words when they were yelling at each other?

A: Yeah.

Q: Was your mother yelling back?

A: No. She was just hollering.

Q: Do you remember what Art was yelling, the words he was saying?

A: No.

Q: Had you ever seen your mother and Art yelling at each other at other times?

A: No.

Q: Was this the first time you remember Art and your mother having a fight?

A: Yeah.

Q: How many times have you seen Art? More than twenty?

A: Yeah. He came over, and we went over there.

Q: Okay. So you've seen Art a lot of times?

A: (Nods)

Q: Was this the only time that you saw Art and your mother fighting each other?

A: Yeah.

Q: The rest of the time they were together, did they seem to get along okay? Did they go places without fighting?

A: Yeah.

Q: Did you go places with Art?

A: No.

Q: Did he take you and your Momma places? Did you go to dinner, go get something to eat?

A: Yeah, he and she did.

Q: Did you use to go to other places with Art? Visit places or drive around, things like that with him?

A: No, not that I know of.

Q: Now, did somebody talk to you before you came in to court today about what you were going to do in court?
A: No.
Q: Nobody talked to you?
A: No. Just he talked to me.
Q: Who?
A: Him.
Q: Who?
A: Over there.
Q: Mr. Negus?
A: Yeah.
Q: Did he tell you what he was going to ask you?
A: Yeah.
Q: And did he tell you what you were supposed to say. You know, what the answer was supposed to be?
A: No.
Q: Okay, did he tell you to be sure and memorize what you should say so that—
A: Yeah.
Q: —you won't forget? He told you to memorize what you should say in your head?
A: (Nods)
Q: You have to speak out loud.
A: Yeah.
Q: And did he tell you that I would be asking you some questions?
A: No, he just said other people would.
Q: He said other people would be asking you questions?
A: Uh-huh.
Q: Is that right? What did he tell you about the other people asking the questions? What did he say to do?
A: He said tell the truth.

I could feel a bright smile warm up my face listening to my son's words. Thank God truth lives in my child.

Q: To tell the truth, right? And did he ask you anything else that you remember about Art and your Momma?
A: Yeah.
Q: What did he ask you?
A: He asked me what they were fighting about and when.
Q: And you're nine, right?
A: Yeah.

MR. BOYD: I have nothing further, Your Honor.
THE COURT: Okay, Mr. Negus.

REDIRECT EXAMINATION BY MR. NEGUS:
Q: Emzie, do your mother and father live together?
A: No.
Q: And before last year, were you living back in Tulsa?
A: Yeah.
Q: Was that with your mother's mother, your grandmother?
A: With my father's mother.
Q: Right. So you have been out in California for about a year now?
A: Yeah.
Q: And during the time that you have been in California, you say that Art never stayed at your house when you were there?
A: He never stayed.
Q: Did he come to visit?
A: Yeah.
Q: So he would come out there, but he never actually moved in and lived there, is that right?
A: Yeah.
Q: During the time that you have been out in California, have you lived partly with your mother and partly with your father?
A: Yeah.
Q: So the whole time that you have been out in California, you haven't been with your mother, is that right?
A: Yeah, I have been with her part-time.

Q: So you'd stay with your father from time to time?
A: Yeah.
Q: And you lived with your father first in Hollywood and then Colton?
A: Yeah.
Q: And you lived with your mother where? In Ontario?
A: Yeah.
Q: Anyplace else?
A: No.
Q: Now, the person that you said was Atujuan's father, his name is Don Juan?
A: Yeah, something like that.
Q: Do you know what his real name is?
A: Who?
Q: Don Juan. I mean, that's one name. Do you know, though, what his full name is?
A: No.
Q: Just your Momma calls him Don Juan?
A: I don't know what she calls him.
Q: You don't know what she calls him, but you call him Don Juan?
A: Yeah.
Q: How often did you see him?
A: I've never seen him.
Q: Oh, you never met him? Do you know where he was working?
A: Atlanta, Georgia, I think.
Q: Last fall, did your Momma go back and visit him?
A: Yeah.
MR. NEGUS: Thank you. I have nothing further, Your Honor.
MR. BOYD: Nor do I.
THE COURT: Okay, Thank you, Emzie. You may go now.
Thanks for coming. What grade are you in?
THE WITNESS: Fourth.
THE COURT: Fourth grade?

It was very quiet on the way home. I guess everyone was thinking. I broke the silence. "Emzie, Momma is so proud of you." I turned around to look at him in the backseat and gave him the proudest smile a mother could muster up, fighting back the tears for what my son had to go through because of me, my choices, my life, and my needs. I began to see life differently now that my children were subject to the penalty and process I was faced with. After we got in the house, I prepared the children something to eat and put them to bed. Then I knocked on Momma's door. I could feel my insides fighting and churning.

"Can I come in, Momma?"

"Of course, you can, darling. Today was pretty hard for you, wasn't it?"

"Yes, Momma, I just wanted them to stop trying to play with Emzie's mind, trip him up and try to set him up."

"But he's a smart little boy. I hope you saw that."

"Oh, yes, I was impressed."

"You instilled honesty in him, Rose, no matter what choices you made. You demanded honesty at all costs out of your children, and that should count for something in you."

Momma's words were so on time, and they made me feel so much better. I never looked at it like that. I couldn't find anything to give myself credit for on that day because I was too bound by shame and regret to even find a glimmer of good or a glimpse of praise in myself.

"Momma, I'm scared. I need you to pray for me. I need God to keep me because my mind is racing. I don't want to go anywhere, Momma. I want to stay home right here with you and my kids. Please pray for me, please pray and tell God to give me the power to stay home."

Momma pulled me close to her like an infant and held me close to her bosom and began to pray in my ear. Oh, how it felt like refreshing water flowing down my total being. The Spirit of God came over me and His peace saturated my soul. I fell asleep in Momma's arms and lay right there next to her until she nudged me to go get in my own bed.

Chapter 7: Rose Parker's Testimonies

Tuesday, September 30, 1986

THE COURT: All right. Thank you, sir.

THE WITNESS: Thank you.

MR. NEGUS: Rose Ann Parker.

ROSE ANN PARKER, the defendant herein, called as a witness on her own behalf, was examined and testified as follows:

THE CLERK: Please raise your right hand. You do solemnly swear the testimony you are about to give in the matter now pending before this court shall be the truth, the whole truth, and nothing but the truth, so help you God?

THE WITNESS: I do.

THE CLERK: Please be seated. What is your name, and will you spell your name, please?

THE WITNESS: Rose Ann Parker. R O S E A N N P A R K E R.

THE CLERK: Thank you.

DIRECT EXAMINATION

BY MR. NEGUS:

Q: Rose Ann, how old are you?

A: Twenty-seven.

Q: And did—have you followed any particular business or occupation in your life?

A: Yes.

Q: What's that?

A: In the entertainment field.

Q: And what were you doing in the entertainment field?

A: Started out dancing, then modeling, and then when I got older, I started acting.

Q: At some point in time, did you meet Art Boga?

A: Yes, I did.

Q: When was that?

A: In the beginning of '82.

Q: And how did you happen to meet him?
A: Some girlfriends of mine that played bass and guitar wanted him to meet me.
Q: And did you start dating him after a time?
A: Can you repeat the question?
Q: Did you start going out with him after a time?
A: Oh, yeah, after a time.
Q: About how long after you first met him was it that you started going out with him?
A: About a year and a half.
Q: Okay. When you first met him, did you know what he did for a living?
A: Yeah.
Q: What was that?
A: He … it was like he was retired. He was retired. That's what he said, "I'm retired."
Q: Okay. Did you find out that he seemed to have a lot of money? My mind was racing so fast as these questions were coming back to back. I didn't even have time to think, especially with the sharp pains in my stomach.
A: Yeah, he seemed to have a lot of money. He showed it to me when I first met him. And that's why I didn't go over there for a while.
Q: Did you learn how he got that money?
A: Yeah, he …
Q: How?
A: He told me.
Q: How did he get it?
A: He was first a bookie.
Q: Okay, and then what?
A: Then he made his first million with heroin. And then he went on to cocaine.
Q: While you knew him, was he doing cocaine?
A: Uh-huh.

While I sat there, the strangest thought crossed my mind. I wished I knew where some of those millions were now.

Q: And what sort of quantities would he get cocaine in order to deal it?

A: Well, the first quantity he had that I saw right after I first met him was about three keys.

Q: When you say "three keys," does that—what does that mean?

A: Well, I found out what a key was. A kilo.

Q: Okay. A kilogram?

A: Yeah, about that much, something like about this much, packed.

Q: A large amount?

A: Yeah.

Q: And how much was he dealing during the time that you met him? Did he acquire three keys at a time, or did it go down and up, or what?

Here I am on pain killers and all, but I wondered what he was on with all this stuttering and repeating himself. I just wanted this trial to be over and done with.

A: It went down, then it went back up.

Q: Now, at the time that you met Art, had you used drugs?

A: Yeah. I got introduced to them.

Q: Okay. Were you addicted to drugs when you first met him?

A: I wasn't addicted.

Q: Were you like a regular user? Occasional user?

A: Just occasional user, you know, hardly ever. But I did it before.

Q: Now, when you were going out with Art, would he give you cocaine?

A: Yeah.

Q: How much?

A: As much as I wanted.

Q: And did that amount increase as time went on?

A: Yeah.

Q: How much would it increase?

A: Well, I always had—but he—I always had my own personal, like an ounce.

Q: Okay. He would give

A: He'd give an ounce at a time or something like that. He would just give me the ounce, and I could smoke it, I could do what I wanted with it. But then he would say, "How much you got left?" And I'd say, "Eight grams." Then he'd give me another ounce.

Q: So he always just kept you in as much cocaine as you could use?

A: Yeah, in the beginning.

Q: Did that continue throughout your relationship?

A: He always gave me a lot, but it—it decreased from an ounce all the way down to maybe like half an ounce or a quarter, because I didn't know that an ounce was a whole bunch of cocaine, because I didn't ever know. I just—I always thought if you have cocaine you always have a whole bunch.

Q: Okay. You found out later that other people, when they are getting cocaine, are not getting it in ounces and half ounces or a gram.

A: Not for personal use, no. Not when you got to buy it.

Q: Did you become addicted to it?

A: Yeah, because I was used to always having it.

Q: After you became addicted to it, did you get it from Art as well as other people at times?

A: Yeah.

Q: When you became addicted to the cocaine, what effect did that have on you personally?

A: I get—well, it depends. Sometimes I would get nervous. I would get nervous that I was doing something wrong. So I would always look at how it was affecting me, because I looked at the way it affected other people. They get dishonest. And when I'm high, I get honest.

Q: What do you mean by that?

A: Well, if you ask me something, I'm going to tell you, no matter how you feel. I don't care if you get mad or not. If you ask me a question, I'll answer truthfully. If Art asked me something, I'd tell him the truth, whereas most people, they'll tell him what he wanted to hear.

Q: How about your career? What happened to your career after you met Art?

A: I—I wouldn't go to work.

Q: Why is that?

A: Well, a couple of reasons. For a period of time, there wasn't enough time for me to get to work because I would be getting high, period. But when I had enough time to make it to a job and I'd be trying to get ready, and I would be going to use one of his cars, then when it would get time for me to go, he'd say out of the blue that I couldn't use the car, which means I'm gonna be late for work, because he didn't care. He really didn't want me to go to work. He'd say he did, but then he'll just say, "You can't use the car." Then I'd say, "Well, I'll take my car." Then he'd give me some more coke, and then I'll want to do the coke. Then I just won't end up going.

Q: During the time that you knew Art, did he ever brag about how dangerous he was?

A: Yeah, when I first met him—well, not the first time, but the—no, no, the first time, as a matter of fact, the first time.

Q: Okay, now, during the time that you were with Art, at times would you live at his residence?

A: Yeah. I stayed there.

Q: And at times would you live at other places?

A: Yeah.

Q: Dr. Root described an old scar on Art's hip when he was testifying. Did you ever see that scar?

A: Yeah. He didn't have no side. His side was shot off.

Q: And did he tell you how that happened?

A: Yeah. He told me somebody shot him with a shotgun, and he stayed in the hospital for three months. And when he got out, he cut their head off.

Q: He cut off the head of the person that—

A: Yes. They ran around like a chicken with their head cut off. Because I asked him did he do it or did he have somebody else do it. He said he did it himself because they —he said you can't hurt him.

Q: You said Art would brag that nobody could hurt him; is that what you're saying?

A: Yeah, and I believed him. He didn't have no side. If you could see somebody with no side, he didn't have no side. It was shot off. He had to get skin from his legs to put on his side, and he —it still didn't match, equal up to a whole side. But if you don't have no side and you're alive, you know, you know you can't—you can't be hurt. He said he can't be hurt.

Q: When you were with Art with other people, did other people ever, like, threaten him?

A: Nobody—no. He—he used to get beat up—I mean, he used to pistol-whip people, you know. But nobody never, never said nothing back to him. They always—he put them on their knees, make them get on their knees.

Q: And he did that to you, too?

A: Yeah. He used to pistol-whip me and just stand up; I'd be on my knees.

Q: Now, did he ever brag about his friends and how dangerous they were?

A: Yeah, he ...

Q: What did he tell you about that?

A: He said people owed him so much money he could have somebody kill me and wouldn't even have to pay them. They could just clear up their debts, because he used to give away lots of money, and people owed him. Or he would say he can give an addict a gram of cocaine to blow me away. He could do anything he wanted to do, and I knew it, because I knew—I saw him give away money. So I knew people owed him money.

Q: Well, were you afraid of Art's friends?

A: I was afraid of anything, period, that had to do with him.

Q: At the preliminary hearing in this particular case, was there a—did he have a friend named Dr. Lowell Augustine?

A: Yeah.

Q: And how close a friend was Dr. Lowell Augustine to him?

A: He was there about 50 percent of the time we got high, because it was—part of the times would be just me and Art. But when people came over, he was always—not always, but 90 percent of the time there.

Q: Did Dr. Augustine ever, like, threaten, or cover up for Art after he would beat somebody?

A: Yeah.

Q: How did that happen?

A: I mean, like, whatever Art wanted the doctor to say—we called him "Doc"—whatever he wanted him to say, that's what he say, you know. And he was a real doctor, too.

Q: Okay. He would, like, write medical certificates?

A: Yeah, but even like with me, when I'd get sick, if I told Art I was sick and I had to leave, he'll ask Doc, and Doc could be high. And I'd say, "You can't take his word for that. He's high. He don't know if I'm sick or not. He ain't even a female doctor."

Q: Even after Art was dead, were you still afraid of Dr. Augustine?

A: Yeah, because he—oh, yeah.

Q: And has he, like, made any threats to you?

A: Yeah. He went like this to me once in court. I wasn't sure if it was a threat. I asked the bailiff. I told him, "What does this mean?" And he got up, and said, "That means somebody—" and he said, "That's bad." He asked, "Who did that to you?" And I replied, "The guy in the courtroom went like this," and I showed him again. And then—

Q: And that was Dr. Augustine?

A: Yeah.

Q: And that was while you were in court?

A: That is while I was sitting in court when I was pregnant during the preliminary.

Q: How about guns? Did Art have any guns?

A: Yeah.

Q: How many?

A: Off the top of my head, he had about—in his house he had about, oh, I can't say, but he had one everywhere—everywhere you walked, you'd run into a gun.

Q: Okay, what different types of guns did he have?

A: From one this big, if you don't mind me using my hands here, all the way to one this long, the long kind.

Q: Like that one?
A: I'd never seen one, a gun. I said, "What's that?" Looked like something that my Momma has in the house, a what-not, you know, those little decorations. And it was this big, if I can use my hands again to show you. I said, "What's that?" He said, "It's a gun to kill, one bullet."
Q: Okay. And then the big gun, what was that?
A: I don't know. One of those kind you see on The Rifleman.
Q: A semiautomatic type of weapon?
A: Yeah, one of those long ones.
Q: How about other things? Did Art ever show you anything else to try and scare you?
A: He showed me a jar of some ears when I first met him.
Q: What kind of ears?
A: People ears.
Q: Uh-huh.
A: He showed it to me. They were in a jar, and it was ears. Now, I didn't ever open the jar and touch them to see if they were real ears, but I saw it was a glass jar, and it was ears. Like I said, I don't know if they were actually real. But he said they were ears, and if I wanted to open it and check, I could. But his word was good enough that they were ears.
Q: Did Art threaten you, and if so, did he threaten you often?
A: Well, he threatened me every time we saw each other.
Q: Okay. After you first knew him, did he begin beating you more often?
A: You—
Q: Do you understand what I'm asking you?
A: No.
Q: How often would he beat you when you first knew him?
A: When I first met him, he beat me; he hit me all the time.
Q: Okay, then did he stop hitting you for a while?
A: Yeah, he stopped for a while.
Q: And when was that?
A: When he was on probation, when he wasn't doing coke, he just hit me, like, just a little bit.

Q: Okay. He had a probation officer that required him to take drug testing, so he was not using coke as much?

A: Yeah. And plus, I was like, about seven months pregnant with Atujuan. So he didn't hit me no more. When I got—when I got real big, he wouldn't hit me no more.

Q: Did he seem to hit you more when he was really high on coke than when he wasn't?

A: Yeah.

Q: Did he start using coke again all the time at some point in time?

A: Yeah. After—as soon as his probation—the day he went to court and got off probation, he wanted me to meet him right after court so he could get high. But I didn't come until the next day.

Q: And when was that?

A: July 20th, I think, last year.

Q: In '85?

A: Yeah.

Q: At that point in time, did he ever threaten to kill you much before that summer of—?

A: He didn't hardly. He would say, "I'll kill you if you do this or if you do that," but, see, he would threaten me when he ain't mad. But there would be threats, like he'll give me some money and say, "If you spend it, I'll—I'll—I'll crack your skull" or "I'll break your arm," you know. He wouldn't be, like hollering. I mean. He'd just tell me what he'd do if I do that.

Q: After Art got off probation, did things get worse between the two of you? Yeah, because I was going to Alcoholics Anonymous. And I would be at his house, and there was an AA place up the street from where he lived at a church. So he had some cocaine, and I told him I was going to go to the meeting. So after I went to the meeting, when I came back from the meeting, he had everything set up so when I walked in the door, it would be the setting that we put forth when we get ready to go get high. Everything would be all set out so when I walk in, I'd see it and forget everything I just learned.

Q: So were you going to the Alcoholics Anonymous for drinking or for cocaine?
A: For mind-altering drugs. I was so happy that the judge interrupted my testimony at this point to take a break.

THE COURT: All right. We will take a morning recess, 20 minutes. Please keep in mind the admonitions previously given.

First 20-Minute Recess
I couldn't believe the hours that passed by while engaged in so many questions. My head felt like it was a spinning wheel. When the judge finally gave us a recess, I looked over at my mother to beckon her to bring the baby so I could breast-feed him. Momma already had a blanket ready, and she handed me Darian. He was hungry, his little mouth was moving so fast. It was a long day, and my baby was starving for his milk. As I nursed him, my life flashed in front of me.

After the baby was satisfied, I had to give him back to my mother. The courtroom was being vacated, and I was escorted to the back room where the bailiffs and guards had their coffee room/snack shop. I sat down at the grey, round table very quietly. I was still heavily medicated from the pain pills, so I closed my eyes for a few minutes.

Eventually, the bailiff said, "Ms. Parker, are you awake?"

"Yeah, I'm going to rest my eyes; I'm not going to sleep, I'm just resting them." I heard a few of the bailiffs laughing.

The next thing I thought about was during the time I was dancing on Soul Train. The small transistor radio in the corner on the bailiff's desk was playing oldies but goodies. "Ain't No Mountain High Enough" by Diana Ross came on. It sounded so soothing. I was drifting in and out. That record triggered memories of my childhood. I thought back all the way to when my brothers and sisters and I would be in the middle of the room clowning, as we would do every Saturday morning, watching Soul Train. We would have a dance contest with soul train lines right in the middle of Rev. January's living room. That was the most we could do as PKs (preacher's kids). Momma would just watch and laugh at us.

Then I thought about when I was 13 at school and told my classmates that one day I was going to be on Soul Train. Another year passed, and I told them this is the year that I'm going to be on Soul Train. And sure enough, it was the year that the Ohio Players had this bad song called "The Funky Worm." I remembered when my brother Peter and Sai were selected to go on Soul Train. I can still see the smile on Peter's face. He was so happy. I remember being happy for him, but I also wanted to be right there with him, dancing near him.

Return from First Break
The bailiff walked over and startled me when he said, "Parker, it's time to go back in." I jumped. I was seated back on the stand, and the questioning picked right back up from where we left off.

BY MR. NEGUS:

At some point in time, did things get so bad that you decided to move out from Art permanently?

A: Yeah, I, you know, I didn't want to do nothing. I wanted to just get away, I wanted to—

MR. BOYD: I'm going to object.

THE WITNESS: Oh?

THE COURT: She answered the question.

MR. BOYD: It can be answered "yes" or "no."

THE COURT: The answer may stay.

BY MR. NEGUS:

Q: Did you have a place to go?
A: Yeah.
Q: Where was that?
A: To my Momma's at first.
Q: Okay. And that's the house on Bermuda Dunes?
A: Yeah.
Q: Now, at some point in time, did your Momma move out of that house?
A: Yeah.
Q: When was that?
A: It was February; the first of February of '86.
Q: And where did she move after that?
A: To a senior citizen's home, so I couldn't come over.
Q: You couldn't stay there?
A: I couldn't stay all night.
Q: Because of your kids?
A: Yeah.
Q: At some point in time in the fall of '85, did you go back East?
A: Yeah.
Q: What was the purpose of that trip?
A: I wanted to be with Don Juan. Don Juan is Donald Douroux.
Q: Okay. And how long had you known him?
A: Don Juan?
Q: Yeah.
A: A couple of years. No, about a year and a half, something like that. I had my little boy, who was a year and a half, so I had known him, I guess, about three years.
Q: Okay. So he is the father of Atujuan?

A: Well, I have two. He is the father of Atujuan and Darian, my two little babies.

Q: Okay. Darian is the baby that was born this month?

A: Three weeks ago.

Q: Now, when you went back in November, was that when you became pregnant with—?

A: Yeah, when I got back, I found out I was pregnant.

Q: In December of 1985 at Christmas time, where were you living?

A: Over at Iris's.

Q: Okay. And on Christmas Day, did Art come over?

A: Yep.

Q: Was he mad?

A: He was hot. He was—he was—mad ain't the word, but you can say mad.

Q: What was he mad about?

A: Because I didn't come over.

Q: And even after you had moved out of his house, did he keep in contact with you?

A: Yeah. I mean, it's like he tells me he would call me and says, "Don't go nowhere," or he'd get me, so if I wanted to go somewhere, I had to call, make sure he was at home so I could go out the door, because he—he—I can—sometimes I come outside and he's right there at the door.

Q: At your place, wherever you were living in Ontario?

A: Yeah.

Q: And did he require that you call him all the time?

A: Yeah.

Q: Why was that?

A: So he would know I'm not out doing something stupid. That's what he said—that I'd go and do stupid stuff.

Q: How many times a day would you have to call him sometimes?

A: It varied.

Q: Depending upon what his mood was?

A: Yeah, well, he called me, and I had to call him back or he would get mad.

Q: Now, at Christmas of '85, when he was mad at you, what did he do to you?

A: He walked in the door and asked where I was. I said I was asleep. And then he just said, "You should have come to me." He was pulling his gun out right when he first came in the door. And he just started—he just started hitting me, just right when he walked in he started hitting me on my head. He just kept hitting me and hitting me and hitting me. And I kept backing up. Then I fell on the couch. I was just lying on the couch, screaming because I wanted my little boy to run out. I wanted my kids to run out because I didn't know what he was going to do. And Emzie, he got scared so he just—you know, I couldn't see. Blood started falling in my hands, it was just everywhere. And I—he just kept hitting me.

MR. BOYD: I object to the narrative answer. The answer is—
THE WITNESS: It was emotional.
THE COURT: Overruled.

MR. NEGUS: Well, after he did that, did you, like, fight back at him?

A: I never fought back with him, ever.
Q: Why not?
A: Because I might hurt him. And if I hurt him, then—you know, you just don't do it.
Q: Is that because you were afraid of him?
MR. BOYD: I object. That's suggesting the answer.
THE WITNESS: You just don't do nothing to make him mad.
THE COURT: Overruled. The answer may stay.

Q: After that incident at Christmas, how many times did you go back to his place after that?
A: I went over there one time just a few days. I went for one day, but I didn't get a chance to leave. So it took three days.
Q: During that period of time, well, by Christmas, did you know that you were pregnant?

A: I knew.

Q: Okay. When did you go to the doctor?

A: I went to the doctor when I first came back from Georgia.

Q: At that point, did you desire to give up using cocaine?

A: Yeah.

Q: Were you able to do it?

A: Well, not totally.

Q: Would you get cocaine from Art?

A: A little bit.

Q: Did you also get cocaine from people in this area?

A: Yeah.

Q: Have you quit now?

A: Yeah.

Q: And when were you able to do that?

A: When I—when I was in jail.

Q: You were in custody for ...?

A: Five months.

Q: ... five months? During the time that you were staying in

Ontario, well, I mean, did you have arguments, like with your folks, about your using cocaine?

A: Yeah.

Q: Were they upset with you for that?

A: Yeah.

Q: And that's one of the reasons why they moved out of the house and went to their—?

A: That was one of the reasons.

Q: After Christmas, did Art still keep trying to check up on you?

A: Yeah.

Q: Still call you?

A: Yeah.

Q: Would he still come out to see you?

A: Yeah.

Q: When he would come out to see you, how long would he normally stay?

A: He would come stay overnight. Well, we'd go to a hotel.

Q: Okay. Here in the Ontario area?

A: Uh-huh.

Q: And just for one night, usually?

A: Basically. Or half a night.

Q: Did you still love Art at that time?

A: I cared a lot about him, but I know that I—I—I love everybody, you know? I have, like, a love for everybody.

Q: Okay. Did you want to break off your relationship with him?

A: Yeah.

Q: Why is that?

A: Because it was too spooky.

MR. NEGUS: Your Honor, I have to get some exhibits marked. Perhaps this would be a good time for a break.

Break for Morning Recess

THE COURT: All right. We will take a morning recess, 15 minutes. Please keep in mind the admonition. I was escorted to the back again and, boy, was I ready to get out of that courtroom. I sat back in the same place I was earlier when I nursed my son.

What was going to happen to my life now, I kept wondering. What went wrong? Where did I miss it? I know I made so many bad choices. They landed me right where I was sitting now, no longer with choices at my disposal and without freedom as my gift. All that jeopardized for what?

The many times Art would beat me flashed through my mind. I wanted to turn the images off, but they kept surfacing. I saw Art kicking me on the floor in the kitchen and his friends were in the other room listening to him humiliate me. I remember hitting my head on the kitchen table as he knocked me down. Oh, the memories hurt to even think about. Part of me was so glad that I was on drugs because I didn't feel the bulk of the pain until the next day. I could still feel the aches, see the knots on my head, and the discolored bruises on my body with blood stains still on my clothes from wherever the injury was that time. I don't know why I stayed with a man that started beating me as a sport. It was all so subtle, and before I knew it, that was part of my life just as routine as waking up and washing my face.

Sadness and nausea overwhelmed me while I sat back and waited for time to pass. I was so happy Momma and Dad were there. They made me feel so safe and loved.

I didn't realize tears were rolling down my face. My thoughts went deep and dark. I was glad that the bailiff nudged me and said it was time to go back into the court.

Chapter 8: Return From Morning Recess

THE COURT: Okay, Mr. Negus.
BY MR. NEGUS:

Q: When you became pregnant with Darian, did you request aid from the County for medical treatment for your pregnancy?
A: Yeah.
Q: When you did that, does the County of San Bernardino require that you name the father of the child as part of the paperwork you have to do to get the aid?
A: Yes, it's a requirement.
Q: And did you name Donald Anthony Douroux as the father of what was going to be Darian?
A: Yes, I did.
Q: Now, when you had Atujuan, did Art know that he was not the father of Atujuan?
A: Well, he—when he was born, he said he accepted it. He—
Q: Okay.
A: He—kind of would think he was but I kept telling him he wasn't.
Q: After Atujuan was born, did you become pregnant by Art?
A: Yeah.
Q: Did you have that baby?
A: Uh-uh. I got an abortion.
Q: How did Art react to that?
A: He'd kind of act different ways at different times. He was kind of hurt, but he tried to act like he wasn't. But he was hurt. And then he just said, well, the time wasn't right. It was too soon. So he says okay, because it's too soon, because I told him I can't take care of two little babies. He said I didn't have to take care of them, he'd have a governess. But I told him I don't want to pay somebody to love my kid. I love them myself.
Q: Now, when you were living in Ontario separate from Art, were you introduced to a man by the name of Barry Pop off?
A: Yes, I was.

Q: Who introduced you to him?

A: Skip—Skip and Dorothy, both of them. Skip and Dorothy.

Q: Did you go out with him?

A: Yeah.

Q: How many times?

A: Twice, just went over his house.

Q: And did he have anything to do with cocaine?

A: Yeah.

Q: What was that?

A: He sold it.

Q: Was he a big dealer, as Art was?

A: No.

Q: When you went over to his house, did Art find out about it?

A: Yeah.

Q: How?

A: Told him.

Q: And why did you tell him?

A: Because I knew that—He kept asking me where I was. And I knew if I didn't tell him, all he had to do was call and tell somebody—he'd give them some coke to tell him where I was and they would tell him. So I always just told him the truth, because I knew he would find out.

Q: Did Barry give you one of his cards?

A: Yeah.

Q: Here is Exhibit 72. Is that one of the cards? He gave you more than one, is that right?

A: Yes, he did.

Q: Is that one of those?

A: Yes, it is.

Q: And at the time that you were arrested, where would you have left that card?

A: In my room.

Q: At 1113 Bermuda Dunes?

A: Yeah. Yeah. On Bermuda Dunes, yeah, correct.

Q: Now, the week that Art got shot, what day of the week was it that he came over?

A: Sunday, early afternoon.

Q: And what happened when he came over?

A: He had a bunch—he had 64 grams of coke.

Q: Is that a lot?

A: Yeah.

Q: And did he have any money with him?

A: Yeah.

Q: Was it a big amount or small amount or what?

A: I don't know exactly, but he normally had at least $5,000. But I think he had less because he had all that coke. So he probably had at least about three or four, something like that. At least, you know, he don't—he always had a lot of money with him.

Q: Now, was he spending money that week?

A: Yeah, making a little bit and spending a lot.

Q: When did Art find out about Barry?

A: Once—early March.

Q: Okay. It was before he came over on—?

A: Yeah.

Q: —that Sunday before he got shot?

A: Uh-huh.

Q: When he came over on that Sunday, was he upset about Barry?

A: Well, we'd gone over to Skip and Dorothy's house.

Q: What was he saying about that?

A: Because Skip and Dorothy were saying that Barry had a lot of coke, Art kind of gets mad if somebody had more than him.

Q: So, well, what do you mean? Why he was mad about that?

A: Yeah, because he didn't want nobody to have nothing more than him.

Q: Well, while were you at Dorothy and Skip's, did Art threaten you?

A: Yeah.

Q: And did he point a gun at you?

A: Yeah.

Q: And was he paranoid about you and strip search you, looking for cocaine?
A: Yeah.
Q: Did you leave him at that point?
A: Leave him?
Q: Right. Did you try and get away from him?
A: You can't do it. He—because every time I go in the kitchen,he comes down to the door and sees where I'm going.
Q: So you just can't get away from him?
A: No. He said a bullet is fast.
Q: Did you get in contact with Barry that week?
A: Yeah.
Q: How did that happen?
A: Art told me to call him, tell him to come over.
Q: And did you?
A: Yeah.
Q: How long was Barry over there?
A: Let's see, from two in the afternoon until nine at night.
Q: And what happened while he was over there?
A: They got high a little bit, talked a little bit, talked about me, and then Art wanted to show Barry that he got a whole bunch of coke and wanted to be the one ahead. So the only way he can be the one ahead is for him to be the one that gives Barry some coke.
Q: And did he do that?
A: Yeah.
Q: Well, were you there when that happened?
A: Not when the actual transaction was made. I was mad, so I went out to him, because I kept telling him not to do it.
Q: Why did you tell him not to do it?
A: Because I knew Barry was going to smoke it.
Q: So Art was, like, giving it to him to smoke?
A: Yeah, he gave it to him, because, see, Art knew better than I did Barry was going to smoke it up, because Barry smokes a lot of cocaine. Seven grams ain't nothing to smoke if you're a smoker.

Q: Well, why didn't you want Art to give Barry that cocaine?

A: Because he was going to smoke it, and then—

Q: So what? So what difference does it make if he smokes it?

A: That means—he charged—told him to pay $700. And Barry wasn't going to pay if he smoked it. And then Art was going to get mad, just another reason to get mad at me. He didn't care about the cocaine.

Q: Why did you feel that Art was going to get mad at you if Barry smoked the cocaine?

A: He just—just—he just do. Whatever happens, he finds some way to get mad at me so he could talk about all the stuff I do and say, "You mess around with no-good people, and they ain't nothing, and you don't deserve to live," and all that kind of stuff. "They can't even pay their debts." You know, stuff like that.

Q: On the videotape that you did with Sergeant John Johnson right after the shooting, you made a statement to the effect that Barry could supply your habit, therefore, he was a threat to Art—some words to that effect. What did you mean by that?

A: Because he didn't want me to take cocaine from nobody but him. And then one thing he felt comfortable with, that I had to have a lot. I—It's not that I had to smoke a lot. If I know that there was a lot there, that if I wanted to have a lot, I could. And Barry would smoke a lot. Barry, he wouldn't get high unless he had a whole bunch either. So therefore, Art knew that if I didn't want to be bothered with him, then I could call Barry if I wanted to.

Q: Did Art stay longer than normal?

A: Yeah.

Q: When would you normally expect him to leave?

A: I expected him to leave Sunday night. He had a little girl who had to go to school in the morning.

Q: What happened with her?

A: He said, "The governess will take care of her." That's what he pays her to do.

Q: How much coke did you use that week?

A: I don't know, about half an ounce, I guess, maybe, something like that. I don't know.

Q: Was that a lot for you or a little or what?

A: Well, actually it would have been normal, the amount that I take in a day, but I didn't. He wouldn't let me go to sleep. I mean, I had to pass out in order to fall asleep. I—my body gave out, and I just passed out.

Q: When was that?

A: On Wednesday, early Wednesday morning.

Q: You mean he would just keep you up?

A: Yeah, and take a Valium or try to make me just pass out, because I would have to just—see, you can pass out if you been up too long. You just fall asleep and pass out.

Q: So how many times were you able to pass out from Sunday until Thursday?

A: Twice.

Q: What days were those?

A: Wednesday I passed out, and he woke me up to eat. My mother and others came over there, and I guess they knew I hadn't had nothing to eat. And being pregnant, they wanted to make sure I ate. So he gave them some money to go get me some food. And they brought it back, so they woke me up to eat it. So I knew after I ate would be the perfect time to take another hit. But then I knew if I took that one hit, I'm going to want some more, so I went back to sleep.

Q: Okay. So just Wednesday was the only time that you got any sleep?

A: Yeah.

Q: Were you up all Wednesday night?

A: Yeah. I got up, I woke up at four, went back to sleep about five, 4:30 or five, and I woke back up at eight o'clock.

Q: So you were asleep then from eight o'clock Wednesday evening until—?

A: I was up from eight o'clock Wednesday evening until I passed out in jail.

Q: That was after you had done the videotape after the—

A: Right.

Q: Now, when you take coke, does that keep you awake?

A: Yeah, for a period of time, because—it depends on how long you been up.

Q: Okay. But normally it will keep you awake until you go so long that you pass out?

A: Right.

Q: When the coke starts to wear off, then what happens?

A: Depends. When the coke wears off, you go to sleep or you want to get more.

Q: So either you get more or you start getting sleepy?

A: Yeah.

Q: Here is Exhibit 73. Can you explain what that document is?

A: It's the letter from the District Attorney's Office that I was supposed to fill out. It's a questionnaire about the baby's dad that came when the mail came Thursday about one or 1:30.

Q: That was a letter from the District Attorney wanting you to tell him how to locate the unborn baby's father?

A: Yeah, right, for child support.

Q: Now, when the mail came, did Art see that letter?

A: Yeah. I said, "Oh, no." And I wouldn't open it. And he told me, "Well, what is it?" you know, "Open it." And then I opened it.

Q: Okay. And that indicated that that the District Attorney already knew that Donald Douroux was the father of—

A: Yeah.

Q: –Darian? Now, did Art say anything that showed that he was jealous?

A: No. He was just mad. Well, I guess that resulted from jealousy, because I didn't have the baby that he wanted me to have and I was gonna have this one. And he said that Atujuan was still too little for me to have another baby, so why I going to have this baby and not the other one?

Q: So he was mad that you were having Mr. Douroux's baby and not having his?

A: Yeah, because he said he wasn't nothing; he didn't have any money like him; he can't buy everything I wanted. But I told Art I don't want everything.

Q: Did Art know that you were going to Georgia in November?

A: He knew where I was. I called him from a pay phone, and he knew because he'd say, "Where you at? In Georgia?" He knew where I was.

Q: Did he know that Mr. Douroux lives in Georgia?

A: Yeah.

Q: Now, did you receive a phone call from your mother sometime on Thursday?

A: Yeah.

Q: Did she tell you that you could come over to her house?

A: Yeah.

Q: What did she tell you about that?

A: She said she got a strange feeling that stuff wasn't gonna be right. She said to clean up my room because I don't keep my room too neat, clean up my room and bring the baby over. She let us spend the night because she said she just had a funny feeling something wasn't right.

Q: Okay. So this was not a place you normally could go, right?

A: No. She never said we could come over and spend the night. You know, it was a senior citizens' place.

Q: Okay. Did you want to do that?

A: Yeah. I wanted to go over there.

Q: Why?

A: Because I knew, you know, my daddy was there, and I felt safe with my daddy.

Q: Now, did you feel that you could just tell Art, "Hey, I'm gonna go over to stay with my Momma?"

A: Oh, you don't know him. You don't tell him that, because he wants to know that you're scared of him. You don't tell him that you want anything other than something that has to do with doing it with him, whatever you want to do. I didn't want to do it with him.

Q: At some point in time, did you say that you wanted to go out to eat?

A: Yeah.

~ 129 ~

Q: Did you really want to go out to eat?

A: I was hungry. But I wanted to go over to my Momma's house.

Q: What did Art say to that?

A: He wanted me to have something in my stomach because he kind of, you know, cared about my system sometimes. It depends, but earlier it was okay. He said it was okay until every time it looked like I'm really trying to leave, then he kind of gives me some more stuff, and I just stay there smoking.

Q: Okay, at some point, did you actually attempt to leave?

A: Yeah, because I knew it was getting close to the time when he was going to do what he said he was going to do, and it was getting too close, and—I knew that I had—that it was time for me to make my move to get out of the house.

Q: What do you mean, the time he's going to do the thing he said he was going to do?

A: He told me he was gonna do something to me. And it was getting close to when he said. So I knew it was time. It was time for me to go because it was getting dark.

Q: When you said that he was going to do something to you, what did you think that meant?

A: Well, he said he was going to kill me. And it was okay at first. I—I was going to just die, because he told me why I had to die, and it made sense to me. I was high. I didn't care. I didn't take care of my kids good, I was pregnant, smoking cocaine, and my baby was in danger in my stomach, and I shouldn't be alive. So he convinced me. Then when I realized that I did love my kids and I didn't want to do all that, then I didn't want to be getting high. So then I decided that I didn't want to die, so I decided I would just go ahead and try to sneak out of the house.

Q: Did you get out?

A: Well, when the police took me out.

Q: But before that?

A: No. At this time, tears ran down my face without me knowing it. It felt like my body was crying. I was tired. I was in pain. And I was confused.

BY MR. BOYD:

Q: Now, why did you say that Art was going to kill you? For what reason was Art going to kill you?

A: Well, a whole bunch of 'em. He just wanted me dead.

Q: Okay. Why did he want you dead?

A: Because—it wasn't nothing that happened. He just wanted me dead. He didn't want me alive no more. I had to die. And I didn't think it was fair.

Q: Okay. Let me see if I understand this right. Art still lived in Woodland Hills, right?

A: Yeah.

Q: And he would drive out to see you every week or two to spend money on you and your kids and your family, right? But he wanted you dead; is that what you are saying?

A: That's what you just said.

Q: This is what I'm asking you. Is that what you're saying?

A: You got to say it over, because I got—see, I—I can't have nothing twisted. I got to make sure what I'm saying is what I know and what I'm saying and not the way you put it.

Q: Okay. Well, he bought you and your kids and your dad gifts when he was out here. He drove all the way from Woodland Hills to spend time with you every week, week and a half, right? Before you got—

MR. NEGUS: Objection. This—

BY MR. BOYD:

Q: —before he got—

A: All that ain't just perfectly right.

MR. NEGUS: Just a second. Can I get to my objection? I object to this line of questioning as argumentative and being defined as a lawyer trying to get a witness to agree with his version of the facts. And I think it's also been asked and answered.

THE COURT: Well—

MR. NEGUS: It's cross.

THE COURT: Not what it's—it is cross-examination. It's going to motivation. Overruled.

THE WITNESS: No. I'm going to say no, because it's got to be, if you're going to word it with all those things in it, it's got to be exactly so. No, that's not the way how—whatever you said, that ain't just right, no.

BY MR. BOYD:
Q: Can you think of a reason today why Art wanted to kill you?
MR. NEGUS: Objection. That calls for speculation on her part. All she can say is what he told her.
MR. BOYD: She has already testified on direct. I think I am entitled to ask the same thing on cross.
THE COURT: Overruled. She can answer.

Q: Why did Art want to kill you?
A: Lot of reasons, okay.
Q: Can you come up with a couple?
A: Yeah.
Q: Well?
A: I was pregnant, and I was having somebody else's baby, not his, and I killed his, so I—I mean, that's part of him. I should die. There wasn't no future. Nothing. You know, I didn't want—I didn't want my kids' father—stepfather—being a drug dealer. And because he thought I messed around on him and he told me not to, he told me not to see nobody if he was givin' me money, I couldn't see nobody. And if I do, he was going to do this and that to me so—and I did I, so therefore—
Q: Okay. Can you think of any other reason Art wanted you dead in addition to those three? How about this one, the one you told Officer Tejas, "Barry's the guy he gave the stuff to—to have a reason to kill me"?
A: Yeah, so that was just to make it all come out. He wanted me dead. Hopefully he wouldn't argue about all those things and then—but if he started getting mad again he—When he gets mad, he brings up things you did to make him mad four years ago. He'll tell me now, "You got pregnant with Atujuan, by somebody." And that was three years ago. He'll start talking about something that happened before. And I didn't want him to do that.

Q: When you were talking with Officer Tejas about what happened that night, you didn't tell Officer Tejas that the reason Art wanted to kill you was because you were pregnant with someone else's baby, did you?

A: I told him all of that.

Q: You did?

A: Told him a whole bunch of stuff.

Q: Has Mr. Negus shown you a transcript of the tape?

A: He did. But when the police and I talked, one of them would say something else. He just didn't let me finish. Every time I would tell him something, he would say something else and then my baby would cry, and then they made me think I'm going to get to hold him, but I ain't going to get to hold him unless I answer their questions and stuff like that. And

my baby was crying. And I just said whatever they wanted me to answer fast, so I can see what was going on with my son. He didn't have any shirt on.

Q: You talked with Officer Tejas until after midnight at the hospital, didn't you?

A: Right. And I told him a whole bunch of stuff, and then he didn't write any of it down.

Q: Did you go over everything that had happened and why it happened between ten and twenty times that night with Officer Tejas?

A: I don't—didn't do all that because every time I'd fall asleep, he'd wake me up and say something. I don't know what he said because I fell asleep, and he'd wake me up.

Q: Were you here when he testified that he went back?

A: I was here when he testified, but he didn't just say everything that exactly was true.

Q: Do you recall him saying that he went over this thing with you, like, between ten and twenty times? Do you?

A: Well, if he did, I was asleep. I dozed off. I had a Valium, I was high. I'd sleep, wake up, and sleep again.

Q: Do you recall telling Officer Tejas that night at the hospital that you didn't know who the father of your unborn child was?

A: No, I didn't—I didn't—I didn't tell that I knew who I was pregnant by.

Q: Okay. Are you saying you don't recall, or are you saying you did not tell him that?

A: I'm saying I don't recall.

Q: You don't recall if you told him or not?

A: I don't think I told him that, but I'll just say I don't recall, since I was high.

Q: When he testified that you told him that you didn't know who the father of the child was, do you have any reason for believing his testimony was not truthful?

MR. NEGUS: Objection. He testified to contradictory things, actually.

THE COURT: I will sustain it under 352.

Q: Now, did you ever tell Officer Tejas that Art wanted to kill you because you had an abortion?

A: Don't remember saying that.

Q: Did you ever tell Officer Tejas that Art wanted to kill you because he thought you were messing around with somebody?

A: Yeah. I—that—I probably said that.

Q: Well, do you recall or not? You don't recall or you do recall?

A: That means I got to think. Let me see. Yeah, I—I know I said—I had to say that.

Q: Now, the night that you were at the house, your two brothers, Peter and Joseph, were with you, weren't they?

A: They were there.

Q: Yes?

A: Just like Art.

Q: And you told Mr. Negus that your brothers weren't going to protect you.

A: I didn't—

Q: Is that right?

A: Yeah.

Q: Why wouldn't your brothers protect you if someone was going to harm to you?

A: Because they—
MR. NEGUS: Objection. That calls for speculation on her part as to why she knew.
MR. BOYD: She gave it as an opinion this morning.
THE COURT: I think she can say why she felt they weren't going to protect her.

Q: Why did you feel your two brothers weren't going to protect you if someone was going to hurt you?
A: Because they were high, and Art convinced them that I was bad. He used to always convince them that I'd do stupid stuff and I needed my ass kicked and all this stuff. And they didn't ever do nothing about it, so I knew that I'd probably just end up being dead and they probably still all be high and I be just laying there.
Q: Now, the night of the shooting, you and Art and Peter and Joseph were freebasing cocaine; is that right?
A: Yeah.
Q: And then Peter started hitting Art, is that right? And how many times did Peter hit Art?
A: I don't know.
Q: More than five?
A: I don't know.
Q: Where were you when Peter was hitting Art?
A: On the—looking for the gun.
Q: I'm sorry?
A: Looking for the gun after he hit him.
Q: After Peter started hitting Art, you went looking for the gun?
A: After Peter hit Art.
Q: "Hit" meaning once?
A: After he made the first strike.
Q: So after Peter hit the first time, you went and started looking for the gun, is that right?
A: Yep.
Q: I'm sorry?

A: Yes, sir.

Q: Who was the one yelling, "You're dead, you're dead"?

A: Peter was talking to himself.

Q: I'm sorry?

A: Peter was talking to himself.

Q: Peter was yelling "you're dead, you're dead" to himself?

A: Yeah, make sure he can hear himself real good.

Q: Now, before you pulled this gun and shot Art, he wasn't coming at you, was he?

A: Before what?

Q: Before you pulled the gun and shot Art, he wasn't coming at you, was he?

A: He didn't have a gun on me, no.

Q: He wasn't coming at you, either, was he?

A: Yeah, he was coming at me.

Q: I thought you said Peter was hitting him.

A: Look, he comes at you in a psychological way. You don't know Art, okay? You don't know him, and you don't know how smart he is.

Q: So it's your testimony that you shot him because he was coming at you psychologically rather than—

A: He was getting—No, not just like psychological, because when Peter hit him, I knew, plus he had a little bitty gun somewhere. I don't know where it was. And when you hit him, that makes him mad enough to just—that's it. I'm surprised I'm sitting here now, anyway.

Q: He didn't come at you, but you shot him anyway?

A: He didn't have a gun on me.

Q: He didn't even come at you without a gun, did he?

A: He wasn't standing over me like that, no.

Q: Wasn't Peter hitting him before you shot him?

A: Yeah, he hit him when I grabbed the gun, so I guess by the time the bullet went off, he probably hit him a couple three more times.

Q: You think Peter hit him a couple times after you shot Art?

A: I—I can't actually say, because I have to be exact, and I—I'm not exact.

Q: Well, this morning, didn't you tell us that after you fired the gun that Peter thought it hit him because it grazed him, so Peter was running out of the room?

A: No, I said after I fired the shot, Art ran.

Q: And what did Peter do?

A: Ran after him.

Q: So Peter ran after him, and Peter didn't hit him anymore in the room, did he?

A: Peter caught him at the stairs. I couldn't see exactly what they were doing.

Q: Did you get a chance to see Art run out?

A: Run out?

Q: Out of the bedroom?

A: Yeah, but all that is like in a strange place in my head.

Q: I'm sorry?

A: Nothing.

Q: By the way, when Art went out of that room after he had been shot, did you see him fly sideways in the banister?

A: I can't remember.

Q: Who is the one that made the statement to you, "Rose Ann, how could you have done this?" Who said that?

A: JoJo said that.

Q: And did he say that after you shot Art the first time?

A: Yep.

Q: I'm sorry?

A: Yes.

Q: Rose Ann, did JoJo make the statement to you while you were in the bedroom, "Rose, get the gun and him"? Did he make that statement?

A: No, I don't think so.

Q: I'm sorry?

A: No, I don't recall.

Q: Do you know of any reason why he would have told the police—

MR. NEGUS: Objection, Your Honor. Counsel is engaging in misconduct.

THE COURT: Sustained.

Q: After you shot Art the first time and he ran downstairs, you yelled at Peter to get him, right?

A: Yeah.

Q: Okay, you kept yelling, "He's not dead!" is that correct?

A: That's what I heard I said.

Q: I'm sorry?

A: I don't recall it, but I heard myself say it. So either they said I said it or I heard me say it. I don't remember saying it.

Q: Is your memory a little unclear today as to what happened that night?

A: Oh, it's unclear of every little tiny detail. I remember a lot of it real clear. But every little detail in my mind I can't—you know, it plays tricks on me a little bit. Not the way you suggest, but I can't remember every— See, when I talk, I have to be totally honest about things. If you ask me, I have to answer perfectly honest. And if I don't remember one little thing, I can't say it, because it won't be exactly true.

Q: You told Mr. Negus earlier this morning, didn't you, that when you used cocaine, it caused you to talk a lot, is that right?

A: Yeah. And I talk too much.

Q: I'm sorry?

A: I said "And I talk too much." I talk more when I'm high. I talk a lot now. I go on and on. When I'm high, I go on and on and on and on and on; I never stop.

Q: Does the cocaine loosen up you inhibitions so that you ...?

A: If I feel high, I want everybody just to talk and feel free. That's what it used to make me do. That's why I used to like it.

Q: When you use cocaine, does it make you lose your inhibitions?

A: What's an inhibition?

Q: Well, if I thought something bad about, say, the judge or something, and am not under the influence of anything or I haven't been using anything, I probably wouldn't say it. But if I had been drinking too much or something, I might say whatever is on my mind. Is that the way you are when you have been using cocaine? You just let your mind go and you tell people what you really think?

A: No. If you asked me, "Do you really want me to tell you?" I won't just openly say anything. I ain't crazy. Somebody might hurt me. I don't get hurt being high.

Q: You just don't make up stuff?

A: Oh, no.

Q: Okay, what you told the officer that night, that was true, wasn't it?

A: Basically.

Q: Well, what part of it wasn't true that you can think of?

A: I—I can't think of—Let me just wait because I want to make sure I tell the truth, so I got to make certain what part wasn't true. When I said, "If I get the chance," I don't remember saying that part.

Q: The part about telling Art in December if you got the chance you were going to shoot him between the eyes—that part wasn't true?

A: I don't know that. I didn't say if I got the chance, you know. I'll just be quiet. I talk a lot.

Q: Is there anything else you can think of you told the officers that night that wasn't true?

A: That's all I can think of right now. I'll just leave it like that.

Q: Do you recall telling Detective Johnson on the videotape, "I told him a long time ago I wanted to shoot him between the eyes"? Do you recall telling the detective that when they had the camera on you?

A: Something like that.

Q: You recall telling the detective when the camera was on you, "I wanted him to be dead in the head"?

A: I didn't say that.

Q: Okay. Do you recall telling Detective Johnson on the videotape, "I was going to kill him, and I can take responsibility for what I do"?

A: I don't remember saying that exactly like that, either.

MR. NEGUS: Objection. That misstates it.

THE COURT: She states—

THE WITNESS: That's a misstatement. That's not exactly correct. That's turned another kind of way.

THE COURT: Strike the comment of the witness.

MR. NEGUS: I believe the statement was—

THE COURT: I'm not sure what the statement was.

THE WITNESS: That is not it.

THE COURT: She gave an answer.

BY MR. BOYD:
Q: Do you recall telling Detective Johnson on the videotape, "He was going to kill me, but he didn't tell me when"?
A: I said that.
Q: Okay, you did say that, right? You recall that?
A: Yeah, I remember that one.
Q: So on March 27, when you killed Art, he hadn't told you when he was going to kill you, did he?
A: He didn't tell me exactly what time.
Q: He didn't tell you what day, either, did he?
A: No, he told me that day. I knew the day. It was getting dark. I knew he was ready to.
Q: So when he offered you the keys to the Excalibur because you wanted to go out and get something to eat ...
A: That was a perfect time.
Q: You responded by saying you didn't want to take his car because it was too flashy, right?
A: Yeah.

Q: Why didn't you just take the keys to the Excalibur and drive away if you thought he was going to do some harm to you?

A: Do you think it was like you just do that?

Q: Well, he offered you the keys, and you said you were going to go get something to eat. Also, he was going to stay there and do more dope. If you really felt he was going to do harm to you and that he was going to kill you that day, why didn't you just take the keys, drive away, drive anywhere, including the police station?

A: You don't—you don't do that. And I would have got up, I wouldn't—you just don't understand.

Q: Didn't you tell Mr. Negus this morning you were trying to get out of the house?

A: Yep.

Q: Wouldn't that have been the perfect opportunity, when he gave you the keys to the car?

A: No. Not his car.

Q: Was his car running? I mean, did it work? Could you have driven away in his car?

A: I don't know. I doubt it.

Q: You knew where Peter had the gun in the house, didn't you?

A: Yeah. I knew. I moved the stuff out of the way. I went where I thought it was.

Q: And after you shot Art the first time and he ran downstairs, you told Peter to get him because he was still alive, then you went downstairs, didn't you?

A: Yeah.

Q: Then you went back upstairs to get Art's gun, because JoJo had taken Peter's gun away from you, right?

A: Yes.

Q: And you knew where Art's gun was because you went and took it out of his bag, right?

A: Yes.

Q: Then you ran back downstairs with Art's gun and you tried to shoot him between the eyes, didn't you?

A: No.
Q: You didn't try to shoot him between the eyes?
A: Uh-uh. If I wanted to shoot him between the eyes, I could have. He was right there.
Q: Didn't you aim to try to shoot him between the eyes?
A: Uh-uh. If I would have, I would have shot him between the eyes. I wanted to be mad enough to shoot him between the eyes. I tried to get mad to shoot him between the eyes, but I just shot him behind his head.
Q: Do you recall talking with Officer Tejas and being asked the question—
MR. NEGUS: What page are you on, counsel?
MR. BOYD: Five.

BY MR. BOYD:
Q: Do you know where the bullets hit? Do you recall saying this statement: "I'm not one hundred percent positive. I think one hit him at first in his back. And I tried to shoot him between the eyes."
A: Yes, I do.
Q: So you did try to shoot him between the eyes the second time, didn't you?
A: Not aim-wise.
Q: What did you mean when you told Officer Tejas, "I tried to shoot him between the eyes"?

MR. NEGUS: Objection. Counsel has not read the complete sentence. Perhaps—
MR. BOYD: It goes on and says, "But I'm—"
THE COURT: Overruled.
MR. BOYD: "I shot him behind the head."
MR. NEGUS: You left out part.
MR. BOYD: It says "Can't understand."
MR. NEGUS: That's what the transcript says, not what the tape says.
THE COURT: Well, overruled. She can answer.

BY MR. BOYD:

Q: What did you mean when you told Officer Tejas, "I tried to shoot him between the eyes"?

A: Oh, I meant that I wanted to focus my mind and I wanted ... I tried to do it like that, but I didn't. I didn't want to do it like that because it would have hurt him. He was already lying on the floor.

Q: So you felt if you shot him between the eyes, it would hurt him, but if you shot him in the back of the head, that would be painless?

A: No. I shot behind the head where it wouldn't get it.

Q: After JoJo took Art's gun away the second time, you went and got the butcher knife out of the kitchen, didn't you?

A: Yeah.

Q: And what were you going to do with the butcher knife?

A: Don't know. Depends on what he would have done.

Q: I'm sorry?

A: I don't know. I just wanted it in my hands.

Q: You can't recall what you were going to do with the butcher knife?

A: I don't know. My baby was right there, and I didn't have nothing, and Art was right there, so I just grabbed it.

Q: Well, Art wasn't moving, was he?

A: I didn't stare a whole lot. I was too scared.

Q: Did he give any indication that he was anything other than dead at the time?

A: Yeah.

Q: What indication was that?

A: Well, at first I, like, looked. And I thought he was peeking at me. So I backed up.

Q: Now, you know Maya Snowden, don't you?

A: Yes, I do.

Q: And tell us who Maya Snowden is.

A: She's Art's sister.

Q: Art's sister. And you called ...

A: Well, I said—

Q: —you called Art's sister Thursday of last week, didn't you?

A: Thursday of last week?

Q: Yes. After the end of court, you called her, didn't you?

A: After ... not after the end of court.

Q: Didn't you tell Art's sister when she asked you—

MR. NEGUS: Could we approach the bench before we get the question?

THE COURT: Do it in chambers.

Chapter 9: Discussion In Chambers

(The following proceedings were held in chambers)

MR. NEGUS: I object to this statement. I haven't received any discovery on it. And even oral statements of defendants are supposed to be provided by way of discovery if the prosecution wants to bring them out. I haven't the slightest idea what it's going to be.

MR. BOYD: What I'm offering is impeachment. I'm going to put it on in rebuttal. I mean, I am not—

MR. NEGUS: I object to it coming in on rebuttal because I haven't got discovery of it. If he knew about it before, he should have provided it by discovery.

MR. BOYD: I found out about it thirty minutes ago. It's his client that did it. His client can tell him who she called.

MR. NEGUS: Wrong.

MR. BOYD: Nobody knows better than the defendant what she's doing. I, at least, hear it secondhand or third hand. Mr. Negus can hear about it firsthand from his own client.

MR. NEGUS: Mr. Boyd is aware of his—

MR. BOYD: That's illegal. That's not a legal objection.

MR. NEGUS: Mr. Boyd is aware of his legal duties to provide discovery, and he is not doing it.

MR. BOYD: I'm not offering it in my case in chief, which I haven't—

MR. NEGUS: It doesn't matter.

MR. BOYD: I'm offering it as impeachment.

MR. NEGUS: It doesn't matter whether it's his case in chief or not. If he still intends to use it, he has to provide discovery, and he hasn't done it.

MR. BOYD: If counsel is suggesting the law says that one has to provide discovery of what they intend to use as impeachment, I would certainly like to see the legal authority on that.

MR. NEGUS: People v. Rutherford, 14 Cal. 3d.

THE COURT: I think, though, that she has testified concerning all her activities and conduct leading up the shooting and her motivations at

that time. This apparently is something that has occurred in the last
couple of days, and I don't know what it is. But what's the cite you're
giving, Mr. Negus? Ruther—

MR. NEGUS: Yes, People v. Rutherford. And there is also a case—I have to
find it—that indicates that the prosecution has to give discovery
statements of the defendant they intend to use even if they are—

THE COURT: Subsequent impeaching statements?

MR. NEGUS: There's never been a distinction that I'm aware of between
subsequent impeaching and whatever. It's just anything they intend to
use. It doesn't say—

MR. BOYD: Discovery?

MR. NEGUS: There's nothing in California law that say that
it's what the prosecution intends to use in their case in chief.

MR. BOYD: That's not—

MR. NEGUS: It's any matter which is relevant.

MR. BOYD: That's not the law. You know, his client gets up all morning
long and blabs about everything, and then every time I ask a question on
cross as to whether she even said it or if it has bearing on anything, he
poses some type of objection. And he wants to run the risk that he is
keeping it out in front of the jury. They are not stupid. But from a legal
point of view, you know she gets up there and says, "I was afraid of him.
He could have still been alive so I grabbed the knife." And I've got
evidence that she knew right then and there he was deader that a
doornail because she went ahead and called someone up on the phone
and told her that.

MR. NEGUS: Well, the problem is that counsel doesn't like my objecting.
But he shouldn't ask objectionable questions. I was going to make a
motion for mistrial again because of another act of misconduct on
counsel's part, using a statement of JoJo January, who he—

MR. BOYD: There's nothing—

THE COURT: One at a time.

MR. NEGUS: —he knows is not admissible against my client. A hearsay,
out-of-court statement that he alleged was made by JoJo asking her
about that. He knows that is objectionable, and I think that that is in itself

prosecution misconduct, which is grounds for mistrial. It shows counsel's ignorance of the law, because anyone that has practiced law for more than a year knows that hearsay is inadmissible for impeachment. If counsel thinks that's the law, counsel better go back to law school.

THE COURT: Okay, well ...

MR. BOYD: Hearsay is an exception to the rule. Impeachment is an exception.

MR. NEGUS: What Evidence Code section is that?

THE COURT: Off the record.

(A discussion was held off the record.)

THE COURT: What's the offer of proof on the statement?

MR. BOYD: She called and talked to the sister. The sister asked, "Did he suffer?" and her response is, "He was dead immediately after I fired the second shot." And that's completely contrary to her testimony this morning that she thought he might still be alive, and in order to protect little Atujuan, she grabbed a butcher knife. It's a complete inconsistency.

THE COURT: Well, that's—

MR. NEGUS: But that's after she knows about Dr. Root's autopsy.

THE COURT: I would sustain it. That's post. That's all post trial, post-incident knowledge that she has acquired. She now knows he was dead. I'll sustain it on that basis of lack of discovery.

MR. BOYD: Okay.

(The following proceedings were held in open court in the presence of the jury.)

THE COURT: Last question is withdrawn.

BY MR. BOYD:

Q: Did Joseph take the butcher knife away from you?

A: Yes.

Q: Why did he take the butcher knife away from you?

MR. NEGUS: Objection. That asks her to speculate as to why JoJo did something, unless he told her.

THE COURT: If she knows. Overruled

THE WITNESS: I asked him. He said because he didn't know—

MR. NEGUS: Objection. That would call for hearsay if she

is asking JoJo why.

THE COURT: Well, JoJo took the butcher knife away from you?

THE WITNESS: Uh-huh.

THE COURT: And did he tell you why he took it away from you?

THE WITNESS: He said because he didn't want me to—

MR. NEGUS: Objection. I object to the statement. Hear say.

THE COURT: Overruled.

MR. BOYD: Art knew you were going back to Georgia to be with the other boyfriend?

MR. NEGUS: Objection. Vague as to time.

MR. BOYD: How many times did you go back to Georgia to be with your boyfriend?

MR. NEGUS: Vague in time as to when Art knew.

THE COURT: Overruled as to the last question.

BY MR. BOYD:

Q: How many times did you go back to Georgia to be with your boyfriend?

A: Once.

Q: Did Art know about that?

MR. NEGUS: Objection. Vague as to time.

THE COURT: Overruled. She can testify about it.

THE WITNESS: He didn't know. He didn't know that I was going to go. He knew that I went.

BY MR. BOYD:

Q: You called him from Georgia?

A: Yeah.

Q: When?

A: He had called. He had been calling me.

Q: I'm sorry?

A: He was looking for me, and he didn't know where I was, but my mother said he was calling.

Q: So you called him and told him you were in Georgia?

A: No, I called him and he told me where I was. So I just said yeah, that's where I was.

Q: You made a comment to Mr. Negus this morning, and your response was Art used to say to you, "What are you scared of?" Did Art used to say that?

MR. NEGUS: Objection. I don't recall that.

THE WITNESS: I don't remember.

THE COURT: I don't remember that.

BY MR. BOYD:

Q: Do you recall answering a question this morning with the response, "Art used to say, 'What are you scared of?'" to you?

A: No, I don't think so, no.

Q: Do you remember what you testified to this morning?

A: Yeah.

Q: You're not making this up as you go along, are you?

A: Nope. (How can they keep badgering me, beating me down the same as Art did? I thought they were supposed to help me. I wish this would stop! Can't you see he wanted to kill me?)

Q: Now, when you came out of the house and the policemen were there, you said you were glad to get out of the house because you knew the police would protect you from Art, right?

A: Yes.

Q: Why didn't you go to the police before if you had fears that Art was going to hurt you?

A: Because he wasn't like that.

Q: You mean he wasn't dead? Is that what you meant?

A: He wasn't stopped.

Q: I'm sorry?

A: He wasn't stopped still.

Q: When you went out to the police and you knew that would protect you from Art, at that time you said you thought Art might still be alive, right?

A: Yeah.

Q: So, in other words, you felt good having the police there because they would ...?

A: Well, they were there. I didn't call them on me.

Q: But they would protect you from Art, right?

A: Yeah, but they came on their own. I didn't call them myself.

Q: But you never went to the police any time, any other time to be protected, did you?

A: No. I'd kind of drop hints. When I went to the hospital and my head was cracked open, the people in the hospital asked me what happened. I told them what happened, and they wanted to call the police, but I told them no. I told them what happened, though.

Q: Let me show you Exhibit 65. This photograph of you has a scratch on the left part of the temple. Can you see that? That picture was taken in December, is that right?

A: Yeah.

Q: Okay. That little scratch on the left that runs about an inch, do you see that? See what I'm talking about?

A: Do that again.

Q: There's a scratch on left-hand side of your head up on the temple.

A: Yeah, I see that.

Q: Right here? Right there?

A: Right there.

Q: Right?

A: Okay.

Q: Is that what you are referring to when you said that Art busted open your head and you almost died? Is that the injury that you were referring to when you made that comment?

A: No. It was all these other—my head was—I still got scars inside my head all over now, right now.

Q: Where are the ones that busted open your head?

A: The ones that are up in here.

Q: Okay. And you almost died from that, is that correct?

A: Yeah. They said I had a concussion. I went to the hospital two weeks later. He didn't ever let me go.

Q: Did that make you mad when that happened?

A: I was mad when it happened.

Q: When you were mad, did you tell Art that if you got the chance, you would shoot him between the eyes?

A: No.

Q: But it made you mad?

A: Yeah. It made me mad. It was kind of uncomfortable being pregnant with my—you know, like that.

Q: Now, you indicated that after the shooting, you were hungry. You wanted to call your Momma and then the police, is that right? In that order?

MR. NEGUS: Objection. I don't recall hunger being part of that statement.

THE WITNESS: Yea, I was.

THE COURT: Overruled. She can answer, if she recalls.

BY MR. BOYD:

Q: Is that right?

A: I was hungry, but I wasn't getting ready to eat like right then. My appetite wasn't too up. I was going to call my Momma, call the police. I wasn't able to think real good. My Momma, I wanted to call her. And I knew the police had to be notified. But, you know, I was pregnant and I was sick and my kids was there and I couldn't think good, so I wanted to talk to my mother.

Q: You testified this morning that you have always been concerned about your children. You were concerned about your children when you were going out with Art, is that right?

A: Yeah.

Q: Why were you using cocaine when you were pregnant?

A: Because I was—

MR. NEGUS: Objection. That's argumentative and—

MR. BOYD: It's not argumentative.

MR. NEGUS: And if I could finish my objection, counsel—merely an attempt to try to convict her of homicide because of bad character.

THE COURT: Overruled. She can answer.

BY MR. BOYD:

Q: That means you can answer. If you were concerned about your children as you said you were, why were you using cocaine when you were pregnant?

A: I don't know.

Q: I'm sorry?

A: I don't know. That's why I had to stop.

Q: You told Officer Tejas at one time, didn't you, that you were going to call your mother and then you were going to call the police because you knew you couldn't get away with it? Is that the phrase you used when you talked with Officer Tejas?

A: I guess. I mean, I—that's what he says I said. I probably said it, though.

Q: What was it you didn't think you could get away with?

A: Just somebody being shot and you don't know who shot him.

Q: Well, you knew who shot him, didn't you?

A: Yeah. That's why I didn't want to act like didn't nothing happen, though, like, you know, I was supposed to just act like nothing happened. But I couldn't act like nothing happened. Somebody was hurt.

Q: When Officer Tejas took you in his police car to the hospital and then to the police station, you had a baggie with cocaine in it which you put in his police car, right?

A: Yes.

Q: Where did that baggie of cocaine come from?

A: The two rocks I took off Peter's plate.

Q: I'm sorry?

A: It was two rocks I took off Peter's plate.

Q: Off Peter's plate?

A: Uh-huh.

Q: And did you put it on your person somewhere, in a pants pocket or something?

A: I had it in my pocket.

Q: You had it in your pocket?

A: Uh-huh.

Q: And on your way to the police station, you put it inside the car. Why did you take it out and put it inside the police car?

A: I didn't know. I was high, and then I realized I had coke on me, so I just took it out of my pocket. And I was sitting down, so I just left it there in the car.

Q: In other words, you didn't want to be accused of or found in possession of cocaine, so you left it in the police car?

A: Yeah, but I wasn't thinking, so that's why I had to tell the police. I told them, I said, "I put some cocaine in your car." I told them I didn't mean to do it, but I did it. They went and got it.

Q: What did you mean when you told Officer Tejas, "I mean, I killed the man. God has forgiven me, okay? I might suffer the consequences of the law"? What did you mean when you said you might suffer the consequences of the law?

MR. NEGUS: I object. I think that calls for a legal conclusion that she may not be qualified to give.

MR. BOYD: I am asking for her state of mind. I—

THE COURT: Post-incident state of the law. State of mind would be irrelevant. Pretty obvious what the consequences of the law have been.

MR. BOYD: I am asserting that it shows consciousness of guilt.

MR. NEGUS: Well, I am asserting that it is absurd.

THE COURT: Sustained.

BY MR. BOYD:

Q: Were you laughing and joking with Officer Tejas about Art being killed?

A: No, not about Art being killed.

Q: What was it you were laughing and joking about regarding this incident?

A: That I was alive. I was happy that I wasn't dead.

Q: Do you recall Officer Tejas testifying you were laughing and joking?

A: Yeah.

Q: That your brothers wanted to go bury him in the backyard?

A: No, I don't even remember my brothers saying that. He didn't—I don't remember him saying that.

Q: Why did you throw the rug over the hallway to cover up the bloodstains?

A: Because my son might have stepped in it. There was some blood on the floor, and I didn't want anybody to step on it.

Q: Is it your testimony that you put the rug that's in that photograph on the board over the bloodstains so that your children wouldn't step on it?

A: No. I just didn't want it there. I mean I had to have something over it. I didn't want to see it, because ... like a whole bunch of reasons. Really, those two.

Q: Would one of the other reasons be perhaps so that you could cover up the fact that there was a bloodstain there?

A: No.

Q: Like from the police?

A: No. I was not going to cover it up if I told them.

Q: Joseph, your brother JoJo, started giving you advice, you indicated this morning, because he had been in trouble. He started telling you things to do, to act normal—

A: Yeah.

Q: Right? To go upstairs, put on your nightgown, act as normal as possible, right?

A: Yeah. Calm down, just relax, just act like nothing happened. Just, you know, calm, cool, you know.

Q: And while he was telling you to act normal, is that when you put the carpet over the bloodstains? Was it after he told you just try to make things appear normal?

A: No, I put it over right when I first—after I saw it, I guess. I can't remember exactly.

Q: Joseph took the guns from you and told you he was going to wrap them up and wipe the fingerprints and hide them, right? Isn't that correct?

A: Yeah. He was saying a lot of stuff that wasn't making any sense to me. I just let him keep talking because I was trying to calm down, because I knew I was pregnant, and I had to just try to calm down.

Q: And you did what he said, didn't you?

A: So I went and changed clothes. I put my shirt on and acted like he was going to take me out.

Q: Did you do what Joseph told you, to try to act normal?

A: No, I was acting like I was going to bed.

Q: I'm sorry?

A: I acted like I was going—

Q: You acted like you were going to go to bed, and you put on your nightgown or your bedclothes?

A: Yeah, we were just acting then because the police were outside. We didn't want them to come in shooting. If they figured we were normal people, they might not just bust in with the SWAT.

Q: So you were just putting on an act?

A: I was trying to just be normal so they wouldn't come in and hurt my kids, you know, and everybody.

Q: After you just shot Art. That wasn't very normal, was it?

A: No.

Q: So you were acting, right?

A: Wait. I don't want to get confused. So we'll take this slow. Now, what?

Q: You were acting because Joseph told you to act normal. You started acting what you thought would appear normal, correct?

A: I was trying to calm down. I was just trying to be okay. I was trying to act normal, not act, because if I would have been acting, I would have done a better job. I'm a good actress. I was trying to act normal under the circumstances, trying to calm down.

Q: As an actress, when you want to act, you know how to act, right?

A: When I'm getting paid for it and I have a job to do, I'm going to do what I'm supposed to do.

Q: How about if you are charged with a crime? Would that be an appropriate time to act?

A: No.

Q: This morning when you were testifying and you were imitating Art by saying that Art said, "Why you go messing around wit' those no-good people?" that was acting, wasn't it?

A: That's just me. I'm just that kind of person. I'm emotional. That's why I thought I should be an actress because I get into it, you know, stuff. But I just was doing like he does. But acting a job and acting conversation kind of stuff are different.

Q: So, you told Officer Tejas and Officer Johnson when you talked with them at various times that you were willing to take responsibility for what you did to Art, right?

A: Yes.

Q: Okay, and you have made the statement during these proceedings that you knew what you did was wrong, isn't that right?

A: Yeah.

Q: And what you did do was wrong, wasn't it?

A: Yeah, it was wrong. But it wasn't wrong for me to save my life; I know that. That's the only reason why I'm okay, because I knew that as long as I was saving my own life that I don't have to walk around feeling sad all day.

Q: Wasn't it wrong to kill Art?

MR. NEGUS: I think counsel is about to—

THE COURT: Let's take an afternoon recess. It's that time anyway. Fifteen minutes. Please keep in mind the admonition.

(Recess) (The following proceedings were held outside the presence of the jury.)

THE COURT: On the record.

MR. NEGUS: Mr. Boyd has in his hands, or did have in his hands when he was questioning Miss Parker, some document which he hasn't seen fit to share with anybody, again, and I would request that before he starts trying to read from it, that he let us know what it is and what he is trying to do.

MR. BOYD: Yes, I will be pleased to do that, Your Honor. It's a transcript of the proceedings on Friday, August 22, at which Mr. Zavidow was appearing for Mr. Negus when the Court was considering various matters, including the OR release, and the defendant spontaneously made a statement indicating that she knew she had done something wrong which, despite the best efforts of everyone—her counsel representing her and everything else—she decided to blurt out in court. I don't know of any particular reason why that's excludable.

MR. NEGUS: Can I—

MR. BOYD: Particularly since it appears to be a—

MR. NEGUS: —have a look at the document?

MR. BOYD: —statement of her mental state.

MR. NEGUS: It would appear to me that it was a statement made when she was in court when I was in Jamaica, so I wasn't aware of it. It would also appear that what has happened is that Mr. Zavidow asked the court for an OR, and what she said is, "I mean, I'm a very honest person. I did something wrong. But I will be where I'm supposed to be."

MR. BOYD: That's right.

MR. NEGUS: Hardly seems like it's very probative. And it's also apparently made as an attempt to get an OR. I would think that statements made as an attempt to get an OR are the same as statements that are made to a probation officer, and they would not be admissible in a court.

MR. BOYD: That's an interesting theory.

MR. NEGUS: Certainly at the time that we had OR officers when representations were made to the Court about OR's, those statements were not admissible. So I would think that is of limited probative value because she already stated essentially the same thing in the exact same words. And counsel cross-examined her. So it is cumulative, 352, and inadmissible because it's made in an OR hearing.

THE COURT: Well, it has certainly limited probative value in light of the fact that through the whole proceedings from the very beginning to the very end her very first statement to Detective Scharf, as I recall early on, was that "Thou shalt not kill" and it is wrong. And this doesn't appear to the Court to necessarily be inconsistent. But I think that it may be something that could be argued. It may. Whether it tends to show a consciousness of guilt or not is something I don't know. I guess the jury can figure that out.

I'll note the objection, and overrule it. She can answer.

MR. NEGUS: Can I get a copy of it, then, so that if he reads portions of it that I can look at the whole thing?

MR. BOYD: I'll read the whole sentence.

MR. NEGUS: "I mean, I'm an honest person. I did something wrong. But I will be where I am supposed to be."

MR. BOYD: Yes, I will read that whole sentence.

THE COURT: All right. Want to bring the jury in?

MR. NEGUS: I would ask that counsel be admonished not, however, to bring up any more statements in front of the jury that he hasn't shared with us.

THE COURT: Yes.

You can come around, Miss Parker. Have a seat. Well, I'll order that counsel provide the Court with notice of other impeaching-type of information before it's shown to the witness.

MR. BOYD: "Other?" you say. I didn't hear.

THE COURT: Other than this.

MR. BOYD: Oh.

(The following proceedings were held in open court after the jury entered the courtroom.)

THE COURT: All right. The record should reflect our jury has returned. Mr. Boyd?

MR. BOYD: Thank you, Your Honor.

BY MR. BOYD:

Q: When Art was running down the stairs from the upstairs bedroom, you indicated you thought he was going to get another gun, is that right?

A: Yes.

Q: Was there anything that made you think that he wasn't running away from you because he didn't want to get shot again?

A: No.

Q: Before you left the house when the police were there that evening, the guns had already been taken away from you and hidden, is that right?

A: Yeah.

Q: And Art's body had been put in a closet, correct?

A: Yes.

Q: And the rug had been thrown over the bloodstains where he had fallen and where you tried to shoot him the second time, right?

A: You say that—wait, the rug was already—

Q: The rug had been put over the bloodstains where you had shot him the second time, or tried to. Is that correct?

A: Yeah, the rug was over the blood.

Q: Now, before we went on the recess, I was asking you about the fact that you had made statements in this case that you believed what you did was wrong. Is that true? Did you make those types of statements?

MR. NEGUS: Objection. That has been asked and answered several times.

THE COURT: Sustained.

Q: Do you believe as you sit here today that what you did was wrong?

MR. NEGUS: Objection. Asked and answered.

MR. BOYD: That has not.

THE COURT: I'm not sure. Overruled.

THE WITNESS: As I sit here today?

BY MR. BOYD:

Q: Yes. Do you believe what you did was wrong?

A: I believe you shouldn't kill.

Q: Do you believe that what you did that evening was wrong?

MR. NEGUS: Objection. She just answered that question.

MR. BOYD: She was unresponsive.

THE COURT: Overruled.

THE WITNESS: I believe that you're not supposed to kill. But as a matter of being wrong, I have to look at it that I should be happy I'm alive and not that somebody else is dead.

BY MR. BOYD:

Q: So, do I take it from that answer that you don't believe what you did was wrong?

A: No, it's wrong for a person to kill. But it's not for me to defend myself.

Q: Okay. Now, remember when you were in court back on Friday, August 22, when we were discussing with the judge in the other courtroom whether you should be released in order to have your baby? Do you recall that?

A: Yes, I do.

Q: Do you recall toward the end of the discussion between the attorneys you made that statement?

A: Yes, I did.

Q: And when you said at that time that you did something wrong, were you telling the truth?

A: I know the Bible says, "Thou shalt not kill," and I was responsible for somebody's death. So I felt that I did something against God.

MR. BOYD: I have nothing further.

THE COURT: Okay. Any redirect?

MR. NEGUS: Just a little bit.

RE-DIRECT EXAMINATION

BY MR. NEGUS:

Q: Rose Ann, what was your father's occupation before he retired?

MR. BOYD: I'm going to object. This exceeds the scope of direct.

MR. NEGUS: It certainly has to do with the word "wrong."

THE COURT: Overruled. The witness may answer.

BY MR. NEGUS:

Q: What occupation?

A: Same as he does now. He's a minister.

Q: And did you receive religious training as part of being his daughter?

A: Yes, I did.

Q: When you're talking about "wrong," are you talking about wrong in the eyes of God or wrong in the eyes of the law?

A: I'm talking about in the eyes of God.

MR. NEGUS: Thank you. I have nothing further.

THE COURT: Okay. Any other recross?

MR. BOYD: Just one sentence.

RECROSS-EXAMINATION

BY MR. BOYD:

Q: With respect to not being wrong in the eyes of the law, did you tell officer Tejas that you killed Art and said, "I might suffer the consequences of the law"?

MR. NEGUS: That's not impeaching, and we have already had that objection.

MR. BOYD: It is, too.

THE COURT: Sustained. That's what we are here about.

MR. BOYD: I have nothing further.

THE COURT: Okay. Thank you, ma'am.

—END OF ROSE'S TESTIMONY.

Chapter 10: Truth Pays

It was finally over. I sat in the witness chair, thoroughly exhausted. I felt traumatized at times having to relive everything with sober eyes. I couldn't believe the questioning that ranged from my life as an actress, dancer on Soul Train, meeting Art, telling how many millions Art made, naming my babies' daddies, revealing abortions, miscarriages, identifying Art's low-down friends, disclosing who Art sold cocaine to in the Hollywood circuit, stating which drugs he sold, how much dope we smoked, recalling how many times he beat me and the way in which he beat me, and reliving the night I shot him and he died. I wonder if I made a wise decision by pushing the trial forward at this time. I said it was okay to continue because I wanted it to be over so I could go home.

When I stepped down from the witness stand, my attorney nodded to me in an almost "feel sorry for me" motion as I walked back toward my seat.

I sat there feeling like I wanted to die. I felt like I had been robbed, raped, and misunderstood—all in the public's eye. I kept telling myself, I can't believe it, I can't believe it. How could the prosecutor, the DA, the State, the people that are supposed to be after the truth, how could they twist everything? I just couldn't believe it. Every word I said, Mr. Boyd gave another meaning. Now I understand why my brothers kept telling me to be quiet and don't talk, or plead the fifth. I didn't know what hurt worse—this cut in my stomach or the slashing of the truth into a thousand pieces so that it became totally unrecognizable. My attorney interrupted my train of thought by asking if I was OK.

"What do you think? How can he get away with twisting everything?"

"Rose, that's his job."

"Well, what's your job? What happens now?"

"Tomorrow we have to do closing arguments. You are finished for now," he replied.

We returned for closing arguments, then the jury were given the instructions. So now we wait as the jury deliberates.

The Final Nursing

On Oct. 3rd, I lay in bed nursing my newborn in one arm and holding my 25-month-old son in the other arm. My newborn, Darian, bit my breast, and at the same time, Atujuan kicked me in the stitches from my Cesarean, causing me to scream, "Momma!" My Momma came in the room and took both babies from me. I turned over in pain, suddenly struck by the realization that this incident would be a major memory that will never die. The phone rang. Rrrrrrring. My heart jumped. I thought it might be the verdict. Please, Lord, let it be just another wrong number like we've been having all morning. I wanted to scream each time I slammed the phone down. But this time was different. "Hello," I said softly.

"Rose, the jury is back with the verdict!" my public defender exclaimed.

"OK, here I come." I put the phone down slowly. My heart was pounding in my throat.

My Momma and dad stood in the doorway, waiting for me to turn around. "The verdict is in, and this time, I want to go alone."

"Rose, are you sure?" Dad asked.

"Yes, Dad, I need to face this day by myself."

I didn't know what I was saying, but I knew this was the way it had to be done this time. "Momma, I can go with you, and it will be just you and me," Emzie pleaded.

"Baby, Momma has to go alone." He was only nine years old and filled with so much confusion and fear. It broke my heart to see his heart hurting. It hurt me to tell him no. I could see his brown eyes growing glossy with tears forming and fear scrunching his eyebrows together. I rushed to grab a little bag to put my medications and miscellaneous items in. Then I picked up my newborn already in his crib and held him close to my breast, trying to impress in him the assurance of my love. Atujuan grabbed me by my leg, staring up at me with those beautiful brown eyes and long lashes. Oh, they were making this so hard for me. It almost felt like they knew something, and deep down inside, I pondered the what-if's as well. What if I don't come back? What if this is really the last moment I will see my kids for a long time before I get out of prison? I couldn't bear to think of it, so I shook my head and tried to hold it together.

I walked over to Emzie, who stood very tense. "I love you, son. Momma's going to be alright, trust me. You are going to be alright, too. Okay, baby?" I tried to convince him. "Give Momma a hug." Somehow when he held me, I could tell he didn't trust letting me go.

"Rose, are you going to call us as soon as the verdict is read?" Momma yelled out as I was closing the car door. I nodded yes, fighting back tears of uncertainty. I couldn't stand to look back and see my family. I drove off as fast as possible. Thank God the court was not far from our house. I sat there in the car, looking at the building that held my fate in the minds of its experts while I listened to my gospel song, "Trust in God." I left all my money in the glove compartment except for $40, took my pain medication, and proceeded into the courthouse. The heat was scorching that day. My public defender was in the hallway, waiting to whisk me into the courtroom.

"They've been waiting, Rose," he whispered.

"I got here as soon as I could."

We took our seats in the front and the judge came in and then the jury entered. My heart was palpitating, but somehow, I felt a sense of peace, too. Then I saw the bailiff come from the jury box and walk over to the judge and hand him a piece of paper. "Will the defendant, Ms. Rose Parker, please stand."

The judge looked at the jury and asked, "Have you reached a verdict?"

"We have, Your Honor," said the jury foreman.

"You may read it," said the judge.

"We, the jury, find the defendant guilty of first-degree murder."

I went numb. My public defender pushed papers in front of me and told me that it was for an appeal and to sign it. Everything sounded like I was in a tunnel and part of my mind was there and the other part kept hearing, "We find the defendant guilty of first-degree murder. GUILTY, GUILTY, GUILTY GUILTY." I couldn't make sense out of it. Someone was asking me to please sign a document which read that the defendant would be remanded back into custody until sentencing, which was scheduled for February 10, 1987, another four months away.

I gave investigator Paranti my keys and purse. I also asked her to call my parents and tell them what had happened and to give them my things. They escorted me to a temporary holding cell. Deputies kept walking back and forth in front of my cell. I couldn't understand why. This went on for several hours until finally, I just couldn't take it any longer.

"Why are you doing this?"

"We don't want you to hurt yourself," an officer answered.

"Look, I love God, and I love myself, and that is the last thing on my mind.

~ 165 ~

God will vindicate me. They transported me back to the county jail."
One of the officers said, "Baby, you're going to prison."

A couple of nights later, I asked for some paper. I needed to write my Momma. I had to get some things off my chest, and I knew I could say it just like I felt it to Momma and not worry about her treating me different. I knew my Momma loved me no matter what.

Momma,
I'm so sad. I want my babies. Help me to trust the Lord. I ache so much in my guts, Momma, I can't eat or nothing. Please, Momma, did you know that I had just breast-fed Darian before I went to the courthouse? I gave him some out of both breasts so I wouldn't be lopsided. I mean, they called on the phone for me to come to the courthouse, but something said feed the baby.

Momma, it hurts and you know what is strange? I'm crying, but I'm remembering that I had just fed Darian and after all day at court and then when we got here, my breasts never filled up. I was so scared, 'cause I knew that in a few hours they were going to hurt. After I got to the jail and saw the nurse that morning, she was going to give me some pills to make my milk go away, but it had been almost 48 hours and no pain and they didn't fill back up. That's God, huh? Momma, I don't know. I know God is with me and I'm going to be OK, but it doesn't feel like it. I'm going to go now. I remember a Scripture that said that all things work together for good to them that love God and are called according to His purpose. I know if God said it, there has to be a reason, but it just doesn't feel good. I'm going to read all that part again. I guess I will begin to read the Bible through again next week. This will make two times for the whole Bible. I'm going to close. I do feel better just writing to you.

Love,

Rose

October 1986

The next few days were extremely painful; it felt like someone had kicked me in my guts and tore out my insides. I could not eat, and I spiraled into a depression thinking about my babies.

For a month or so, my Momma kept reassuring me that God would help me and that she would take care of my babies. Momma then asked me if I would take care of her baby. Puzzled, I said "yes." Then I thought, Oh, I'm her baby. So I tried to eat, only because I had agreed to take care of her baby.

Visit from Investigator Paranti

The next morning, Investigator Paranti came to see me. She was sad. I know she was sad for me and my children because she knew we had just got back together again as a family. I picked up the phone.

"Hi, Rose."

"Hi. Did you give my Momma everything I gave you? Did you give it to her exactly the way I way asked you to?"

"Yes, I did, Rose. I honored your request to the letter."

"Thank you. Where is Mr. Negus? Didn't he want to see me?"

"He's working on your appeal and will be here in the next couple of weeks."

"Is that all? I'm just here? What happens now? I mean, they said they found me guilty of first-degree murder. Isn't that what they said, Ms. Paranti?"

She put her head down then looked at me with tears welling up in her eyes.

Then I started praying right then, "Father, I thank You for Ms. Paranti and Mr. Negus. I know You're going to give them the strength and the wisdom on how to get me out of here."

She smiled as I was praying.

"Rose, I have to go. I have another case I'm working on. I wanted to reassure you that I took care of what you asked me to do. I believe your family is coming to see you tomorrow, because tomorrow is visiting day. Your Momma said she's coming the first opportunity."

The telephone turned off on us. I tapped on the window and she looked as I waved bye.

I could think better now. I thought about my children most of the day. They let me stay in my room and sleep. I needed to write my son, Emzie. He had been heavy on my heart ever since I left the house.

That evening I had a lot on my mind, but I wanted to write my son. I needed him to know some things just from Momma.
Hello, Honey,

I love you and I really don't want you to have to be brave. I don't want to put any more on you than necessary. You are a very brave nine year old. I couldn't have asked for a better son. I'm so sorry that my choices were bad and I allowed Art in our lives. I hate that all this has happened, but we can't go back, only forward. The money I gave you, just use it for whatever you want. For some reason, I knew that I wasn't coming back, that's why I did not want anyone with me.

I do believe and expect a miracle from God. I'm just not sure how He is going to do it, so for now, you and your brothers need to be together. Hopefully, you don't mind being with them for a while and your dad will let you stay down here. Plus, I know that Grandma and Grandpa will make sure that I get a chance to see you guys. Honey, when you get the opportunity to hold your baby brother, hold him close, with lots of love. I know he is real little right now, but that makes you able to hold him. You hold him just like Atujuan, but more delicately, OK? Grandma will show you what I mean.

It's OK to cry. Never let anyone tell you that you can't cry for your Momma. I love you, and I will write you from time to time. You write to me when you feel like talking to me, OK?

I love you, Momma
Psalms 34: I will bless the Lord at all times. His praise shall continually be in my mouth.

With the Psalmist's words on my mind and in my mouth, I decided to write God as well.

Dear God,

I don't understand any of this. Please help me to have peace in my mind and take care of my babies. Lord, my Momma sang a song that said You would be a lawyer in a courtroom. Will You please be my lawyer, Lord? Will You be my friend, my Momma, my dad, my doctor, and my everything? Amen.

Thanksgiving Season, 1986
It's Thanksgiving! I have always spent this holiday with my parents, my siblings, and their families. Today, I am surrounded by strangers, people that are not thankful for anything as far as I can tell. These ladies don't even seem to believe in God, much less thank Him. Sometimes, Father, I'm afraid to close my eyes. Some of these people are so mean! One of my cellies slapped the other because she was snoring too loud. Now, how do you like that? She was asleep! There is one nice one, though.

My roommate, Betty, said that she always liked this day. She said, "I shouldn't be in this place, Rose. I was raised better than this. My mama always told me to watch who I hang out with. Did I listen? NO! I used to hang out with a real rowdy crowd. We smoked dope and partied hard. If we didn't have what we wanted, we felt no qualms about taking it from anybody that did. I really hurt my parents. They have cried many a tear over me, and it took my coming to jail, getting a 20year sentence, for me to come to myself. Because I can now see, I'm thankful. How about you, Rose?"

"I know what you mean," I told her. "I feel the same way. I shouldn't be here either, and I'm glad that God has gotten my attention, too. But I'm grateful for the little things, too. I'm thankful that today in the cafeteria, we had a real Thanksgiving Feast—turkey and dressing, with all the trimmings. We even had sweet potato and pumpkin pie for dessert. Everyone else said that it was good, but I swear to you, I couldn't taste a thing. I'm thankful for my parents and what they have taught me, for my kids, and my brothers and sisters. I'm thankful for another chance to do things right. It may be a while, but I promise that whenever I get out, I will do it right this time."

I rested and stayed off my feet like Sgt. Miller suggested, day in and day out. I would only get up when I was calling home to talk to the kids or my attorney.

My visits were infrequent because I had to let people know that I was still recovering from my surgery. Around Thanksgiving time, I had more abdominal pain than usual, and there was only so much medicine I could be given. The facility arranged for me to be taken to the hospital because I was having more pain and discomfort than I should have. As soon as the doctors checked me, they told me I needed surgery.

"Again?" I snapped.

"Yes," a soft-spoken white doctor responded, looking over his glasses. "I don't want another surgery."

"Don't worry; it's only an exploratory surgery. We need to just open you up and look inside to see what's going on."

"I was just opened up to get a baby out of me, and I'm trying to heal from that. If you open me up, I'll have to start all over again."

"Rose, this will be different. We have to find out what's causing you so much pain."

Another day, I had a follow-up appointment with my doctor to check my progress. Another early morning bus ride to look forward to.

As I was walking slowly down the bus aisle, my eyes ran across this man who was reading his Bible. I was immediately impressed. Everyone was going to the doctors on the van. I wondered what was wrong with him. On the way back to the jail, the same inmate asked me if he could send me a poem. I said, "OK."

Doctor's Results
Rose, you're fine," the doctor said after the surgery. "Perhaps with the stress of having a baby and going through your legal battles your body overreacted temporarily, but physically, you're in excellent shape."

"So I don't have a disease. I asked.

"That's absolutely right," he assured me.

That night, I didn't sleep too well. A woman inside the dorm just lost her dad to leukemia. She wailed all night long. I guess the most painful part was that she would not be let out to attend his funeral. I just prayed for her.

My Son's Birthday
The days had flown by so fast, it's scary. I can't believe it's December 10, 1986 —my son's 10th birthday. I wish I could get him a cake and a present and throw him a party. Father, keep my son. Maybe Momma and Daddy will bring him out here to visit so I can wish him a happy birthday.

Two days after Emzie's birthday, my parents brought him out to visit me. I was so glad to see him, even with glass between us. I saw my son turn two digits —The Big Ten! He blushed as I kept making a big deal out of his birthday. I knew he hated that I wasn't there to celebrate with him, but he still smiled, making me feel like it was okay.

"Did you get the Walkman from me?"

"Yes, thank you, Momma. I really wanted one of those." He was such a grateful child.

Reminiscing about Christmas Beatings by Art
I can't believe nine months have gone by and it's now Christmas time. It felt strange and weird. Memories of last Christmas entered my mind. It was Christmas Day that Art came over and pistol-whipped me in front of my kids. He knocked me to the couch and called me every bitch-name in the book. A sad and angry feeling came over me suddenly. I had to write, I had to pray, and then I had to read. It wasn't only last Christmas that bore horrible memories. There were other Christmases that Art gave me brutal beatings, followed by great gifts afterwards. It was as if I had to take a beating before I got whatever else he was going to give me.

I couldn't wait until Christmas was over. I thought about my kids. I know they are coming to visit, but my heart aches because I have nothing to give them. The following week leading into the New Year brought many of my family to the County Jail to encourage me and give me strength. Lord knows I appreciated it. I saw many inmates that cried because their families and friends wrote them off. I didn't know their stories, but I believe even the most difficult person should be forgiven by at least one person. My family was always there for me. They weren't judgmental and didn't write me off. I was so thankful for them. I guess that's the blessing of being a part of a large, loving, and forgiving family.

A Different New Year, 1987

As the New Year arrived, it brought much difficulty and pain. I can still hear David tell me that my sister Carol had a stroke. She was trying to care for the kids and it was too much for her. After my visit with my Momma, David, and Diane, my heart was heavy with uncertainty for my kids. But somehow, I could hear Momma say, "He is an ever-present help in trouble," and man, was I in trouble!

Letter to Daddy

Dear Daddy,

Hi, Daddy. I just want to remind you that my sentencing is on the 10th. I'm hoping that they give me a stay, Daddy. Don't forget I need the letter letting them know I will be at your house. That way, I can come home for a couple of weeks and get prepared to go to prison. I think my attorney needs a copy and the judge gets the original. I know God is going to work a miracle, but I just can't figure out how He's going to do it. Thank you, guys, for taking care of my baby. Daddy, it was so hard 'cause Darian was only four weeks when I left. He's getting so big now. Just think, he'll be six months old next month. Everybody teases me that he is Art's, but I know that he looks just like his grandpa. I'm going to close for now. There is another letter enclosed for Momma. You know she sometimes wants her own letter and I do want to make Bertha Lees happy.

I love you
Rose Ann
February 1987

P.S. Happy early Valentine's Day

Chapter 11: Sentencing Day

Sentencing Day, February 10, 1987

I didn't sleep at all the night of February 9th. My mind would not shut down. When they called for court time, I was already up and ready to be transported. It rained hard that night.

After we arrived at the court, the same familiar faces were there—my family and friends and some of Art's family. This appearance was the shortest appearance of all of the proceedings. The judge had my future in his hands, written on a little white square piece of paper.

"I hereby sentence the defendant, Rose Ann Parker, to a sentence of 27 years to life, to be served out at the California Institution for Women (CIW) as soon as she obtains medical clearance." A cold quiet was in the courtroom and then an immediate crescendo of noises from counsel and onlookers. His words had an immediate, numbing affect on me. I looked over and saw my family was totally devastated.

Art's sister looked alternately pleased and upset. She couldn't quite make up her mind how she felt because she knew how badly he had treated me. Still, he was her brother and I had killed him! Oh, well, the gavel had fallen.

My attorney immediately put in an appeal. Inexperienced, he felt awful about the verdict, but he had done the best that he could.

The Transfer

I will never forget the eve before I was transferred out to CIW. I went over to Sgt. Miller's office area to make small talk with a couple of the deputies. I soon discovered that Sgt. Miller was out to lunch and noticed an older officer whom I had never seen there before. In the corner was

Sgt. Miller's assistant, working on the log book, pretending not to hear me come in so she never turned around to speak to me.

I read the name tag on the officer who stood by the door as I entered. Mary Fletcher was her name. She smiled at me. I greeted her and asked where Sgt. Miller was.

"She's at lunch and will be back in about half an hour," the woman replied.

She began small talk with me and asked what I was doing in a place like this. I really liked her spirit. She reminded me of my mother's personality, kinda of soft and sweet.

I told her the same things I told Sgt. Miller, and I also told her I was going to CIW the next day and that I was coming to say good-bye to Sgt. Miller in case they transported me at some ungodly hour before she got to work. The lady looked over at Sgt. Miller's assistant and whispered, "Come over here for a moment and let me speak to you about a few things." She walked toward the door and stood on the other side of the entrance. I followed.

"Rose, may I offer you a few tips of wisdom for you to consider doing when you get to CIW?"

"Sure, you may. I need all the wisdom I can get. It seems like they are trying to send me away forever, but I know it won't be that long," I assured her.

"I know a lady who is serving 30 to life up North. Believe it or not, she is a sweet lady, just like yourself. And just like yourself, got caught up in the wrong crowd. Anyway, she was convicted for a double murder."

Ms. Fletcher wouldn't go into details, but said the woman would probably never see the light of a free day. My heart failed.
"How is she doing?" I asked.

"Well, I can tell you that her spirit is stronger today than ever." She smiled, "Oh, yeah ..."

I sighed. She continued, "Let me tell you how she lives on a daily basis. She treats everyone with respect. She prays to her God day and night. She journals every day as a discipline to get the junk out of her mind that tries to stay there. You will need to do this too."

"Journal?" I interrupted. "What would I journal, Ms. Fletcher?"

"Everything—your confusion, your questions, your anger, your fears, your joys, and your needs—and more than anything, journal your dreams. Never stop dreaming."

I smiled and thought to myself—my dreams. I can still dream. A life sentence doesn't have to rob you of dreaming.

"Well, my first dream is to get out of here for good."
"In due time, young lady."

"Ms. Fletcher, please, please, do you have a pencil and paper that I can use to write down what you are saying to me?"

"Sure." She quickly grabbed a narrow notepad out of her back pocket, along with her pen.

"Anything else, Ms. Fletcher?"

"Yes. Once you get into regular population, keep track of your daily schedule for the entire quarter so that you can see yourself as a productive citizen and not a criminal."

I was already feeling like a secretary.
"In other words, I'm going to let the time serve me, and not me serve the time, right?"

"Oh, you're not as naïve as you appear."

We laughed together.

"I appreciate your wisdom, and I will remember it."

Ms. Fletcher looked at her watch and said, "Oops, it's my lunch time now. I should have been gone." "Okay, nice talking to you."

I started going back to my dorm, thinking about Ms. Fletcher and thanking God for sending her to encourage me. I put my note in my private things under my bunk bed so that I would have it with me tomorrow. Before 5 P.M. went back over to Sgt. Miller's area to say goodbye, and she was there closing her log books.

"Hey, Rose, how are you today?"

"Oh, I'm OK. Tomorrow's the day I leave and so I wanted to come say good-bye."

Sgt. Miller felt like the big sister that I never had and didn't know I needed. I loved my own sisters, but there was a special bond between Sgt. Miller and me that we had created this past year.

"I met Ms. Fletcher and she was so nice. She's probably somebody's favorite grandmother, huh?" I asked Sgt. Miller.

"Ms. Fletcher?" she repeated with a puzzled look on her face.

"Yeah, Ms. Fletcher, you know, the older, pretty, gray-haired woman with the cutest dimples."

"Rose, we don't have a Ms. Fletcher with the cutest anything," Sgt. Miller insisted.

"Sure, you do. She probably works the night shift."

"Well, I do the schedules, and I think I would know if I had an employee by the name of Officer Fletcher."

Sabrina, her secretary, was about to leave. "Sabrina, remember when Ms. Fletcher was here earlier?" I asked.

Sabrina sighed with impatience, adding to my confusion. "No, I remember that you came by for a moment, Rose, and then you left right after you saw Sgt. Miller wasn't here." With that, she left. At least she did see me even if she didn't see a Ms. Fletcher, but I got nervous and then something wonderful leaped inside of me.

Sgt. Miller was smiling at me as I kept this puzzled look on my face. "Rose, take care of yourself and watch your back."

"I will. Ms. Fletcher gave me some good tips and instructions."

"Rose, there is no Ms. Fletcher."

"Oh, yes, there is, and she's walking around here with a Brown County of San Bernardino uniform on."

"Okay, Rose, if you say so." Sgt. Miller grabbed her purse.

"Sgt. Miller, I wanted to thank you for your—" before I could finish my words, my eyes started welling up with tears. I continued, "You didn't have to be nice to me. You really took care of me and my baby when I came in here as a hurting, pregnant woman, and I want to thank you."

"Rose, I have seen some hurting women, but you stole my heart for a few reasons. Your witty, funny, and upbeat attitude was great, even though you were in mental and physical pain." Good bye Sgt. Miller, thank you.

Welcome to CIW

On March 4th of that year, I was transported on the big black and-white bus from County Jail to CIW to do my time. I used to pass those buses all the time and try to look in at the inmates, wondering what it would be like to be shackled and on your way to prison. Now I knew. I was totally numb and feeling nothing. Never, even in my lowest state, had I allowed myself to believe that I would really be going to prison. The night before I left for CIW, I kept hoping for some kind of a stay—you know, time allowed at home with my family before going to prison for the rest of my life. That was kinda silly, huh? I looked around at my fellow inmates, hoping for a familiar face, but found none. I was sad but still, God gave me peace.

The bus taking me to my new home, CIW, rolled into the yard around 9 A.M. I remember looking out the window thinking, Oh, Lord, can I do this? What is this life going to be like? Are these women going to be threatening me? Do I have to worry about being raped? Is there a female "Art" just waiting for me? My only frame of reference for prison life came from the movies and what my brothers had told me. I hoped deep inside that both of them were exaggerating.

As the bus began to slow down while turning onto the CIW grounds, a brick or stone display with a lot of words on it introduced the grounds and the ground rules. Then, we pulled over to a large gray building called the Reception Center (RC).

Then I was faced with another journey of dehumanization as they told me to strip naked in front of the guards. I had done that in County Jail, but it's something that I don't think you ever get used to or comfortable with.

For the first time in my life, I know what our ancestors—African mothers, fathers, and children—felt like when being treated like cattle—mere property. After that, we each received one thin blanket and a pillow for our beds. I normally like piles of covers on my bed and so this just confirmed my suspicion that I was in for a lot of suffering. I felt like a little kid wanting her Momma. I was crying inside, "Momma, Momma, I don't want to be cold!" I was among the last to be processed, because it was count time. That's when they count the inmates to make sure they are all where they should be.

Once I got to the door of my cell, the most offensive, disgusting, polluted, and foul smell I had ever encountered slapped me in my face. I gagged. I was about to throw up.

It was so horribly filthy, I refused to vomit. "Abominable" does not even begin to describe what I saw. This is inhumane. I didn't even want to open my mouth for fear the stench would come inside me. Just then, an officer came to our door to do the head count. "I don't feel good," I told her. She left and came back with what I assumed was a pain pill, which I promptly swallowed.

I told my new roommate, Tracie, that I had been assigned the bottom bunk that she was sitting on due to my recent surgery. She started to cry and pleaded with me to let her have it because she was blind and afraid of high places, fearing that she might fall during the night. Because Tracie looked so pitiful in her dark shades, I decided to struggle with the top bunk.

How could they put a blind woman in here and make her fend for herself? I thought angrily. This was madness! How could she see to clean the toilet and those bloody clothes? My God, the guards should be reported for this. I immediately started trying to clean up the place because I just couldn't stand it.

"Chow time!" came a booming voice over the speaker. Inmates started running for the lines from everywhere. I filed out of my room rather quickly because I just wanted to get out of there. I wanted to talk to somebody—anybody—about this horrible room.

I began to talk to the inmate next to me in line about poor Tracie. "That's a shame that they make that poor blind girl live on her own like that. She can't see to take care of her clothes or her body. That room isn't fit for a dog to live in!"

Taylor, the inmate that I was talking to, fell out laughing. She said, "Janie, look! Traci got another one."

Janie said, "Girl,you don't know? How long you been living wit' her?"

I said, "I got here today."

"If I was you," she laughed, "I'd be afraid to close my eyes in the room with that fool. Traci ain't blind; she just crazy. You in the room wit' a psycho!"

"What!? You mean, she ain't blind? I went through all that pain trying to clean that nasty toilet and she ain't blind?" I was yelling at the top of my voice now. Calm down, I told myself. "She must be one sick lady to live in that filth. I'll pray for her, but I don't want to be her roommate," I told Taylor.

Fainting Spell
Several minutes later, my head started to swim and I felt like I was gonna fall. Still thinking about Tracie, I said, "I can't believe they put me in a cell

with a crazy woman! How could they do that?" I asked. She needed to be in a mental institution.

Taylor said, "They can do whatever the hell they want to. You ain't got rights now."
"Hell, you're a non-citizen, m-f--in" Janie added.

"You're right, I ain't a citizen here! My citizenship is in heaven; I'm a stranger in this land, baby. And we got a King as the head of our government—King Jesus."

"Well, you got 27 to life in this land, Baby," Taylor said.

"A King? Where you from?" Janie asked.

"I told you that I'm a citizen of heaven, and God will protect me no matter where I am."

"Oh, my goodness," Taylor rolled her eyes at me. "Don't tell me you're one of those religious nuts. Yeah, you and Tracie belong together."

At that moment, I could feel myself falling against the wall almost in slow motion. An intense heat swept over my body and sweat began to pour off my head. Like in a far distance, I could hear Taylor calling for help as I hit the floor.

Infirmary
When I came to, I was in the infirmary. "What happened to me? What happened to me?" I kept asking the nurse.
"What medicines are you on?"

"Well, I don't have any more prescription medicine, but this morning when I arrived, I asked for some pain pills and Officer Judy brought me a pill."

The nurse said, "Officer Judy? Oh, no, not again." "What do you mean 'not again'?" I asked.

"Well, we just had another incident where Officer Judy supposedly administered some Tylenol to an inmate, and she also fainted." I could tell the nurse was disgusted by the frown on her face. She said, "What you were probably given was a psych drug instead of a pain pill."

"What?! A psych drug? Am I going to be okay?"

The nurse replied, you're going to be fine. I was transferred that same evening to a different cell.

Lying in bed that night, many thoughts flooded my mind. I thought about all the women that were in this one place and wondered what happened to them that took away their freedom. I had such an eerie feeling about my new surroundings. My worst fears emerged. I kept saying, "Lord, help me! Help me, please! How can I do this, Lord?"

At that Moment, a Voice answered, "One day at a time, daughter. You do it one day at a time … with Me."

Startled, I jumped up and looked all around because I thought for sure somebody was in the cell talking to me.

"Sleep in peace knowing that I am watching over you. Rest."

Sleep overcame me after hearing those soothing words. I dreamed that I was in this awful, smelly, and dirty little cell with a mean cell mate that wouldn't leave me alone. In my sleep, I heard "CHOW TIME, ladies." Still sleeping, the words became a part of my dream, and I was trying to figure out where I was. Then, I heard it again, "CHOW TIME" as I drifted closer to consciousness. This time, I became instantly alert.

Daily Commands
In my journal, I wrote down vital information that they had given us the previous morning, like lock-in and count time. We got most of our commands collectively. At 4:20 P.M. and 9:20 P.M., we heard the words, LOCK-IN TIME, over the loudspeaker. This was an announcement made by the staff standing outside to inmates that it was time to leave the yard. When the yard closed at 4:20, it was lock-in time. When the yard closed at 8:30 P.M., it was time for all inmates to return to their units. People could shower, use the phone, or whatever, until 9:20 P.M.

DAY 1 - MY NEW HOME
I looked around the cell and remembering the hellish events of the night before. I got up, went to the shower, and got ready for breakfast in an amazing 15 minutes. When I was on the outside, it would take me hours to just get up, get ready, and go to the store. But here, I had to shower and dress in under a quarter of an hour. This morning, I read Psalm 91 and rested in the warmth of the promises there. I needed to journal some more. Ms. Fletcher knew what she was talking about.

Dear God,

I'm so grateful that You kept me through the night, that You didn't allow that girl to harm me. I'm going to make a memorial here so that I can remind myself of Your goodness and mercy and how You take care of me, Father. Thanks, again. I placed my journal back under my bed with my private things.

After eating, I went back to my cell at 7:30 A.M. wondering what a day at CIW was going to bring. I hated getting up so early. This was an awful place to be. Man, I planned to tell everyone I met to avoid it at all costs. This is truly no way to live. We had to get up in a chilly room and walk down an icy hallway to shower with complete strangers. I was washing myself and noticed a couple of women looking at me like I was a piece of peach cobbler or something. Thank God they didn't say anything to me.

Lord, help me today! No wonder it took me less than five minutes to shower. I practically ran out of there, and it's not like I could go back to my room and dress in privacy, either. OK, I'm dressed, now what do I do? I thought. So I just sat on my bunk. At that moment, my new cell mate walked in from her shower. She was a petite, gray-haired black lady named Marilyn. We made small talk for a minute, exchanging light-hearted observations and complaints about the shower and some of the women. Marilyn looked like someone's sweet mother who couldn't hurt a fly—until she opened her mouth. She walked very gracefully, kind of like my mother.

"Why are you here, Marilyn?"

"I was walking one day and got lost, turned on the wrong street, and ended up in here with you." At first, I thought she was serious until I saw her smile.

"Naw, I cut a niggah up," she said. "I caught him with my baby girl in the middle of the night. She was only six years old!" Her eyes hardened with anger. "She had been telling me that Leroy touched her too hard. I didn't know what she meant, but one night it clicked. That niggah tip-toed out of the room and was supposed to be going to the bathroom, but he was gone a long time. I got up and passed my son's bedroom, grabbing his favorite metal bat, and found my husband. He was in her room. I hit that SOB so hard, he fell to the floor and was out. Then I walked to the kitchen, grabbed my meat cleaver, and cut that niggah's thing right off and flushed it down the toilet like it was shit." "Oh, Jesus," I said under my breath.

"I figured that since he didn't know what to do with that thing, it was a danger to him. It could get him killed, so I decided to help him out and cut it plum off. I padded the area, helped to stop the bleeding, and then called the police. They couldn't stand still 'cause they were all men. They hated what he did to my baby, but they hated what I did to him more. I could see on their faces that they could feel his pain."

"They even looked around for it, but they couldn't find it and I wasn't about to tell them it was down the toilet. Wasn't no doctor gonna sew that thing back on. He better buy himself a prosthetic thingamajig a, 'cause he's finished with that one unless God grows it back."

I laughed out of sheer disbelief and shock. Then I sobered up. Ah man, Art cut off ears and this woman cut off men's things. Oh, boy. Hmmm … "Alright, Ms. Mary," the name I called her, "I got to respect you for that."

Then it got quiet. Ms. Mary's face changed from anger to drowning sorrow.

"They took my children from me." Mary dropped her head in a real sign of remorse and shame.

"The only thing I regret is that my children are in the system because of my impulsive actions. I had no other family for them to go to, and so, because of me, they'll be raised in a strange system. I can't write them to tell them I love them. They can't write me."

I felt so grateful to my family. My children had somewhere to go. Marilyn was in a lot of pain. I could hear it in her voice. I knew deep down inside of me, underneath my denials, I, too, was in a lot of pain. She made me miss my children so much.

That night I wrote God and told Him how grateful I was that I have family that love my children—a family that's standing in the gap for me (at least most of them) until I get out of this place.

Also, remembering what the angel, Ms. Fletcher, told me to do, I asked God to help me make out my schedule for the rest of the time I would be in RC (the Receiving Center). This was going to be easy. I wrote about reading my Bible and I prayed and sang during lockdown.

About 11:30 A.M., the loudspeaker belched out, "COUNT TIME," I heard that announcement two more times that day, 4:30 P.M. and 8:30 P.M.

"Lord Jesus," I cried, "don't let the heavens be silent! If there ever was a time that I needed to hear from **You**, it's now." And my first day went by much quicker than I had anticipated.

Chapter 12: General Population

SINGING OUT LOUD

I was really beginning to feel the Lord near in my life. I experienced His favor every step of the way. First of all, I was moved to General Population, with a new cellmate named Jennifer, a freckled-face, small Jewish girl. She spoke with cool street vernacular and seemed to be well versed in slang.

"Hey, my name is Jennifer. What's your name?"

"Rose, and you're my second cellie in one week. I have a high turnover, I guess."

"Yeah, I hear you've had some pretty crazy people around you."

"Yeah, I don't know if it's them or me."

She looked at me and we both started laughing.

"So, you're a lifer?"

"Yeah, that's what they say, but I'm going home soon."

Jennifer looked at me as if I were crazy. "What do you think you have on your side that nobody else does after they've been convicted and sentenced?

"I got God on my side, Jennifer." I then started singing out loud. Jennifer finished straightening up.

"You have a beautiful voice," she said.

"Thank you." I pulled out my Bible and lay back in my bed and began to read.

THE SMELL OF RAIN

Oh, how wonderful the fresh scent after a rain. I thought that would have been an unpleasant experience, but it wasn't! Then I was taken by surprise because I saw a familiar face totally unexpected. It seemed that God was whispering, "See, I've got you covered." One of the guards was a family friend! I couldn't believe it. Shirley knew my brother David and she kinda liked him. Once, she was trying to get me to put in a word for her.

"Give me his number and I won't tell him where I got it," she smiled.

"Shirley, you know I can't do that!" I protested. "When I hear from him, I'll ask if that's OK."

She laughed and said, "Do that."

We talked for a while and then Shirley walked me to the front of the chow line, telling the kitchen staff to make me a tray. I didn't take it because the other inmates were already giving me the eye. As it happened, there were several other staffers that I knew there. Maybe the time was not going to be that bad after all. "So far, so good," I said to myself. It's amazing what a familiar face can do to brighten up your day.

Write Momma

Dear Momma,

Hopefully, I'll be able to be in the real visiting room when you guys come. I'm in a little room about a little larger than my bedroom closet where we used to live in San Bernardino. Momma, I think I get a courtesy visit so you and dad can come see me.

I'm praying for the day and Moment you bring the boys so I can hold them and touch them. After a while, you can bring the kids and I can keep them in this place called the Children's Center. I need to ask my counselor how it works for those of us on close custody.

Anyway, I have a pretty good roommate, I think. This is different from the County and RC 'cause in the County, we only went outside 'bout three times a week. In RC, that's the reception center, we got to go outside and stay two hours every day, except at certain times. This time, I'm in the main yard, but they have me in close B, or close custody, 'cause of my time, and for the adjustment. I really don't mind; I need to know how this place works. It looks like a campus or something, not like on TV, where they show those dark, dingy-looking prisons. Momma, it looks like a school campus. Guess what? A lady named Sis Lillian teaches bible study on Monday nights. I just missed it. But it gives me something to look forward to.

How is Carol? She is too young to have her blood pressure so high. I keep remembering when they came to the county jail with all the babies, Darin and Lil Carol were newborns, Candace was one yr. and Atujuan two years. Thank God Emzie IV was old enough to help them, I know it was hard for her. I think Boonie might take Emzie IV or send him to Tulsa, I will hate for him to be so far. But anyway Mom I have to go, I love you and will call when I can.

Oh, my scripture is Isaiah 40: They that wait on the Lord shall renew their strength, they shall mount up with wings as eagles; they shall run and not be weary; they shall walk and not faint.

Dancing Feet
It was my first Saturday on prison grounds after RC. I saw a large group of people after lunch in the area called the "circle", I went over there and was shocked "it was a dance" all women, by themselves just everything. I loved to dance, something in me wanted to dance so badly. I hadn't

danced since 1985 before I started hanging out with Art and staying so high I couldn't even stand up on my feet, let alone go to some studio to dance. I didn't care who was dancing. I just wanted to dance. Something inside of me rose up, and I couldn't wait to get there.

The music started, my feet started taping and then my fingers started popping and by the time my head started bobbing, I was on the dance floor with everybody else. The music felt like electricity in my bones. I wanted to dance forever and ever. I was spinning and turning and doing the moves like the "click" that I created when I danced on Soul Train. The floor started getting thin with dancers and when I looked around, I saw everyone was just standing and watching me in fascination. I danced song after song—from Kool & the Gang, The Whispers, and the Gap Band, Shalimar, to Michael Jackson, Funkadelics, Heatwave, Rolls Royce, to Earth, Wind, and Fire, Stevie Wonder and more. Every song I thought I might want to hear played from that box which had great amplification. After a couple of hours, something happened to me and I stopped in my tracks in the middle of the dance floor. Others kept dancing, but I froze. Then very slowly, I walked off the dance floor and sat down next to the window, gazing at the other side of the campus. Jennifer, my s20 Jewish roommate, came and sat down next to me. She worked in the kitchen. I had noticed that she was nice and smiled at each person that she served. She made me feel like it was OK to smile, even in such a dark place.

"Rose, are you alright?" she asked.

I continued to stare out of the window in front of me. The longer I looked, the more I was able to make out images. I began to see people inside a glass building clear across the campus, and I wondered what was happening.

"What's going on over there?"

"Oh, that's just church," she replied.

"They have church on a Saturday?"

"Yes, every Saturday."

I stood up and immediately began to feel convicted. "I need to go over there," I told her.

"Now?"

Without answering, I walked toward the door and felt the eyes of everyone following me as I was leaving. Jennifer finally caught up with me.

"Wait, Rose! Wait up!"

Church on the Way

I open the door and peeked in, trying not to disturb the service. Entering, I stood near the side. Some were praying over others at the altar and some were just leaving as I walked in. Many had smiles on their faces and others were crying with thanksgiving to God for hearing their prayers. I felt so convicted because I could have experienced what they were experiencing instead of shaking my booty.

I asked Jennifer if they have this service weekly, and she replied, "Yes, at night too, around 7 P.M."

I groaned within myself because I was on close custody, which meant as a lifer, I have to be in at 4 P.M. and can't come out unless I'm escorted by the authorities.

Jennifer asked "do you have to stay on close custody for a year?"

"Yea, "God knows what He's doing," I told her. "He's just keeping me safe."

I knew in my heart that people feared for my safety in this prison. Art had connections not only outside the prison, but also inside it. But I knew God was in control and would keep me safe.

Horns Are Blowing

The horns of the prison started blowing and Jennifer ran out the door toward the dorm, telling me to come on. I ran out of there and got to my cell as fast as I could.

Once I got in my cell, Jennifer told me that I was the talk of the grounds with my dancing.

"Oh, yeah?" I had to admit part of me really enjoyed the attention.

Jennifer told me that people were commenting how it looked like I was on stage. Everybody was amazed. She told them that I had been on Soul Train. "After count, they want you to come down and dance some more," she said.

"Is that what they do after count? Everybody goes and dances?"

She said, "No, we just go in the laundry room and bring the boom box. The officers really don't say anything to us; but, girl, everybody wants to see you dance, and I told them I could get you to dance."

I hesitated, recalling how I had struggled with conviction at the church service, but then I convinced myself there was nothing wrong with it. "Sure, I'll break them off a little sum'en-sum'en. I love to dance."

As we were leaving our cell, women were walking by, some shouting to Jennifer, "Is she your roommate?"

I could tell Jennifer puffed up her chest a bit now having star status.

When Jennifer and I walked over to the laundry room, we could hear the music from a short distance away. One girl asked if it were true that I had been married to one of the men in the Gap band.

"Yes, it's true."

Then the guard said, "I heard you were on Soul Train, but I don't believe it. I need to see it, so I'm gonna let those girls crank that music up."

My song came on—Michael Jackson's "Pretty Young Thing." They formed a circle and called me in. I asked if somebody wanted to dance with me or was I doing it by myself. Somebody did want to hang with me, a girl name Rita in the back. She said she could dance. She came in the circle, and we started dancing. Everybody went crazy when I did the camel lock and the robot. We danced and everybody was cheering and happy and then they brought us out of the laundry room into the TV room because we needed more space. They thought I was Janet Jackson or somebody. I could hear the screams and the wows, and I just ate it up.

"Alright! Alright," the officer finally shouted. "OK, ladies, it's count time; time to lock-in."

My roommate, Jennifer, tried to talk to me all night. She kept firing questions at me, like, "Where did you learn how to dance like that?" "How did you get on Soul Train?"

"Do you want the short or long version?" I asked her.

"The long version. We ain't going nowhere soon." We both laughed at that. I told her, "I'm going to give you the short version because I'm tired.

"Let's see, it started when I was about 13 years old. I remember the day I was at school and told the kids that I wanted to be on Soul Train. It was the year that the Ohio Players came out with a really great bad song. We were in the hallway talking about the episode on Soul Train that weekend and I told them one day I was going to be on that show. "My brother, Peter and Sai Evans was accepted to go on the show. I wasn't. I thought I was so special that surely when they saw me, they would just let me in."

"Well? Did they?"

"Naw, I went up there with my brother and his partner and they let him and his partner in, then they looked at me and told me 'NO.' He was on the list and I wasn't.

"I was left standing there with my mouth hanging open. I couldn't believe it. I waited out there for about an hour and then Don Cornelius drove up in his shining Rolls Royce. Apparently they had called him and let him know that there was a shortage of dancers. When he saw us, he said, 'Let these kids in.' And that is the story of how I got on Soul Train."

"How long did you dance on Soul Train?"

"I danced for six and a half years. It was one weekend out of the month, and we taped for four weeks at a time. I had many dancing partners, but my favorite one was Mr. X. He was a regular and made me feel special because he wanted to always dance with me. He even looked for me, and that made me feel good." He either carried me down the line or did other crazy things, like having golf balls come out of his mouth.

I was growing tired and was being drained by experiencing so many mixed emotions reflecting on all this, so I told Jennifer that we would talk a little later.

"Rose, I feel like I'm talking to a celebrity. I mean, you've been on TV, in movies, hung out with stars—can I get your autograph?"

"Yeah, tomorrow, now lights off."

I was exhausted. I drifted off to sleep, hearing her still talking in the air.

First Prison Church Day

The time was 6:30 A.M. Click, click, the doors began to pop. Time to go eat. I got up, went to breakfast, and came back and got dressed for church because it was Sunday morning. It was my first day in prison church, which was in the same building I saw yesterday, the opposite side of the cafeteria.

When I walked in church, it felt like everybody was looking at me. They were the same people that I danced with last night. I took my seat and Chaplain Fortier called for the song from Sister Monique. She sang from the depths of her heart. Not once did she ever open her eyes. Her hands were lifted and pointed towards heaven, and she had an angelic smile on her face as she sang "To God Be the Glory."

Once Sister Monique sat down, I heard sniffles and folk gathering themselves together, including me. She had touched me all the way down to my toes.

Chaplain Fortier stood and opened up by saying, "My subject this morning is 'Cold, Lukewarm, or Hot.'"

"OUCH!" I said to myself.

He continued, "Do you have one foot in the world and one foot in the church?"

I just knew God was talking to me, or somebody must have told the chaplain about me. I prayed, "God, You are going to have to help me because I love to dance."

The chaplain continued to preach, and I asked the Lord why I felt guilty for just dancing. "You know I love to dance, Lord. What should I do?"

After the chaplain delivered a powerful message, he gave an altar call. I hesitated because I had already asked God into my heart and I wasn't sure if I should go up. I thought about it a long time, then I got up with tears in my eyes. It seemed like many people started getting up and began crying. The chaplain prayed for us. I knew from that day on that my life had to represent something different here and be consistent.

As church was dismissed, the young lady who sang that powerful song came up to me and introduced herself as Monique. "I saw you peek in the door last evening when service was over. Are you new here? When did you arrive?"

I said, "Yeah, I got here not too long ago. Today is my first Sunday."

"I've been here about a month over at RC, but a week in the yard now. Say, I'm not going to beat around the bush. I heard how well you can dance. Everybody was talking about it this morning at breakfast. You live in Killer Miller unit, right? We all eat together but are spread around on different levels depending on time and crime. They want life to adjust without incident. That's why they separate us the way they do."

Monique continued, "I have something that you just might enjoy." Then she gave me a cassette.

"How am I going to play this?" I asked.

"Ask Chaplain Fortier. He'll let you check out a cassette player."

The cassette was a group called the Winans I had never heard of them.

"Listen, Rose, we're having Prison Fellowship Ministries in a couple of weeks, if you're interested. It's a lot of fun, and we learn so much."

"What is Prison Fellowship Ministry? Do they show you how to get out of here?" We laughed together.

"It's a ministry that comes into CIW to teach a series of Bible-based subjects, like What the Bible Teaches, Journey through the Bible, and Lessons on Assurance, and then at the end, you get a certificate."

"Oh, OK. That sounds cool, thank you."

"You'll see the flyers posted around. Keep an eye out for them."

"I will, thanks again, Monique."

God sent Monique to me. I felt a bond with her. When I saw her in chapel, I always noticed her attention was upward. Whenever she worshipped or praised God, her hands always reached toward the heavens.

When I walked out of chapel into the prison atmosphere, I was rudely jolted back into a grim reality. The chapel experience made you feel like you were out at somebody's church—not in somebody's prison. My spirits were lifted when I left there. I couldn't wait until Prison Fellowship Ministry began. That sounded really good. The next day, I asked the chaplain for a cassette player, and he was more than happy to lend it to me once he saw my cassette. I hurried back to my cell, plugged it in, put the cassette in, and played it. I was amazed at the beat. This would have never played in Daddy's church.

1987 Mother's Day Blues

Dear God,

Today, I struggle. Lord, I feel less than a mother. I know my family loves me, and I know my sons love me. I only wish I could have thought about them more while I was out there getting my way. I wish I could have thought about You more and came to You before now. Why do mistakes and tragedies cause people to run to You? I guess these things remind us Who is really in charge and Who we really need.

God, You are going to have to be my heavenly father and earthly father. I know it's hard for Dad to see me in here—his baby girl. He doesn't come as much as Momma does and sometimes that hurts, but when Momma explains how it breaks his heart, I do understand.

I pray for my mother who is always so loving and sweet. I hate that I didn't see all of her wonderful attributes and excellent qualities when I was younger. She actually thought I didn't love her at one point. You know, Lord, she was so sick once and the doctors told us that she was going to die. But Dad said if it happened, she would be in heaven. I remember in my stupidity asking Momma how come she wasn't dead yet and gone to heaven. I think from that moment on in my childhood, she thought I despised her. I couldn't explain then what I meant, but I sure have the opportunity to tell her how much I love her now and how glad I am that she didn't die and leave us to go to heaven.

I'm so glad I have You to talk to, God. Thank you for always being there.

I love You, Your daughter, Rose.

First Day of School (GED)

May 20, 1987, my first day of school. My real assignment was school. I signed up for my GED, and my day was full. My Adult Education class ran from 8 A.M. to 11 A.M., and my Business Education class was from 1 P.M. to 4 P.M. This schedule lasted from May 1987–October 1987. The registration staff told me that my Business Education class would last through February 1988 and after that point I could apply for a job. I couldn't wait. I didn't know how school would be for me because I had not been in awhile. I was determined to re-invent my identity in this place with the help of the Lord. Somewhere deep inside of me, I wanted to be a positive role model for my kids and others.

Getting prepared for school that morning felt strange and then adding the reality of going to high school again years after I had dropped out was even weirder. I could say the good side was that it started at 8 A.M., unlike regular school that always interrupted my beauty rest.

I walked in the classroom where about 30 other women sat, not knowing what to expect, a nice, brown-skinned man with some cool glasses on greeted me. I decided that I would sit in the front row to make sure I was not distracted and used my time wisely. I wanted the teacher to know that I was ROSE PARKER and I was SERIOUS, so I brought him an apple and I sat right in the front. Everybody looked at me like I was crazy, because they sat way in the back.

"Mr. Martin, an apple a day keeps bad teachers away. Have you had your apple today?"

He chuckled to himself and said, "Thank you, and what is your name?"

"I'm Rose Parker. Nice to meet you."

"And nice to meet you too."

At the end of the class, Mr. Martin assigned everyone homework that was due the next day.

"Hey, Mr. Smith," Mr. Martin said.

A man had walked into the classroom and was standing near the back of the room.

"Class, this is your next instructor, Mr. Smith."

"Hello," everyone said at the same time.

The teachers made small talk before Mr. Martin left. This gave the class a five-minute break to talk with one another.

Here I am in ABE III, which stands for Adult Basic Education. I was a little intimidated and hoped that I could relate to what the teacher was about to teach us. The materials were pretty basic and the more he talked, the more things began to sound more and more familiar. Mr. Smith was an expert because he went over things and equations at least seven times, and even if I didn't understand it, I certainly remembered it because of the repetition involved. When I left that day, I felt like I had just picked up from where I left off when I dropped out of school in 1976 in the 11th grade. Things are not all that different, I thought to myself. Thank God I didn't smoke all of my brain cells away.

Journal
Dear God,

I am so glad to have the chance to go back to finish what I started. Thank you for letting me do this. I pray that You give me the strength and the enthusiasm to do it. Lord, I don't want to quit anything without finishing any more. I want to show other women that it can be done no matter what. I like how Mr. Martin said winners don't quit and if I quit, I can never win.

June 3, 1987, My National Holiday Birthday
Early that morning, I was as happy as I could be. It was my birthday and my birthdays always brought me so much joy, so why not here too.

"Alright, it's a national holiday, ladies! I'm giving everyone the day off. No work assignments and no school. Everybody, you are off from work assignments and school today!" I yelled down the halls.
"What holiday is it, Rose?"

"My birthday is what holiday it is."

This was followed by laughter, some smart remarks, and a lot of swearing and screaming at me to shut up and let them sleep. I laughed so hard because I was so filled with joy I didn't care what they hollered back at me. God let me see another day.

I couldn't wait to get to school so that my peers could sing happy birthday to me.

Mr. Martin had already been informed that it was my birthday and in unison, the entire class started singing "Happy Birthday" as soon as I walked in. I was purposely tardy so I could surprise them with my birthday, but I ended up getting surprised.

After they sang, Linda, the girl that always sat next to me, told me to come and sit down while each student came up to me and gave me gifts. I began to cry and laugh at the same time. The love I received was more than I could handle—and way more than I expected.

Then to top it all off, it was Progress Report Card Day. I received my report card and screamed, "Thank you, Jesus!" I got all "A's." The first thing I thought about was writing my parents and sending them a copy of my report card. It's been a long time since I got a good report on anything. Letter to Momma and Dad

Hey, Momma and Daddy,

I couldn't wait to write you this letter. Thank you for your beautiful birthday card. I am so happy today. I thank God for giving me so many chances with Him. He has given me a second and third chance to start all over again. Remember I told you I was going to get my GED? Well, I'm enclosing my first report card. Momma, I told you that you have your daughter back for your Mother's Day present, and I am where I left off in 1976 when I dropped out of school. I'm picking right back up and going forward. I hope you are proud of me.

I got all A's and I'm doing good in school. I have six months to complete my GED, and I'm going to finish this time. Every month we get a progress report card. I'll be sending them home to you every time I get one, Momma. I have joined so many volunteer projects to keep me busy that by the time my day is over, I'm exhausted, and when I get back to my bed, I fall asleep. I love you and Dad. Remember, I'm redefining myself for the good up in here. Momma, keep praying for me, please. Give my love to my sons and show Emzie my report card too. Tell him to finish all of his homework. If I can do it, he can too.

Love,
Rose

Jeremiah 29:11: For I know the thoughts I have for you and the plans I have for you; they are good and not evil; they are to give you an expected end and a hope.

Chapter 13: Hope

March Telephone Call

I looked at the clock and got excited. Oh, it's my phone time! I dialed those numbers as fast as I could and hoped Peter was there. I couldn't wait to tell him that they're going to let me have a family visit.

"This is a collect call from Rose in a California Institution. Do you accept?"

"Yes, I accept," the person on the other line answered.

"Hi, Peter, I'm going to be able to have a visit with Momma, Daddy, and the boys next month. I just put the paperwork in."

"Will they let me come?" he asked.

"Yeah, any immediate family member can come."

"So, you don't have to be married, huh?" Peter sounded so relieved.

"No. Actually, I think the kids can come by themselves later, when I get off close custody. This is a trip! I'm so thankful. I'll be able to be with my babies all night, eat breakfast with them, spend the day together, everything."

"I'm so glad for you, Rose Ann. Momma will be glad, too. I hope Daddy is able to make it."

"He will. Well, I'll talk to you later. Love you."

April Telephone Call
"This is a collect call from Rose in a California institution. Do you accept?"
"Yes, I will."

"Hi, Momma. Guess what? You can bring the kids, or have someone bring the kids, and they can stay here with me. It's like I'm the babysitter."

"Oh, for real?" Momma said, delighted at the news.

"There are some forms that I sent in the mail that have to be notarized so that the state will not be held accountable, but as long as the birth certificate says I'm the mother and you have temporary custody, the visit will be authorized."

"Yeah, we got those in the mail today."

"It's going to take a few weeks for the whole process to be completed, but from now on, whenever you don't have anyone to watch the kids, they can just come here."

"Rose, it's amazing that they do that."

"See, Momma, that should take a lot of pressure off you and Dad, because the visiting is open from 9 A.M. – 9 P.M. every day except Tuesday and Wednesday.

"Oh, I also enclosed the form that I had notarized here that gave all of you temporary legal custody, so make a bunch of copies and give one to Diane, Peter, Carol, and David." Momma didn't have a chance to get a word in. I know I was talking faster than a speeding train.

"Oh, yeah, Momma, another thing which is really cool. They also have a visit where the kids can spend the night. Did you hear me, Momma? The whole night!"

"That's good, Rose," Momma said, barely getting those three words in.

"While I'm on close custody, I have to have someone come with them from my immediate family. I know I've been rambling on. How is everything at home?"

"I just want to make sure my baby girl is OK."

The officer shined a flashlight signaling me to get off the "I have to go now, but I'll call back in a few days or so, OK? I love you."

"I love you, too, Rose."

A Touch of Thankfulness

David brought Momma and the kids to see me. I couldn't believe it. How I longed for this moment and for this day to come. I could actually hold my own flesh and blood in my arms. No glass between us, no phone receiver and cord as a mediator. I could whisper in my babies' ears and touch their skin. My heart wept with thanksgiving to God. I sat there speaking to everyone and engaged them in conversation, but deep, deep within me; I was overwhelmed with emotions because of the physical touch we shared. Oh, God, how I've missed this. What joy and delight to simply touch and hold my children.

"Momma, thank you for my package. I'm really enjoying everything."

"Hey, Rose," Officer Carla said, "are these your handsome princes that you've been talking about?"

"Yes, they are, and they're getting more and more handsome as they grow."

"Listen, did you know that we have a Children's Center where children can play and mothers can be together?"

"No, I didn't, but thank you for the information." That was the day I learned about the Children's Center, and I decided on my next visit that I would take my kids over there so that they could play while I watch them.

Before my family left, I asked them to send me some journals booklets. Momma looked puzzled.

"Journals, Rose?"

"Yeah, Momma, so I can write to God and write my feelings down."

"Oh, OK, baby girl. You got it."

"Rose, you seem to be in great spirits. I'm glad to see that." David put his arms around me and held me tightly.

"David, I can't let this place keep me down. I know that I won't be here forever. I'm just waiting for the day that I leave this place. I know it won't be long."

I will forever be grateful and thankful to God for keeping my mind and allowing me to touch my family and for them to touch me.

That night, I thanked God for allowing my family to see the joy that He had given me so that they would not worry about me.

Chapter 14: Joining LTO

Long Termers Organization

"Hi, I'm Karen, and we, the LTO, would like to welcome our new members today to our group. Sorry that you qualify, but we are glad to have you. Since we have so many of you, let me tell you a little bit about us. (The room was packed.)

"Our membership is comprised of lifers and prisoners sentenced to long prison terms. Our goal is to stay on top of any new legislation and inform you regarding legislation that might affect you. We seek to educate you as it relates to court commitments, prison rules as they exist now, and any subsequent changes. This group could show you, and me, how to best fight our cases in order to get out of here.

"Occasionally, Short Termers do stupid things that cause the powers that be to want to change the rules. We have opportunity to serve as a buffer between the institution and the inmates because we are the ones most seriously affected.

"We also want to advise you of what I consider the ten most crucial points to embrace while you are here:

1. Make sure that you attend the programs and group activities that have been set up for your benefit.
2. Get your education.
3. Keep your mind sharp.
4. Get a job.
5. Don't allow yourself to vegetate in here.
6. You are still a viable and functioning human being.
7. Always remember that you matter.
8. Don't give up.
9. Don't do stupid stuff and get into trouble.

10. Avoid write-ups at all cost, because you don't want to add years to an already-long sentence.

I walked away from the meeting saying I wanted to be one of the LTO Executive Board members. I knew I could do what Felicia just did. That was so cool. After Lynn gave me the schedule for the volunteer program, I rushed back to my dorm. Later that night, I couldn't wait to write in my journal because I felt it was such a promising week and a positive day. I wanted to tell God about it as soon as possible by writing, as if He didn't already know.

Dear God,

I'm so glad the LTO exists. I wonder why most of the people in the class are so dry and non-responsive. The leaders were trying to be positive and hopeful. I could tell by the way they made their reports and congratulated the lifers for their participation in the various fundraisers and events. I would love to work in that group. I think I could do a great job. I want to join other groups, too, like Felicia encouraged us. Lord, help me be ambitious and hardworking while I'm here for as long as I will be here. I don't want to do like Lynn pointed out that other women do, just stay in their rooms and rot away or get in everybody else's way trying to block them from progressing. God, protect me from people like that and may I not block anyone from moving forward. I love You, God. Thank you for being there for me always. Take care of my boys and my family please, Lord.

Good night.

I put up my journal and lay back thinking over the events of the meeting.

I'M VITAL

I could still hear Felicia's sultry voice when she was encouraging the old and new Long Termers to stay positive. I wanted to do everything she said we should do. I had to keep my mind sharp, and going to school helped. I decided to go see Lynn in RC in order to get started with volunteer work over there and as soon as a job opens, I can earn some money and begin to pay my way. I picked up the notes that I was writing down while Felicia had been talking and read them out loud.

"I will not allow myself to vegetate in here. I am a vital and functioning human being." Tears rolled down my face as I repeated those words. "... because I matter. I can't give up." I was so glad I wrote those notes down while she was speaking because they were just what I needed to hear.

June 1987 Family Visit

"Rose Parker, you have a visitor."

Oh, thank God. This is my first visit with just the kids and me privately. I got ready and ran as fast as I could to the visiting center because I knew my sons were there waiting.

"Hi, I'm Rose Parker. My kids are here to see me."

The guard beckoned for me to come through the door. "Come this way, Inmate Parker. Your kids are in the visiting center with the childcare staff. You have until 8:30 P.M. tonight."

"Oh, I see them from here!"

After they patted me down in the visiting room, I proceeded into the children's visiting area. My kids saw me and began to run toward my open arms as I stretched them out to them. Darian just started walking, so he was struggling as he was coming toward me. Oh, how blessed I felt to have another special moment with my kids. We colored in the coloring books, and I clapped for them as soon as they completed coloring a page. Then the boys stopped coloring and started playing with the race cars.

There were moments when I had to turn away from them so they would not see me crying. I was so thankful for their presence and their unconditional love for me. Even though it was early in the day, inside I was already counting down the hours and dreading the Moment we would be separated until the next time. Only God knew how important these moments were for a Momma to be able to hold her babies. Whoever fought for this opportunity for Mommas to still be in contact and spend this type of quality time with their children was a God sent. My boys didn't know how much strength and years they added to my life.

After Atujuan played on the scooter, he jumped right off and climbed on a bike. "Momma, look, look, Momma." He and that little tricycle were going in circles. I guess that's a kids' world for you.
"That's great. You're riding the bike. Wow. Where did you learn how to ride a bike? You're so smart."

Darian kept getting in the way trying to catch him. Darian ran so much and played so hard that he fell asleep so I put him in the playpen.

Later, I started to read Atujuan a story from one of the children's books that was the property of the center. Before I knew it, we both had fallen asleep.

"Count time, ladies."

I jumped awake. It was already 11:30 A.M. I couldn't believe I had been here for two hours.

I laid Atujuan down next to Darian and went to stand with the ladies for count. After the count cleared, I went to get the assistant from the visiting childcare to get some change for the vending machines (inmates were not allowed to have any contact with money). I needed to get something for me and the boys to eat for lunch.

"Momma, Momma, give me some," pleaded Atujuan. I was drinking my orange soda when he woke up. It was such a joy to feed the boys and watch them eat. My heart melted every time they said, "Momma." These were stop-time moments for me.

The clock now said 8:20 P.M. Time passed so quickly. I gathered my boys together next to me and put Atujuan's hands in Darian's hands and told the boys to always say their prayers at night, then I prayed over my sons.

"Father, thank you for my children. Thank you for the time You have ordained and allowed us to have together. May these Moments stick in our hearts that we may never forget them. Lord, protect my boys from evil and temptation. Protect their lives, please. God, be with Emzie and strengthen and protect him too. God, I know You can keep my boys, and I trust You with them. Bless Momma and Dad and all of my family. Thank you again, Lord, for making a way for me to spend a day with my boys. I love You. In Jesus' name."

Atujuan repeated, "In Jesus' name."

"Momma loves you. Remember that always, okay, Atujuan?"

"I love you too, Momma."

Darian was trying to get at the tricycle again.

The guards stood there to take my sons to my waiting family. I hugged them over and over again, following out as far as I could go and watched them. Oh, God, help me, please.

Prison Fellowship Ministry Week: Loving Others
"Well, Rose, how did you like it? Wasn't it wonderful?"

"Yes, I learned a lot about myself," I told her.

"Okay, now you know I'm going to drill you to see if you were paying attention," Monique warned.

"How come I can't drill you first?"

"Because I invited you, and the truth of the matter is that I think you are very special and I just want to make sure they were clear enough for you."

As I looked into Monique's eyes, it occurred to me for the first time that she had a glass eye. I had heard rumors about someone stabbing her in the eye, but I didn't believe it because of the type of person I perceived her to be. Then I recalled that she always had on tinted glasses whenever I saw her. This was the first time I was close enough to see her eye. How she got a life sentence for a home invasion murder I will never understand.

"Well, the seminar was entitled 'Loving Others.' What I learned in this seminar was that relationships are important and we need others. Not just any other, but healthy others because that's how God made us. Also, that the key to right relationships with others is a right relationship with God first."

Monique interrupted, "Wasn't that an eye-opener?"

"Yeah, that was a hit right to the center of your stomach," I joked. "Well, next, we are supposed to make it our goal to love others as Christ loves us and to lay down our lives for them. Now, Monique, this one was a little hard for me because I had a lot of mixed emotions here." I looked at my paper where I had notes from the lecture. "We should try with God's help to mend broken relationships." Many thoughts came to me about this one because when the minister was talking about broken relationships and the need to make sure you mend them with all your ability, I thought about the man I shot and how I can't mend that relationship since he's gone.

Monique took me by the hand in a really comforting way as if she knew my heart was heavy. "Rose, God has forgiven you for your actions. You have repented over and over again and you need to know that God has forgiven you. The only mending that you needed to make was between you and God and you have done that, sweetie. God has given you another chance to do what number 5 says. Did you write that one down?"

"Yes, I sure did. It says the way we relate to others can help them want to know God. And he quoted John 15:12–13, where Jesus said, 'My command is this: Love each other as I have loved you. Greater love has no one than this, that he lay down his life for his friends.'"

"Girl, I'm glad you kept great notes because one day, you are going to have to teach this to others and it looks like you have your material already mapped out. Just make those notes part of your everyday goals. Healthy relationships are possible, Rose, no matter what," Monique encouraged.

"Yeah, this was really, really good. I needed it. Lord knows I had my share of unhealthy, toxic, and crazy relationships, as they call them." I was sitting there, at times embarrassed and ashamed. I was so glad they encouraged questions at any time during the teaching segment. I was grateful to learn that the key to right relationships starts with a right relationship with God. As I reflected on my past, I realized that I left God out and went after everything I thought I wanted and needed.

The line filled up quickly as we waited to thank all the facilitators who participated in today's seminar. I was kind of glad because it gave Monique and me time to talk and bond some more.

"Rose, remember, there is another seminar next Saturday, 8A.M. Don't miss it." A Heart-to-Heart Talk with Jen

I had the radio going and an upbeat song called "You Brought the Sunshine" came on by the Clark Sisters. Oh, was that on time or what? I was dancing in my cell while folks were passing by. I didn't care. I started clapping my hands and singing along with the music after I caught on to the words. Thank God the words were repetitive. God sure did bring the sunshine and the light this morning.

Jennifer walked in as the song was almost over. She wasn't sure if I was partying to a secular song or a gospel song.

"Rose, you ought to join the choir. You really sound good," she complimented me.

"You think so, Jen?"

"Yep."

"I'll join if you join," I told her.

"OK, let's do it, but I can't sing. I can move my lips and pretend."

"It'll have to be after I finish school and get my GED in October."

"Damn, you're busy. Let's see, you volunteer for RC; every time Prison Fellowship Ministry comes, you are there; you are at weekly Bible study; you just started attending LTO; and now you're in school. How are you doing all that?"

"Like I told you a long time ago, Jen, I ain't serving time; I'm going to let time serve me, and I'm about to be somebody and change my life up in this joint!"

"Well, sh--t—excuse my language, but I can barely handle my job and the little church I do go to."

"Jen, you can do more than that."

"For what, Rose? Hell, I'm going to be here fifteen damn years to life."

"Not me, Jen. I'm getting up out of here somehow, someway."

"Rose, you got 27 to life! I don't think you're getting out of here anytime soon."

"Oh, yes, I am. Wait and see. And when I do go, I got to have my stuff together. I promise you, just as you see me standing here, I ain't gonna be here no 27 years to life."

"Rose, I'm sorry. Just because I can't believe doesn't give me the right to rain on your faith. You know what? Secretly, I wish I had the attitude that you have and the faith that you exhibit in all that you do. You do everything so damn good. I just can't believe you ended up in here. You're such a nice person it's hard to believe you were involved in everything you've told me."

"Jen, I have to get involved with everything because inside of myself, I'm not here in this prison. Girl, this feels like career training on prison grounds. Hell, I ain't never been so damn committed to anything the way I am now. And I made a point to try to be the best at whatever I'm going after."

Jen was in for three counts of murder. Ever since I met her, she told me that she was in for mistaken identity. But she said this is the only place she has ever been where she has had a family. She was abandoned as a child on someone's doorstep and then grew up in foster care where she acted out and had minor misdemeanor accounts on her record, but she swears up and down she did not kill three people over drugs. It was a transaction that went bad, and she was in the wrong place at the wrong time.

I know Jen thought I was crazy part of the time, but just like God's man, Pastor Roger DeCuir, said, "I got to believe God! I can't believe nothing else but God!!!"

Empty Satisfaction

In the wee hours of the morning, we heard what seemed to be crying or whimpering. It was hard to make out the sounds and where they were coming from. I whispered to see if Jennifer was awake. She was.

"Jennifer, what's that?"

"I think that's Cindy."

"Is she okay?"

"I'm sure she's okay. She used to do that sh--t in RC."

"Used to do what?"

"Girl, she's masturbating."

"What!? Masturbating? Oh, hell, I thought she was sick, hurting, or crying."

"Yeah, she's been written up for that dumb sh--t before. She obviously ain't learned her lesson still."

"That's so crazy."

"How do you think her cellie feels? She's right in there with her."

I turned over and put my pillow over my head, holding it close to my ears.

The next day I told one of the guards that I didn't want to hear that every night. I didn't care if Cindy knew I told either. Jen teased me and said Cindy was going to get me and make me come in her room and watch.

"Jen, you can be one of the nastiest talking people at times."

"Keep praying for me, Rose. God is going to change me. I hear you praying for me all the time."

"I sure do because God sure is able!"

More Radio Encouragement
Church was really good today. I truly enjoyed hearing the Word and singing in the choir.

After a long day, I returned for the night. I wasn't really sleepy but wanted to hear some gospel music. I learned about the KMAX radio station from Monique in the chapel, so I walked over to my radio to find something. I tuned to a station that was gospel and heard a calm, fatherly voice. It stopped me in my tracks 'cause I was missing my dad something fierce that day. During the entire program, I paid no attention to what the man was saying because I was so mesmerized by his voice. I hated to see the program come to an end, but I quickly wrote down the address, time, and station so I could listen again next week. I entered this information on my weekly calendar so that I wouldn't forget to listen. The man reminded me so much of my dad.

Right after that program went off the air another man came on that almost scared the daylights out of me. He was screaming, "Don't touch that dial! You are listening to GOD'S MAN, Pastor Roger DeCuir! I'm God's

Man! I believe God! I believe God for somebody tonight!" He kept repeating this. I lay back and got fired up because he was talking about believing God like Abraham did for the unbelievable—the unthinkable—the unreachable. "I'm talking to you out there in Radio land, you who are in a bad fix and you don't see no human way out. But God can and He will, if you just trust God!!! Believe God!" I started thinking about being in this prison, and I wanted out so badly. I knew God would get me out. I believed Him for it.

Jennifer woke up while the pastor was praying and prophesying. "Rose, does he have to holler at God so loud?" she asked, irritated.
I laughed because he was a bit wild, but he didn't bother me. "I'll turn it down just a little, okay? I'm sorry. Go back to sleep." (Jennifer worked in the kitchen and had to be up and out by 4:30 A.M. for the first shift.)

You Must See Your Way Out!
Mr. Martin stood before the class after everyone was seated and quieted down. We were all so excited about our accomplishments in finishing. His face lit up with a huge smile, just like the sun. "I know each of you is excited. It's good to see the joy in your eyes. But I have one thing to say."

He waited long enough for us to think something was wrong and then continued, "You made it! Look at you! Turn around and look at your classmates next to you and behind you and see a champion!"

As I walked back to the dorm, I sang "Victory Is Mine" all the way. I thought about my writing time with the Lord. I hadn't journaled like I normally did. Of course I talked to God wherever I am and I continued to say my prayers at night and when I was awake, but my time in writing was not as consistent as it had been in the past. I decided I would start back as soon as I got to the dorm.

Volunteered For Chapel

I recognized one of the women in the Chow Hall waving at me. She often attended chapel service.

"Hey, Rose, how are you today?"

"It's Rachel, right?" I asked her.

"Yes, that's right. I was wondering if you would be interested in the Administrative Clerk/Cleaning position for the chapel. Basically, it's cleaning, straightening out things like the chairs as they get moved at the end of a service, putting hymn books back on the shelves, making sure the piano is clear of extra things that usually get placed on top of it, and then do the bathrooms. Make sure they're cleaned from the stalls to the mirrors, get rid of the trash by placing it outside the door, and put in new trash bags—"

I interrupted her, "Boy, you sure have the duties down pack."

I started laughing. I didn't know she had been watching me.

"Well, have you seen me walk around the tracks in my quiet time?"

"No, I haven't. I might have joined you had I seen you because Lord knows, I need to walk and exercise more."

"Well, that's my quiet time and I often talk to God during those times about things. I'll ask Him in my quiet time if this is something I can do now."

"I respect that, Rose, wholeheartedly. Please let me know at your earliest convenience, OK?"

We embraced and said our good-byes. Rachel is a hard worker too. I have been in the bathroom when she had just came out from washing things and changing bags, being the first one there, making sure everything was ready for the service, and the last one to leave. I walked back to the unit to rest from a long day.

The Three T's
That night, Pastor Joseph brought a soul-stirring message to Radio land. Tithing was his topic: Giving to God a Tenth of Your Resources. I was struck when he said it doesn't always have to be money. You can also give a tenth of your time, treasure, and talent.

I give what I can in the offering at chapel, which is very little, but Lord, but this is refreshing to hear him say it's possible to give other things, like time, talent, and treasure. I never thought about tithing like that, I guess. He went on to say you can serve God's people, God's agenda, and God's service. People of God should find out where God is moving and working and get involved there.

October 1987 Journal Entry
Dear God,

I know I have not written You in my journal in a long time. Please forgive me for getting so caught up in the day-to-day school activities, volunteer work, prison fellowship, and LTO work. I don't mean to be neglectful, that's why I try to watch TBN and listen to the great men and women of Yours on KMAX. Again, thank you for Pastor Gardner, Pastor Roger DeCuir, Pastor Jean Perez, and Pastor Rueben Anderson.

I know sometimes I go to sleep without praying because I have worked and studied so hard all day and I fall asleep. But with the gospel channel playing in my ears, I know You are still speaking to me. That's why I try to keep the TV on TBN all night.

God, I have never been so focus-driven in my life like now, Lord. You know that already. I am so grateful to You for helping me get through these five months of school and allowing me to get my GED. THANK YOU, JESUS! I did it—or shall I say, "We did it."

At first You know I was scared when I started, not knowing if I could actually do it. God, You restored brain cells that I had smoked out; You gave me the ability to concentrate and remember. Father, I dedicate this GED to You because only You deserve all the glory, and honor, and praise. And Lord, I want to do like Dr. Martin suggested. I don't want to stop here; I want my Bachelor's degree, my Master's degree, and a Ph.D. Father, now that I have graduated, please direct me to a job where I can earn my way and have some funds to send my children.

Meeting with Chaplain Johnson
'The choir is nonexistent. I don't know what is going on and what broke everybody up."

"Rose, sometimes the churches everywhere go through a split because of differences."

"A split? What can you be split on in a prison choir just singing songs?"

"You would be amazed at what can divide people struggling to serve God with their gifts."

He told me that he loved the solos that I sing right before the spoken Word, and that he also realizes that we need a choir.

"Rose, I believe you would make a beautiful choir director. I see how you embrace the newcomers and encourage those that are struggling. That is a beautiful spirit, Rose.

"Now this position won't be too much for you with your other volunteer assignments, will it?" he asked with great concern in his voice.

"I don't think so, but I've been talking to God about it on the tracks. And the burning desire has remained, and my passion has grown even more."

"Rose, let me have a word of prayer with you before you leave, okay?" We held hands and prayed.

The chaplain told me to let him know what the Lord said to me about it. Bonding in Bondage

After getting back to the unit, Jennifer was putting some things away. "Hey, Rose, what's up?"

"Not a whole lot, just have some things on my mind," I told her. "Do you need to talk about them?"

I explained about the meeting I was just in with the chaplain discussing the choir. Jennifer yelled out, "Did God tell you that one was a no-brainer, Rose?"

We laughed.

"Girl, you are crazy."

"No, for real. Remember I told you that if you join the choir, I would too?"

"Yeah, but you didn't keep up your side of the bargain, Jen."

"Sure, I did, I just didn't say how much longer after you joined that I would join and now I'm ready, Sister Director, if you are." "Oh, Jen, are you serious?"

"Yeah, I'm serious. I've been selfishly enjoying all the praises to myself and believe it or not, I know half the songs you sing just in our unit. So I don't come not knowing anything." She gave me a big smile.

"Thank you, Jen.
"Jen, do you think I would make a good choir director? I mean, do you think people would follow my lead?"

"Didn't I just tell you that I'm joining? No, seriously, yes, Rose, I think you'll do a great job. You love God, and it's real with you. I feel your sincerity and your genuineness. You don't play when it comes to God, His Word, or your little media ministry over there. I think a person that's tied up in God, whatever they do for Him, it will be fine 'cause it comes from your heart, not your head."

"Jen, you're a good friend. Thank you."
I lay in my bed that night and was comforted. Then a thought hit me, and I began to laugh within myself. I thought about my Momma and how she was the choir director of my dad's church. I would be following in my mother's footsteps after all. I immediately felt honored. Like Momma, like daughter. I was excited and couldn't wait to write and tell her. Maybe she could give me some pointers. Within a couple of weeks, the word got around that I was starting up a new choir.

Letter to Momma
Dear Momma,

You will never guess what I am doing now. I am the director over the prison choir in RC and for the chapel services. Yes, I'm responsible for providing all the music for each service. See, Momma, your work was not in vain. You know I thought about when we were kids and you had all of us in the choir. Sometimes we didn't want to sing, and sometimes it seemed so hard to learn those songs for Sunday morning service. But I remembered how loving you were, not only to us your children, but to the other kids that were in the choir too.

I plan to take my experience that you gave me many years ago and with the help of the Lord, become a wonderful director. Momma, please pray for me that I do well.

Love,
Rose

African-American Women Prisoners Association (AAWPA)

Inmate Lynn invited me to the meeting that would change my perspective about myself and my race forever. "Girl, it's the most exciting thing going in this prison to me. I never knew anything about my black heritage before I became involved. I had a self-hatred going all of my life. Where I'm from we never saw that many black people owning businesses or any area of community leadership for that matter. I love this group.

Visit from Daddy

It was so good to see my dad. I hugged him for five, long minutes and just cried in his arms. I was so happy. "Hi, Daddy, I miss you, Daddy. How are you?"

"I'm fine, Rose. How are you doing?"

"I'm keeping busy and productive, like I told you I would."

"What have you joined now, Rose?"

"Remember, I told you the last time you came that I joined the LTO organization?" I nudged his arm.

"Yeah."

"Well, now, I'm a part of the AAWPA." I gave him a big smile.
"And what does that stand for, Rose?" he asked.
"The African-American Prisoner's Association. I learn about me, my culture, my people, history, my rights and contributions, and how to be a better citizen. They also show us movies about our history."

"And how are you doing with your piano and voice lessons?"

"Oh, that leads me to tell you something else, Daddy. I'm the new music director, responsible for presenting music ministry for chapel and the Receiving Center, where newcomers enter."

"Wow, that sounds great, Rose. Did you tell your mother that?"

"Yes, I wrote her a letter about it. She'll probably get it tomorrow, if not today."

"Rose, again, I'm very proud of you for getting your GED." He reached across the table and squeezed my hand. "Thank you, Daddy. Then I'm also going to be working with the Mental Health Unit and teaching patients aerobics and leading Bible study. I feel for those in the Mental Health Unit. They really don't have any activities."

"Where do you learn all this stuff from?" Dad asked.

"Daddy, I have been through so many seminars and training sessions; they prepare you for it. But you prepared me for Bible study when you planted all that Word in me when I was a child. It's been watered, and now God is giving the increase and pouring the increase back out to others."

"You have always had a big heart, but don't overload yourself. I know that sounds strange, but don't overdo it."

"Dad, it doesn't feel like I'm in prison because God has opened so many doors for me to help other people as well as help myself too. Oh, Oh, I have to run, Dad. I love you."

"I love you too, Rose."

That night I sat up in my bed, thinking about Dad and seeing his cheerful and supportive face. He has always been my hero. He has always spoiled me and denied me nothing. I wonder if he really regrets it now. My mind changes thinking about how God is going to open these doors for me. People keep saying go to the Law Library...well I know for now I need to go to sleep.

Education Building/Library

The next morning I walked over to the library. A large sign reading "Legal Service" stood on an easel as I gazed beyond the frail-looking, short white lady standing behind the counter. I saw exactly where I wanted to go. I learned a lot of things that day. One was that the state has mandated that the prisons provide law material for the inmates so that they can work on their cases. They also have computer access with the restriction of printing privileges. A large sign which read "For viewing only" was near the computer. I had an exciting time in the library as I went down aisle after aisle.

October 1987

After listening to Pastor Gardner every Sunday night for the past couple of months, my faith was even more strengthened. I eventually wrote him and asked him to pray about me applying for clemency and asked that he and his church would pray that God would grant me mercy, strength, patience—and a miracle.

X-Rated Shower

I woke up late this morning and ran to the shower, hoping I was not using someone else's time slot. Everyone pretty much has a pattern that they basically operate in. This particular morning, I walked in the shower area and caught two inmates kissing and holding each other. That vision jacked me up. I stumbled back in shock! I heard that sort of thing goes on in here, but to actually see it really messed me up. I believed it was wrong, but the fact that they had love for each other did something deeper to me. I don't know if I was mad because they were sinning or if I wished so desperately that I had someone to hug and kiss me. I turned back around and went back to my dorm, rebuking what I had seen.

Pastor Gardner Writes Back

After a few weeks, I received a letter from Pastor Gardner. I was very surprised to hear from him. His letter was encouraging and put me in high spirits. He told me that God was going to do it in such a way that only God would get the glory out of it! He also told me that God would show me favor and change the mind of the king. Then he ended by saying that he was going to come visit me soon. I waited for that day.

The Word Is Out

Word got around that I might be considering becoming the next choir director. I can only blame Jennifer because she was the only one outside of the chaplain who knew I was even considering it. Maybe she

was trying to boost my ego. Soon, many of the cellies started asking me when we would begin rehearsals.

Choir Dynamics

Everyone grew to really like choir, and it became the thing to do and the place to be. Often, we were the talk of the prison. The ladies enjoyed learning songs by Hezekiah Walker, LA Mass Choir, Chicago Mass Choir, and every other mass Choirs I could get my hands on.

Chapter 15: A Strange Year

"Happy New Year, everyone!" I yelled from my cell as soon as my eyes opened.

"Happy New Year" echoed back from my cellies that were still in the unit. Many others were already gone for breakfast, including my roommate, Jennifer.

I just lay in bed and reflected about the past year. What could possibly be ahead of me for this year? "Lord, is this the year You'll set me jailhouse free?" I spoke out into the atmosphere.

I grabbed my pen and paper and began to write to God.

Lord,

I'm looking forward to my long, busy days dwindling down because my Business Ed classes will be completed at the end of February. This New Year seemed to have gotten here so fast. As I reflect on last year, I certainly accomplished a lot. I looked at my chart that I completed each quarter and saw nothing but productivity. Completion of GED, joining LTO,
participating in weekly chapel, directing the choir, attending Prison Fellowship, conducting Bible studies, joining AAPW, volunteering at RC, being blessed with my family visits and spending time with my children. Plus, I enjoyed frequent telephone conversations with family members.

Lord, if I was to summarize 1987, I would have to say again as I have said before, it has been the most productive year of my life. God, I thank You for changing my heart, my spirit, my outlook on myself and my life. I feel the change in my mind, Lord, and I just want to be out to prove to You that Your daughter loves You and is willing to live a life before people to prove it.

God, I appreciate the wisdom that You have given me, the courage and the boldness to stand on Your Word without wavering. Did it have to take coming to this place to get to really know You? I guess it did, but I'm glad I know You like I know You now.

At times it feels like this has been a career assignment where I work on these grounds day and night without going home. It almost feels like being away and enlisted in the Army of Life and I'm in Boot Camp and in position to help others as well as being helped by others. I've faced the enemies in my own unit; I've seen friendly fire explode right in front of me, crazy sexual relationships. I'm grateful that You allowed me to meet new friends like Pastor Gardner, who visits me every week.

Lord, even though I am busy sun up to sun down, I still had moments of loneliness. Sometimes at night, before going to sleep, I just want to hug and hold someone or just be held. There are some things prison life just does not afford you, I guess.

Psychotherapy and 12 Steps
I have group psychotherapy and the 12-Step Program to attend this quarter. Officer Carla suggested that these programs would help me learn more about my addictions and the role that my mind plays in them. I had some fears of
psychotherapy because I was afraid they would misdiagnosing me and tell me I was crazy. It's only for three months, so it shouldn't be too bad.

Telephone Call with Momma
"Hey, Rose, how are you doing?"

"Momma, I'm doing really good. I'm excited about the New Year and just waiting on God."

"Well, baby, this could be the year, you know."

"I know, Momma."

"So what's new? There's always something new with you, Rose."

"Oh, yes. You know I told you I'm going to the top of wherever the top is in this prison."

Momma and I laughed together. I loved to hear her laughter, and I was so glad I could be a part of making her laugh again.

"Well, I'm going to be the chaplain's clerk since I have my business classes completed and my GED finished, and I can't wait. I consider this to be a dream position; not only do I get a chance to worship and praise God, I get a chance to work directly with the chaplain." "What will you be doing?"

"I'll be his administrative assistant and doing a lot of typing and filing and organizing events. And Momma, this was prophesied to me when I was incarcerated before I came here while I was in County. What an honor."

Valentine's Day

Early this morning, I called my parents and wished them a Happy Valentine's Day. I loved on my children and told them they were my heart.

I wrote letter after letter to everyone that I could think of to pass the time away.

This day usually does not bother me. But this February 14, I had a jones for love. I don't know where it came from, but I craved someone to hold and love, someone to love me and hold me. I don't think the inmates bothered me too much with their obvious affairs in my face, but I felt a void inside of me that my Word could not fill.

I thought about past men that had been in my life that I felt genuine love from. There was really only one person that I believed loved me and cared for me. That was my old boyfriend Vincent. I could see his face as if he were standing in front of me. We had experienced so much together as a couple. Tears began to well up in my eyes, and I didn't understand why. I reached over and turned on the radio loud to drown out my thinking and my longing. I lay there until I fell asleep. I tried to stay in bed all day and not move, and before I knew it, depression crept in and I didn't want to be bothered with anyone.

New Position
I sat down with the chaplain to discuss the responsibilities and duties that I was expected to perform. I was glad that it involved a lot of administrative work, including typing, scheduling appointments, and posting special guest ministries. I loved typing in the business classes and could type up to 80 words per minute.

This was a great paid position in prison as far as I was concerned. Fifty-eight dollars a month may not be a lot to some, but it was just enough for me to buy stamps and little knickknacks. Plus, I could send my sons some cards and buy them some things for family visits when they came to see me.

Election Day
I was elected as the Women's Advisory Council-Liaison, a position which worked between staff and inmates. Another change came as a result of the promotions. I was being moved to Miller A – The Honor Cottage 136-. This meant I would be getting another roommate. I didn't like that at all because Jennifer was like a sister to me.

Kathy's Brother
I met a lady in chapel that was hurting and scared for her brother's life, who happened to be in Twin Towers. He was being threatened by a gang leader because he was scheduled to testify against them. She came to me

after chapel for prayer and seemed like a nice lady. I took her by the hands and led her in prayer. I prayed for her brother and asked God to put His angels around him. I told her if she gave me Jerod's, her brother's, address, I would even write him and give him some scriptures to stand on. I could tell she was relieved.

TBN

Trinity Broadcasting Network (TBN) became my closest friend. I began to be very familiar with the evangelists and even began to pick out my favorites. I liked Carlton Pearson & Higher Dimensions Evangelistic Center, Joyce Meyer, Dwight Thompson, Pastor R. W. Shambach, Carman, The Tripp Family, Kenneth Copeland and Clarence McClendon. (Boy, he was too fine to be preaching anything!)

After a while, I found that watching TBN each night almost felt like another addiction, but at least this was a good one because I was becoming more and more hooked and addicted to the Word of God. I grew to need to hear more covenant promises as I went to sleep at night.

Letter to Momma May 1988

Hi, Momma,

I tried to call, but just in case something happens and I can't get on the phone, I got the appeal back from the appellate court today. They are going to send me back to court. They have to wait for me to get transportation or something. Also, my lawyer said the attorney general could try to appeal it. If he does, I have to wait on the outcome. Actually, I think he said that it was like a procedure that they have. But anyway, hopefully, I should be home before Christmas.

Anyway, Momma, one good thing about being on the Honor Cottage and working for the chaplain, some of the staff don't automatically think you're a screw-up. I hate that some of these ladies have given up hope in here. I know when I get out, that should boost their faith. Oh, Momma, did Peter and Anita move? Can you ask Carol if she can come visit me soon? I'm glad that she let Darian stay over there a while. Anyway, Momma, I'm tired now. Tell everyone what God did and that when they take me out to court, to wait on me to give my new booking number and to just write me at the County. I'm not sure if I will ever come back to this place once I leave. The people at the County will be shocked. Momma, it was so hard when they had brought me back to the County when they let me out to have Darian. Some made fun of me and my God and said I would be in for life. They will now see God helping me, huh?

I love you, Momma, Rose Ann

Scripture for you:
I John 2: Beloved, I wish above all things that you prosper and be in good health, even as your soul prospers.

Threat from New Cellie
I was finally going to get a new roommate. I was hoping that she was another Jennifer—nice, sweet, and friendly. I walked in the unit and placed my hymn book on my bed. Then I saw a piece of paper sticking on the floor near my bed. As I stooped down to pick it up, I noticed some black dots on it. At that same moment, the door to my unit swung open.

"Hey, what gives?" said the stranger. "That's my stuff, and who's this 300-lb, bold, ugly woman looking like an ugly man?!"
"Who the hell are you and what is this?" I asked.

"Ah, I'm your new cellie, and I see I dropped my school papers, baby. You wanna learn some lessons in black dots and how they can make you feel?"

"What the hell are you talking about? Are these drugs? Because if they are, I'm gonna report yo a--ss."

"You got to sleep in this room tonight, and I ain't playing with cho ass. I will cut you and serve you for dinner."

I walked up to the girl. "Let me tell you something and hear me well. The last g–dm time I was afraid was March 27, 1986, and it landed me in a lifetime prison. So yo a--ss betta get me moved out of here like yesterday 'cause I don't want you for a roommate! And don't you ever threaten me again!" She snatched the paper out of my hand and stormed out of the unit. After she left, I started talking to the wind. "I'm not living with no homosexual and no drug dealer. It ain't happening!" I know I lost it. My spirit was so grieved, and I was so convicted. I don't remember the last time I cursed somebody out. "Oh, God, please forgive me. I didn't represent You in this situation. But it was hard. It
was so hard, Lord. Father, I repent!"

Visit for Holiday Season
I had so much fun preparing for an early Christmas visit with my family.
I arrived early at the special apartment used for the overnight family visits, and hid Christmas decorations for my sons to find later. The Angel Tree Ministry had also delivered my children's gifts. The Lord blessed me with a tree and the trimmings. I had made Christmas stockings (by hand) with the boys' names on them and ordered gift wrapped Sees Candies. I had even cooked dinner in the small kitchen and that night, I had my kids look in the closet. They were so surprised. Later we decorated the tree.

I Expect a Miracle
After the visit, I packed all of my things and prepared to ship them home. I knew I was leaving. I could feel it! I told those closest to me at the prison this was my last month here, and after I go to County for my court hearing, don't expect to see me again. I was glad I was able to befriend some of the staff from Prison Fellowship, RICO, and The Walter Hoving Home because they wrote letters to the judge for my release back into society and sent me copies of what they sent. I was so grateful. I prayed

that as the judge read those letters that God would touch his heart and tell him to "let my Rose go."

As I waited until the court date, I worked hard and made sure I was caught up with all my typing and assignments for the chaplain. I continued my services and work in various self-help programs, aerobics, WAC, and RC. The day before I was scheduled to go to court, I wrote Momma and told her the same thing. But I shared more with her that God was going to open the prison doors for me just like He did for Paul and Silas.

Leave for Court
I was up by 4:30 A.M. for the early breakfast for those leaving CIW to go and sit in County for my court date. I noticed right off that certain staff people were not at County. Sgt. Miller and Massarotti were on holiday vacation. A couple of days passed and my attorney came by and briefed me on what I could expect out of this appearance. The following day at 7 A.M., I arrived at the same place where I was given a life sentence in prison. I wanted to be free. My sentence was reduced from 27 to life to 17 to life. God is good.

Back to CIW
While in Court, I had hoped every second for the judge to turn to me and say, "Rose Parker, go home to your sons. They need you. You have served well. You have proven to me that you are not a threat to society and that you were justified in defending yourself." I had thought about every phrase the judge could say to me, then he would throw up his hands and say, "You are free to go." He never said that. He really didn't look at me much. It almost felt like he was avoiding me. I just wanted him to pay attention to the longing in my eyes for my boys and my desire to be home with them. Maybe God will shake the jail like He did for Apostle Peter in the Bible. Maybe that's how He's going to do it. That night I cried myself to sleep.

Transcript Did Not Say It Right!

Sometime later, I received a copy of my hearing results. I wanted to see in writing that God moved the system to reduce my sentence. As I was reading the document, I noticed something right away. I grew red hot and immediately called my attorney. At first, he didn't understand why my jaws were tight!

"Well, Rose, what's wrong now? Your sentence was modified."
"I read that, but it still reflects the old language of first-degree murder charge and not the current opinion of the court. Do you have a copy of this in my files? Did you read it?" I snapped.

"Uh, yeah, I read it," he replied, his voice lower.

"And you didn't pick up on this? You make me sound like I'm not justified to be angry."
"No, don't get me wrong, please. I'm impressed that you caught it."

"Well, what are you going to do about it?" I pressured him.

"Let me look into it. I'm in a meeting, but I will get back with you."

"Yeah, okay. Bye!" I slam the phone down.

Chapter 16: New Hope

Journal

Dear God,

Good morning, Father, and Happy New Year to You. I'm grateful for another year. Father, I need you to lead me this year. I'm grateful for the sentence reduction, but I also know this is not the end for me. You are not finished with my sentence. Thank you for 17 to life, but God, I was hurt because I just want to be with my boys and my family. Lord, I know your timing is the best timing and You know what You have in store for me, but I want to be free again so bad.

God, lead me this year as I plan my quarterly calendars. I want to only involve myself in those programs You have ordered my steps for. Lord, it seems like I've been forever in this place. Thank you for giving me the strength to stay in County and the safety from all dangers, seen and unseen. Father, last but not least, use me this year for your glory. I pray for all my cellies, that they would know you and come to love You. I pray for their families and their children, God. Keep my family and bless them this year.

Reassignment

I was reassigned to my job as the assistant clerk to the chaplain. I was so happy they didn't give away my job. In fact, the chaplain told me I had nothing to worry about, because he would hold that position open for me as long as it took to get back from County.

I was informed that they stopped the Bible study in the laundry room over in Closed Custody while I was away because of an incident involving somebody trying to escape. This, unfortunately, resulted in no opportunities for outside ministries to come in.

The first week I got back, I contacted all of my family members and was able to hear all of their voices. I was so glad. The last person on the phone was my brother David. He told me to read Jeremiah 29:11–14, and it changed my life. He read it to me over the phone and told me to read it once I got back to my cell.

It was like God spoke just to me. David said, "I know the thoughts that He thinks toward you, thoughts of peace not of evil, to give you an expected end." David said that God was going to deliver me from the place which HE caused me to be carried into as a captive and He would bring back home again. WOW!

I had believed I would be home by December 31. Now it was 11:45 P.M., December 31st. I had told everyone I was going home. Then I heard a still small voice that said, "Satan presented himself before Me, and I said, 'Have you considered My servant, Rose? She loves Me like no other, and I am going to release her from prison.' And Satan said, 'If You don't release her, she will curse you to Your face and give up.'" I understood. Now I said, "Thank you, Lord. I'm OK, just be with me." My days were quiet and focused on what my job assignments were and groups I had signed up for on a week by week basis. My focus on going home had not ceased. But my heart was so broken I could not attend to the groups just yet. It felt like a blow to my ambition. I kept fighting against the will to settle into prison life for any amount of time. I refused to accept just being satisfied with a reduced sentence, but for now, I was unable to fight any longer. I decided to immerse myself in my projects.

Visits were consistent. Pastor Gardner made his Thursday trip out every week like he said he would and that would be the highlight of that week, and then my dad would come right behind him and give me another dose of strength and hope. Even when I had my visits with the boys, I would not let them see me sad or depressed. I had to stay up for them. After a couple of months, I began to feel like my old self again and I was back in the fight for my freedom. I went to the library at every opportunity to seek new ways to try and get out by contacting the powers that be.

Spring Time

I was asked to spearhead this year's Victims Services Child Abuse Prevention Month. I enjoyed last year's and had some other ideas of my own on how it could be better. The inmates were able to participate in hosting this walk-a-thon to give back to the community, and especially those that were victims of the crimes.

I created and posted flyers around the grounds and put packets together along with a team of inmates and staff. I was given limited access and an assigned staff member to contact companies to donate and sponsor our cause. We received lots of water, snacks, bags, T-shirts, food bars, and other goodies for the fundraiser.

I encouraged the inmates and staff to pledge as if they were pledging for their own children and family members. Everyone gave. It was really great and seeing the community come on the grounds and cheer us in our walk for another cause other than our freedom was good, too.

Because I was in charge, I made sure that I gave others a lot of responsibilities if they requested some. This was such a great cause, I enjoyed it and it became the highlight of my year so far. When it was over, it was reported that walk-a-thon earned more money than it ever did. It also had more inmates participate this time than ever before. That made me feel so good. The officials gave me a certificate and a big applause for my hard work. I gave Jesus an applaud in front of them.

Some of the staff said, "We're going to let Rose work all our fundraisers, because she's a real go-getter and hustler for a cause." Many were laughing, but some were actually snarling at me. I could feel their venom.

People kept saying I was a natural. I had never done anything like that before. But I remembered the group training that I received earlier in the year. I have to admit I used everything I learned from that six-week VIP Personal Development and Life Management Self-Help program which was designed to "give insight and provide a positive attitude and promote self-esteem." I tried to promote everyone's self-esteem that was on my team.

Writing Kathy's Brother, Jerod

Kathy's brother, Jerod, wrote back and thanked me for keeping him lifted up in prayer. He sounded like such a nice person. He wrote about his girlfriend, his goals, and what he really wanted to do in life. I adopted him as another brother of mine, and he adopted me too.

The more Jerod talked about his love and his heart toward his girlfriend, the more I wished I had someone in my life that talked about me.

The months passed by so quickly when you work sun up to sun down. I loved my schedule because it kept my mind on work, chapel, and volunteer assignments. I couldn't understand those that never wanted to work or become a part of volunteer services. But I guess it's like some say: What difference will it make?—I ain't going nowhere.

Thank God for the Holy Spirit

As I continued to journal, read and do all that I purposed to do, the more I longed to be filled with the precious Holy Spirit. I knew I was sealed, but I wanted that filling with the evidence of tongues I had heard about. Then I remembered one of the volunteer groups called Carson Community Deliverance Center that came in on the second Thursday of each month, they always spoke about the being filled and with tongues.

I studied Dr. Fred Prices' book the about different types of tongues: the gift of tongues (that came directly from God) and about tongues (heavenly language) that is give to "them that believe" they shall speak with new tongues...I wanted that.

The second Thursday night finally came, Pastor Grate Shipp made an appeal to be filled with the Holy Spirit at the conclusion of his message, I was so excited, the ladies were being filled but not me, I looked at the clock and it was just about time to leave. Pattie Shipp, the pastor's wife looked at me to make sure I received the Holy Spirit and I shook my head "no" and pointed to the time, she rushed over to me, put her hands on me and God moved in those two minutes. Thank you Lord

Chapter 17: Breaking Barriers

Breaking Barriers group is starting this week. I heard wonderful things about how inmates were helped by this particular group. Officer Love from RC encouraged me to get involved with Breaking Barriers and also Monique from chapel reminded me to go the morning session. I didn't know what to expect, but I was excited about it. I wanted all barriers in my life broken.

The flyer talked about how we need to change our ways of thinking about things in general in order to heal from our past. It said that our thought life was what gets us into trouble most of the time. Hmmmmmmm. I got my old cellie Jennifer to sign up with me so we could compare notes as we did in the other groups we attended.

First Meeting
In the first meeting that we attended, the leaders told us that we were going to be given tools that would be effective in breaking some of our reoccurring negative life cycles. They would also help us to confront the challenges we faced emotionally, spiritually, mentally, physically and even psychologically. The facilitator was Ms. Jackson.

Reading from the Breaking Barriers manual, she started the ice breaker by giving an example of a little boy that wouldn't eat liver. When asked if he had ever tasted it before, he said, "No, but I know it's nasty, because my brother told me so." This started me to think about my life choices. How many things had I done, or opinions that I still held, because of what someone else had told me? We were encouraged by the leaders to write realistic goals and identify the barriers that had prevented us from seeing and achieving them. We set realistic time frames in which to break the cycles.

Then we were given our first assignment. Ms. Jackson warned us that it would take us a while, but hang in there and we will understand it as we go along. She said, "I want you to go back at least 15 years in your life, to a time before you got here, and trace and track your footsteps, if you can. Do the best you can and then write it down. We will provide you with the tablets you need. I want you to pay close attention to the relationships in your life and be sure to try and remember the most intimate relationships that you thought meant something to you."

Before I sat down that evening to begin my assignment, I had to pray to God to help me remember. "Lord, as I seek to do this assignment, please help me. Bring back to my mind the things in my past in order to get the most out of this group.

BREAKING BARRIERS ASSIGNMENT
Facilitator: Ms. Jackson

"MY STORY"
As the youngest child they brought into the world, my parents, and grandparents, taught me how to dream and believe that I could obtain whatever I asked for. And then my godparents, who had boys but never had a daughter, treated me like I was their little princess. My godparents would dress me in the best clothes they could purchase, which made it kind of hard on my parents. As a result, my godparents taught me to have high standards and my parents encouraged me to dream.

Meet Emzie III AKA Boonie

I met Emzie Parker III in December 1975 at Mavericks Flat he had just arrived here from Tulsa, OK. He was very unique and was the lead guitarist in his band. I just had to meet him. I saw him from across the room rocking to the music. He reminded me so much of my old boyfriend, Robert Wilson.

I asked my friend Hanley who he was. He said his name was Emzie, but everybody calls him Boonie. He was Robert Wilson's best friend. I started laughing. "Hey, I want you to introduce him to me." He walked me over and did just that.

Emzie remembered me when I was Robert's girlfriend, but I quickly let him know that Robert and I were history. He said, "Well, sit on down then." We left with each other's numbers. Part of me was laughing because I knew this would make Robert so mad.

The next day I talked to Emzie for hours. We just hit it off so naturally. We saw each other again on New Year's Eve. I left Watch Night Service at our church and went to Mavericks Flat to see Emzie, and we danced the rest of the night away. For some reason, we just couldn't stay out of each other's presence.

Las Vegas
Emzie and I made a plan to be together forever. It didn't matter to us that I was 16 years old. We still wanted to get married, so we drove to Las Vegas, taking Momma with us, but had a rude awakening when they told us that we needed both parents' consent. Momma called Daddy, while my brother Peter, his wife, and I waited and prayed.

I guess my father saw something that I couldn't see, and he didn't want me marrying Emzie. I knew that in my heart. But Dad went through a lot to get the consent form notarized and sent to us by airfreight. I knew he was steaming, but he didn't want to disappoint me.

New Addition
We lived with my parents for the first month of our marriage. Emzie III was on the road most of the time with Soul Train Gang Band, but he never missed a day calling me.
Shortly after discovering in June 1976 that I was pregnant, we moved to St. Charles Place in Los Angeles. Emzie was so thrilled when he found out. He was at every doctor's appointment all the way to the delivery time. He

missed the baby coming out though. He had just left to get something out of the car and by the time he got back, little Emzie Emmanuel January Parker IV uttered his first scream. He was so disappointed. Little Emzie was born December 10, 1976 at 11:45 A.M.

Both sets of parents and other family members were very supportive. His mother and father flew from Tulsa to visit. When Daddy and Momma came, they made my day. They were so happy for me and so supportive and loving.

First Separation from Emzie
I remember that the good times didn't last too long. Emzie was always on the road now with the band. And when he would come home, he was always short with me. I knew I didn't have to take that from him so we separated for the first time in November 1977, and I went back to Ontario, where I lived in the house next door to my parents. I still let him come over to see his son because I didn't want to sleep alone.

Attempted Rape
I'll never forget June 1978; I had a job at Jack-in-the-Box. Momma would keep my six-month-old son, Emzie, when I was working. One night in particular, I got home really late from work. I was so happy that Momma lived next door 'cause I was extra tired after working a few extra hours past my shift. I got to her house a little after midnight, picked up my baby, and quickly went home and showered before going to bed.

I knew Boonie was rehearsing and I thought I would probably be asleep before he came over but we were still separated. His routine was always the same. He would jump right in bed next to me and sometimes wake me up for sex. That was fine with me, even when things were bad for us.
I had just dozed off when I felt him getting into bed, but the next thing he did was different. His hand was covering my face. I tried to say, "Stop! Boonie, stop it!" And it was then that I realized that this wasn't my husband. I started screaming and the baby was crying. The man got up

and ran. I immediately called the police and went next door to my parents. The police confirmed that the intruder got in through the back window. I was so scared. I called Boonie and left a message at the club where he was playing that night to call me right away. He got home around 6 A.M., two hours after I had called him. When he came in, he took off his clothes and got in bed just like the other man. I woke up screaming. He yelled, "Baby, baby, it's me. Don't worry." Not long after that, I knew I had to get out of there and start a new life for myself somewhere else.

July 1978
I remembered that my friend Blue resurfaced at the right time at the club. I decided to take my life back and move on from Emzie. After talking to Blue, we decided that we would move to L.A. and be roommates. She knew a landlord who had property all over the place and would rent to us dirt cheap. The first six months we had a blast together. We lived downstairs in this large apartment that had beautiful huge living room.

Enrolled in School
September 1978, I enrolled myself in school at Trade Tech College and my son in Victory Baptist Nursery School. After completing one year in school, I sent him to Tulsa, Oklahoma, for two months to spend time with his grandparents during the Summer of 1979.

Soul Train—Blue Meets the Fellas
I took Blue to Soul Train a couple of times as a spectator to watch us dance and be a part of the audience. She liked to be around the singers and guest artists.

One Saturday, when guest artist Michael Henderson was on, he brought his friends, Ollie and Ray. They stood by the riser before he came on stage. Blue whispered, "Wow, I would love to meet him."

I asked who, and she said the one named, Ray. I told her, "I'll introduce you."

The next thing I knew, Ray was coming over to the house the next day. After a month of hanging out with those fellas, Blue started slacking up on the home-front responsibilities and then she started coming up short with the rent. I couldn't understand it because the guy she was seeing was making money.

I didn't want to get in trouble with the landlord, so I went to tell him that Blue did not have the rent but that I had my part. He told me that he would let me have the smaller two -bedroom upstairs $165, if I could manage that by myself.

That night I told Blue I loved her, but I was moving upstairs into my own place. I continued to go to school.

Demanding Seasonal Visits
After the summer, my son returned home and his father really increased his visitations at our house. Boonie became more and more demanding. He didn't like the idea of me going to Maverick's Flat, the Soul Train Parties, or anywhere else, for that matter. He didn't even like me going to school. "You're already out of school, so why do you have to go back? Staying home and taking care of your son is what you need to be doing!" He put so many demands on me, but not once did he ever offer to pay for his son's school or even part of the rent.

One evening when I was leaving to go out, he started an argument with me. He told me I needed to stay home and be a mother to our son. I went off on him. "After I've gotten my own apartment, enrolled in school, provide for me and my son—on my own—and put him in private school, you have the audacity to try to tell me what to do?"

Boonie said, "Look, you just need to be here with your son at night. He don't need to be at any babysitter's. If you're going to be a damn mother, then be a damn mother." I ignored his comments and walked out the door.

That whole morning I thought about how I was back in the same old rut again, with the same old nut. How did I let this happen? Anger welled up in me so strong. I began pacing the floor and talking to myself. I didn't know exactly what I wanted to do with my life, but I knew that a dominating, controlling, ex-husband was not in my future. I got dressed up, got in my car, and drove around.

At first, I was looking for a place in mid-Los Angeles, but I have always wanted to live where the stars hang out, which is in Studio City. I turned my car around and said, "I'm going after it." I headed to Studio City.

Bank of America

I parked at the intersection of Laurel Canyon and Ventura Boulevard and walked into four businesses, putting in applications. The last place was Bank of America. I met the Operations Manager, who was very impressed with my one year of accounting from Trade Tech College. She hired me on the spot and said that next week, I would start training. I couldn't believe it. God is good. Wow! That meant I had to find an apartment quickly before I started training next week. I left the bank and immediately went apartment shopping in Studio City, the same area. A few blocks from the bank stood a beautiful Victorian, three-story peach apartment building. The sign read, "First month's rent free and second is half off." It was a summer steal special. The only drawback was that the sign also read, "Adults only." I told him I have a son, but he was staying with his daddy and would visit me from time to time. He asked if I could handle the move-in fee and the monthly rent. I said yes.

Boonie, You Can Have the Keys

In the meantime, when I was preparing to leave the old apartment, Boonie walked in the door having finished a road gig. I told him he had to move all of his stuff immediately. I didn't want to let him know I was moving, let alone where I was going. He looked at me and said, "I ain't going anywhere. I'm still your husband, and this is our place." I didn't argue. I simply said, "Well, here are your keys. You can have it. Take care of yourself and your son." I knew he thought I was playing. I walked out with the clothes on my back, and he had no idea that my bags were already packed and in the trunk. Studio City, here I come.

First Day at Work

I learned very quickly that the Studio City Branch serviced most of the Hollywood elite. In my first week, I met many celebrities that came in to cash their checks. I made connections like you wouldn't believe. I knew how much money they had, their mother's maiden name, and the type of accounts they had. I made a point to make everyone feel special and in return, they loved Rose.

Many of the producers and stage managers invited me over to the MTM (Mary Tyler Moore) studio lot where they were filming. After mingling and getting to know the different camera crew, directors, and studio people. I went to after-parties where there was always lots of food. I took so much food home on a daily basis I never had to buy groceries. I was invited to the studio, and went through doors with no hesitation. This day, I visited the sets of White Shadows and The Bob Newhart Show.

The bank manager insisted on putting the merchant sign at my window. He knew I was good, but I told him, "Hey, back up, hold up. I'm counting." I used that and other reasons, after three months with the bank, to quit.

Documentary

I got a called to do a documentary called Wack Attack. It was a dance scene they were filming at the Total Experience using the Gap Band's latest hit, "Shake at the Disco." I wore my green cowboy outfit with matching boots and hat. I was able to afford a few more months' rent from that gig and could stay in the apartment for almost a year!

An unforgettable memory for me was on my 21st birthday when I met this cute, tall, 24-year-old handsome man named Vincent. After Vincent and I talked a few moments, I found out that he was in the original group Raydio, with Ray Parker Jr. We discovered that we knew some of the same people. Vincent told me that he could see himself with me and that I seemed to be a lot of fun. I blushed. Vincent was the first man I felt safe with and that I totally trusted. He was not like anyone I had ever met. He was kind, courteous, and hardworking. He was a musician, but also worked for a law firm to make sure his rent and other financial obligations were secured. He impressed me a lot. I got the news that my divorce was finalized. I ended up living with Vincent for two months until my apartment became available at the end of 1980. I thought we had a wonderful relationship. We partied together, ate dinner together, and just had a good time. Vincent was a musician at heart. I just love to watch him play. Pregnancy At the age of 21, something very wonderful happened. I was pregnant with Vincent's baby. At the same time, I got the news that my divorce was finalized.

While at my mother's house one day, I put my hand on my throat and could feel two heart beats. I jumped with excitement. My mother appeared happy for me. I couldn't wait to go over to Vincent's to tell him. I walked in, and he was standing in the kitchen making us dinner. He had already set the table with two candles and a single rose for Rose. He was always romantic like that.

"Rose, what's going on? You seem very antsy."

"I've got something to tell you, where I begin.

"Baby, just say it. You got me excited." He said.

"OK, Vincent." I squeezed my eyes together and blurted it out. "We're having a baby!"

When I let it out I was so relieved, but when I opened my eyes, Vincent's face had dropped. His countenance had changed completely. He was very emotional as he said, "Rose, hear me good. I love you, and I'm not going to leave you, but I am not ready to be a father."

I must say, I have never been let down so softly, but oh, the pain of soft rejection. I was devastated and disappointed because I truly trusted Vincent with everything, including our mistakes. I secretly thought to myself while looking directly at him that he was just like all the others. This was another bitter-sweet message of double talk as far as I was concerned.

To save my dignity, I told him, "I know you're not ready to be a dad, but are you asking me to have an abortion?" He was silent and didn't say a word. I stood up quietly, got my purse and my keys, and left.

I remember myself asking, what would this mean for me? I don't believe in abortions. Was it me that he didn't want to have the baby with?

A whole month went by and I tried to act like I was getting an abortion, hoping Vincent would change his mind. At times I would say to him, "maybe I should just get an abortion," hoping he would stop me. He never said a word.

April Abortion, 1981
I brought the subject of the abortion up for the third time and Vincent snapped at me for the first time, yelling, "Rose, people get pregnant all the time. It don't mean you have to have the baby." When I heard those words, I thought I was going to lose my mind. I kept hearing his words echo in the back of my mind everywhere I went. Rose, people get pregnant all the time. It don't mean you have to have a baby.

On April 3, 1981, I went for my scheduled abortion. The waiting room was packed with all types of women. The side door opened and a petite lady that looked like an angel called my name softly.

"Ms. January, have you eaten anything in the last 12 hrs?" The nurse said.

"No, I have not," I answered." I need you to write in our own words that you are having this abortion of your own free will, and I will come back and get your note." She turned around and walked out of the door.

I began to cry. Instead of writing what she wanted me to write, I wrote "Somebody help me. I don't want the abortion."

The nurse took the note from me, and I watched her place it in a folder without looking at it. I thought to myself maybe they will read it before they start.

"Rose, follow me," she said. The room was cold and icy. "Please take off all your belongings and place them in the plastic bag on the bed, then please put on the gown."

The next person that entered the door was the anesthesiologist.

"Hi, I'm Tom Geyser, your anesthesiologist. Just relax; you won't feel a thing but an initial pinch from the I.V.
Now my heart was really pounding because I wondered why they're hooking me up to an I.V. Tom told me to count backwards starting with ten. Before I began, I asked him, "If I said 'STOP,' would you stop?" He said, "Yes, we
would."

The nurse turned to leave the room with my folder under her arm. I thought maybe she was going to read it now because she has to verify what I wrote. Tom walked closer and instructed me to start counting. So I did. "10, 9, 8 ..." is the last number I remember counting.

My Baby's Dead

The next thing I knew, I woke up, wondering if the nurse had read the note and when she was going to come in the room and stop this whole procedure. I didn't realize I had already been through it. When I saw her, she came to my bed and asked how I was doing.
"Didn't you read my note?"

"What note, sweetheart?"

"The note I wrote on the blue paper you gave me."

"No, dear. I just filed it away, but your procedure went fine."

"Procedure? What procedure? You didn't kill my baby, did you?"

"Rose, you already had the abortion."

"No, wait." I lost it after that. I started screaming at the top of my lungs for my baby.
The nurse calmed me down, and I realized there was no return from this. I asked if I could use the phone to make a call. I had to call Vincent and tell him to come get me. Within 20 minutes, Vincent was walking through the door. I could hear his voice faintly asking, "Which room is she in?"

A chipper nurse said, "Just follow me. She's right in there."

I turned my head toward the entrance of the door as Vincent was walking in with a supportive smile on his face. The first words I said to him were, "They took my baby, they took my baby. They didn't read the paper, Vincent; they did it anyway!"

Vincent eyes were getting huge as he watched me evolve from this limp position to crazy hysteria. He began rubbing my back and saying, "It's going to be okay, baby. Baby, I'm so sorry you had to go through this."

While we were driving to the pharmacy, all I could do was stare out the window looking at nothing. I was physically in the car with Vincent but emotionally still at the clinic, where they took my baby. Vincent stopped at the pharmacy to fill my prescription while I remained in the car, staring with tears wetting my face.

Time for a Change
A few months went by and life started being different for Vincent and me. I don't know if I lost total respect for him, but something was missing. To some degree, I know I lost total respect for myself. As far as I was concerned, I was a baby killer. I could feel something in my heart change. I wasn't the same. I could feel a hardness develop within me.

I know Vincent sensed something different in me, too. This affected us, but we tried to move on and make the best out of what was left.

My depression over losing our baby was deeper than either of us knew. I lost motivation to go out, and when Vincent would ask if I wanted to go to the jam sessions that he knew I loved, I declined. I felt like I could never smile again.
I tried to make an effort to be affectionate and cordial with Vincent because I still loved him. We still talked to each other but were very careful of the topics we discussed. One night, Vincent came home from a jam session and I couldn't sleep so I was watching The Tonight Show with Johnny Carson. This was a strange night because I hadn't laughed so much in a long time. I couldn't stop laughing, even after Vincent got out of the shower. He walked in the bedroom and said, "It's so good to hear that magical laugh."

"You always complimented me about my laughter," I replied.

"Yes, because it's contagious, and you always look so beautiful when you laugh."

"Thank you. I miss laughing, I miss smiling, and I miss you, Vincent."

"Not as much as I miss my Rose." Vincent began to walk over to the bed. Bending down, he softly kissed me on my forehead and just stayed there for a moment pressing his firm lips into my skin. Oh, how that turned me on. Before I knew it, my arms went up and began to pull him down towards me.

He followed me as I scooted back onto the bed making room for him. He hungrily continued kissing me, but now he was kissing me all over my face and up and down my neck. I began to fill our bedroom with moans of ecstasy and desire. We no longer heard Johnny Carson's laughing but felt each other's passion for one another. It felt like I had been awakened. I was alive again.

A week later, I got up early Saturday morning to cook some breakfast. Vincent was already gone; otherwise, he would have cooked it for me. I wanted the entire spill: scrambled eggs, bacon, and toast. Boy, the bacon smelled good, but the minute the eggs hit the skillet, I had to run for the bathroom. I was nauseated and totally bent over in the toilet. I had no idea what brought that on. Then like a flash, it hit me: COULD I BE PREGNANT? Oh, no! Oh, God, please, no. I started praying. Please, Lord, don't let it be.

Thanksgiving

Vincent and I had reservations at Carlos and Charlie's for dinner. We had gone there a day before Thanksgiving because we were not going to be together on Thanksgiving Day. Vincent had an out of town gig, and I would spend it with my parents.

After the waitress sat us at the table, I asked for a 7 Up with two cherries and Vincent ordered just water.

A white couple passed by the table with a crying baby. I turned to Vincent, and he looked back at me to see if I was going to have a reaction. I smiled and said, "You know I've come a long ways. That crying baby would normally have made me crazy."

"I know, Rose. I never knew what the abortion would do to you. I felt so bad as I watched you these last seven months going in and out of depression.

"Again, I'm so sorry, Rose. I wish I could make it all go away."
"I just might be pregnant now. I won't know 100 percent for another two weeks, but I know my body."

Vincent said to me, "Let me know as soon as you know."
"Vincent, I just have to tell you now, an abortion is not an option. I can't go through that again."

He said, "Look, baby, I don't want to see you go through anything like that again. I'm here this time, and I'm here for good. We'll get through this together, whatever the results are. We will be together. I want it, too."

That's what I wanted to hear come out of his mouth the first time. Two weeks later—yep, it's positive, and Vincent was a man of his word. He didn't change on me. He wanted it, too. It was different this time. Even though the pain of losing my first baby was still tearing me apart, I prayed my new baby would fill the void.

Blindsided—Poor Choice (I'm the Blame This Time)
In December, Boonie called and wanted to take me and little Emzie shopping for Christmas hopefully, before Vincent got home. As we were driving, little Emzie yelled out to his father, "Daddy, Momma's going to have me a little brother."

Before I knew what was happening, Boonie hauled off and knocked me in the mouth with his fist. "b--t-ch, I'm taking you and your son out shopping, and you're a-ss is pregnant by another man?" I saw stars and felt dizzy and stunned, unable to answer.

I tried to shake it off quickly so I can think about how to leave him as soon as he got out of the car to go cash his check. In the meantime, I'm playing it off and crying, but he don't know his a-ss is history once he steps out of my car.

I drove directly to the nearest police station and filed a police report. I told them that my ex-husband just jumped on me. They took the incident report down and put out a restraining order in case he tried to get at me again.

Vincent was not cool with it when I told him what happened. I was eight weeks pregnant now.

He started going off. "How in the hell can he go hit my woman?" I tried to calm him down.

"Vincent, let the police handle it," I insisted.

I got so emotional with Vincent and thinking about Boonie coming after me that my stomach started hurting really bad and cramping. I was bent over, crying, and before I knew it, I was holding the bottom of my stomach where the pain was starting. Vincent tried to calm me and tell me to just be still and not worry about anything. The next morning, I started spotting. As soon as I saw the spotting, my heart started beating fast. "Oh no, oh no, please, God, don't let anything go wrong."

I stayed in bed all day, trying to stay calm, but the more I did so, the more my heart raced. Vincent brought me food in bed and made me promise to stay off my feet. He said I was a nervous wreck and I needed to calm down. I couldn't calm down because I knew Boonie was crazy.

After hearing me moaning all day, Vincent packed my purse and took me to the hospital. I kept thinking to myself, I killed one baby and it feels like I'm losing this one. Oh, no, God, are You punishing me because I took a life? This kept running through my mind as Vincent was driving as fast as he could to the hospital.

Hospital—DNC
I'll never forget that as soon as the doctors saw me, they ordered me to be admitted right away and took me to the labor room, where they took blood tests. The doctor came in and examined me and informed me that I was definitely having a miscarriage. They needed to do a DNC.

They put me to sleep and after I had awaked, it was over. I lay there limp and once again, childless. I couldn't keep writing my past. I noticed myself growing tired and depressed. Some of the memories awakened something else in me. "Lord," I prayed, "I have to take a break. Reflecting back over my life is so painful. Lord, I can't believe some of the stuff I've been through and a lot of the stuff I've done I need to take a break from, Lord, because the pain feels as fresh today as when it happened."

I thought to myself, I need to talk with Ms. Jackson, my boss, to ask her if everyone completes this task or if she had anyone to quit on her. If she would have said someone had quit, I was going to follow suit. I didn't want to return back to writing my past. After talking with Ms. Jackson, I learned that there were no quitters on this assignment. She insisted and pushed everyone to finish because she knew the outcome and how much it would help them. I told Ms. Jackson my fears, and she reached over and gave me a big hug, or, I actually took the hug from her, she whispered it was going to be okay. "Rose, you can finish this project." I needed that hug, but I stormed off, pouting that I had to finish.

Back to Writing Assignment

"Okay, Lord, I'm back to my writing project, but I need You just like I needed You before to help me to finish."

New Year's Eve was different for Vincent and me since the pain, abortion, and different challenges that we had been through. Vincent suggested that we try to do something to bring in some holiday cheer. He was going up to Josephina's. This is where Vincent would go to practice or fine tune his craft. Most of Vincent's musician friends go to these jam sessions at Josephina's. He asked if I wanted to go and expected me to say no, but I followed him there and actually had a great time all night. I met a lot of interesting people. Then before the night was over, a couple of girls from an all-girl's band walked in. Talking to them reminded me of my dream to sing with a girl's band. I was introduced to Sara and Tanya and told them all about myself—without them asking, of course. I told them how I had wanted to become part of an all-girls' band.

Meeting Audrey

I met a girl named Audrey; she complimented me on my jeans and my cowboy boots and hat. I didn't normally take to women too easily. For some reason, all my friends were guys. She introduced herself to me as Tanya and Sara's niece. Audrey seemed to be about 19 or 20 years old. She was from Chicago, the Windy City. She was kind of outspoken, but listened intently to every word anyone said.

She didn't live too far from Vincent and me. She asked me to come by one day while Vincent was at work. I went over and she was kickin' it by herself. Next thing I know she's pulling out a tray and snorted a line and told me to help myself. I didn't know what to do with it. She could tell and asked me to just do what she did. I tried it, but it stung my nose at first. I immediately started feeling something in my throat and my chest. Boy, it felt like a quick rush. I wasn't comfortable with it because I couldn't control it.

0pThe next week, I find out that this nice girl had opened her mouth and talked to some of my friends. It's a small world and people aren't dumb. She was telling about a girl she met that hadn't been exposed to dope before. Since they were my friends, too, I was upset and embarrassed.

Strained Relationship with Vincent

The rest of the year was a strain for Vincent and me. Our relationship was casual, but not romantic. I guess Vincent didn't want to take a chance of getting me pregnant again, only to be disappointed by another miscarriage. I loved him, but the fact of the matter was, I killed my baby and so I just didn't care about anything anymore.

Meeting Art for the very first time

January 16, 1982, I received an unexpected telephone call. If I could have seen where this call would cause me to end up, I would have never answered it. I looked over at the clock and it read 12:52 A.M. Vince and I both were shaken by the ringing phone.

"Hello," I said.

"Hey, girl, what's going on?" There were two people on the phone. I could tell this was Tanya and Sara, the girls from the all-girl band that had hit the circuit and, boy, did I want to be a part of their group.

"Can you come over for a rehearsal?" Tanya asked.

"Are you serious? You want me to come over?"

"Sure," Sara replied.

"Tomorrow?"

"No, silly, tonight. Right now! Get a pen and write the address down." They both said it together as if they had practiced everything. Perhaps they did. I thought about it for a minute. Well, I see Vincent going to the studio all hours of the night and staying all night at times, so the request wasn't too unusual.

Vincent was asleep by the time I hung up the phone. I left him a note and the address I would be at with the telephone number on the kitchen table. As I drove along, I noticed that the streets were empty. Tanya answered the door. "Come in, girl." From the door, I could see through to the living room where two other people were sitting. One, I assumed, was Sara, bent over the coffee table. The other was a man just sitting and staring. As we walked closer, "Girl, this is Art, the mastermind with all the great plans," Tanya said. "Go on over next to him and have a seat and introduce yourself."
I was dumbfounded. "Are we going to rehearse?" I asked.

They all laughed. "Sure, baby, just sit down for a few, moments, and enjoy yourself before we go to the back to the studio," Sara said, struggling with the pipe in her mouth. She sounded like she had a lot of cotton in her mouth. I stood there at first, embarrassed. I was looking for a rehearsal, and they were sitting here getting high. I felt myself getting pissed off and more embarrassed thinking they chose me and supposedly wanted me so bad to be in their band that they called me out of my bed at this time of morning. Art stood up to meet me and lifted up a pipe.

"I don't do that," I said.

"You're a damn liar. Listen, we just want you to have fun with us like you did with Audrey. Here, we want you to have all you want."

"Why? You don't even know me like that."

Art interjected, "You haven't had anything like this, baby. It's sweet, it's pure, and the best. It's just cocaine. I said. He described his entire cooking process to me as if it were a delicate dessert. "I put one drop of 7 up and Perrier. It's Vitamin E. Get it while it's soft and watch it turn hard, baby."

After his sales pitch of how good and different this was, I folded. I reasoned to myself, I'll do it for a while with them and, hopefully, they won't be too high to rehearse so it won't be a total lost night and they might decide they want me to be part of the band.

Art, the mastermind, had the classiest setup. You could tell he was chief of his castle. He used an expensive torch, not a lighter or burning paper, nor did he use rum. The torch replaced the Bacardi. He said, "Low life's use ghetto tools to try and smoke dope. You can tell the ghetto ones from the sophisticated, classy ones." He used that word so many times. This is special; you get all you want, because there is plenty of it to go around—as much as you desire. That way it doesn't create desperation in a person, baby, you hear me?" I just nodded. I really didn't see the difference, but whatever. He leaned back in his plush sofa as he watched us participate and bragged all night long about who he was and about his money, about all the entertainers that come to him for drugs, and all the stars that depended on him for supply and demand. The more they smoked, the more I smoked. But I was tired and wanted to go to sleep. They laughed at me and called me weird.
"Cocaine don't make you sleep, girl. It keeps you up. What's wrong with you, baby?"

"Well, I am sleepy and hungry. I can't believe it's almost 6 A.M. in the morning."

Art went to the kitchen and brought me back a boiled egg because I kept saying I was sleepy and hungry. They called me weird because apparently it's not normal to get hungry or tired when you're getting high on cocaine. He told me to go upstairs to one of the bedrooms and take a nap. As I was going up the spiral staircase, he followed closely behind me, almost on the same step as me, which irritated me. As we were walking by different rooms, he took the opportunity to explain each room and who had slept in them. Then he walked me into a room with wall to wall closets, showing me expensive clothes, shoes, silks, and satins that he bought for his women. He also showed me his closet filled with shoes, suits, hats, and furs. I felt myself getting so mad. I was not impressed with this stuff. I wanted to go to sleep. I went to sleep and later when I woke up, they were still at it.

After I got up, I remember going downstairs and telling them I had to leave. They made me sit down and take two more hits. I argued with them because I didn't want to, but I knew I wasn't going to win the fight.

Finally, I stood up, grabbed my purse, and walked toward the door. Art came behind me and said, "Let me walk you out, baby."
"Hey, girl, we'll reschedule the rehearsal for tomorrow, okay?"
"We'll see Tanya, just call me when you're ready."

Art walked me out a different way than I came in. It was through his enclosed garage. We stood there in the dark garage, then he flicked on the light. Parked were two cars, a Porsche to my left and an Excalibur to my right.

"These are my little cars that get me where I need to go." He raised up the garage door and his Seville was sitting in front of it.

"Nice cars," I said.

"Hey, baby, everybody has bills that need to be paid. You have any?"

I asked, "Why are you asking me that? He said, "I would like to be real close to you."

"You don't even know me. That's gross. You just met me a few hours ago." You sleep with just anybody.

He shrugged his shoulders like a 13-year-old boy.

"Art, you take me through your place, show me all of your expensive stuff, but why are your fingernails so dirty. Can't you get a manicure?"

I got in my little car and spun off. Driving home, I didn't know what story I would tell Vincent. He would not believe what I did all night. What a waste of time ...

Chapter 18: Life Reflections

Writing Project

February 1982, Depression

During the next six months, I suffered from many crying spells and deep depressions. I felt as if I were losing it and knew I needed help. Vincent was supportive, but he couldn't help me with my emotions.

I picked up the telephone book and located Michael O'Neil, a counselor in North Hollywood. After making an appointment, I went and shared everything with him. He told me that I was on the right track and we didn't need any more meetings. I walked away from there feeling like "OK, am I
better just because I poured out my heart? Is this how it works? Is it this simple?" I convinced myself that Mr. O'Neil probably didn't like me anymore.

I knew how I could distract my mind and bring me out of this slump. In order to cope with my depression, I decided to get busy. I auditioned for every role I could. I knew I could escape my pain by being someone else.

My first callback was from Central Hollywood casting for a show called Hill Street Blues. I was excited and drove over to the lot where I knew a lot of people. They all called me Jazmyn.

For the next few months I got work, met a lot of people, and stayed very busy. My routine consisted of getting dressed up, attending all the hot awards ceremonies like the Grammy's and American Music Awards, and stay out all night at the after-parties. I repeated this lifestyle over and over again. Even though I was preoccupied with mingling and walking that red carpet like I belonged there, I was growing more and more empty inside.

June 1982, Art Calls Me

I was shocked when Art called one morning after Vincent had gone to work. I called him back and let him know I would come over for a "quick visit," then I drove over to his Woodland Hills town house. When I arrived, we walked up the stairs to the tri-level area to sit down in the dining room where he offered me something to drink. I asked for my usual, 7 up, as I heard noises and voices coming out of the kitchen. I sat there and thought about how I didn't like Art constantly excusing himself and leaving me, then coming back. I assumed he was going to take a hit. I told myself I didn't want to do drugs, I didn't want to live this type of life. The last time he returned, I said, "Maybe I can come visit you when you're not so busy." The truth of the matter is I needed full attention. I needed to be needed and I wasn't the center of his attention that day, so I left.

Visit to Art's House

Art kept hounding me. He said all he wanted to do was treat me like a queen. After lying to Vincent for the past two years, Art finally got me in bed. The first time I saw him naked, I almost screamed because I saw that he didn't have a side. His side had been shot off and patched up with skin from his knees. I later learned that he got even with the shooters and cut their heads off. He was so arrogant and didn't realize that his body was an eyesore. Since I was hanging out there every day, Vincent thought I was working for Art in the band or was doing something involving entertainment. He didn't know I was getting high.

Art would send me to the store with $500 to shop for Bounty paper towels, filet mignon, lobster, and shrimp. One time I came home with a cup dispenser and put it on the wall. He was like what the hell is that? I said "people keep using all your paper towels and these cups will save you from a lot of dishes". He did a lot of drug activity in the kitchen and everyone's hands were nasty.

Laker's Game

Art started acting paranoid after awhile. I remember the time we were going to the Laker's game and he thought I was looking at somebody in another car. He was so angry that he reached over his young daughter and smacked my head so hard that it bounce off the passenger door window. I liked going to the games and sitting close to the floor. I also knew it was time to get away from Art for awhile and visit my family.

Reunited with Family

I got in my car and drove to my Momma's house. Everyone was worried about me because they had not heard from me in so long. I had to see little Emzie, and I was so grateful that my parents kept him for me. I'm not sure if Momma really understood why I couldn't keep my own son since I lost the baby. I could only hope she did. Dad was so happy to see me. After he hugged me, he lectured me about keeping in touch and letting people know I was alright.

I Need Art Again

After a few days at my parents' home and playing with my son, I began to crave drugs. Art called that same day when everyone was busy around the house and the kids were outdoors and asked to pick me up. I sneaked out so nobody would see me. As I got in the car, Art handed me a loaded pipe. When we got back that evening, we went to our favorite room. Art set up everything. I was in the same place for that entire week, with the exception of taking showers, eating something, and making a fake call to Vincent.

It Started Getting Bad

I finally realized that it was getting pretty bad for me. I started tripping, like I was seeing stuff. At times, I acted like I smoked all my dope, but I had actually put some in my pocket for later on. I had screens with lots of hits of free base cocaine on it because I knew how to turn the screens over. Art had a ritual. We would smoke for three days straight. He would sleep for a day, eat and sleep, and after he ate and rested, he started the party all over again. Somewhere down the line, I would get my a-ss kicked. It never mattered who was there. It happened like clockwork. He kept me high for three years when I was with him because I would wake up with a hit.

From Bad to Worse
Art started doing something that was the lowest of lows. He created a game for us to play. Whoever could hold their hit while they counted to 60 seconds, or whoever held it the longest, was the winner and whoever lost had to sleep with the person Art picked. I lost and had to have sex with Doc who was 38 or 40 years old, big, fat, and ugly. I hated it. The next time I lost the bet, I had to go upstairs to have sex with Phil Elliot. After we got to the bedroom, he sat me on the bed and said, "Little girl, we are going to pretend we are having sex. Afterwards, go take a shower. Then we'll both go back downstairs and pretend everything was fine. Don't worry."

Beatings by Art
Every now and then when Art would go off on me really bad, I would run away. For instance, after he made me go upstairs for sex with Phil Elliot, I came down smiling and feeling good. Then I saw rage in Art's eyes and as soon as they left, he goes off cursing me and calling me every b--t-ch name in the world. He yelled, "You are cheating on me in my face! Sh-t, you ain't supposed to like it!" I was so confused.

Art Busted My Teeth
Then the beatings increased. Day in and day out, I did the same thing—smoking all day and getting my a-ss kicked. I knew that somewhere down the line, he was going to hit me and convince me that I deserved it. Three days later, he hits me in the head with the phone and wrapped the cord around my neck trying to drag me. I remember one time he busted my teeth and then a couple hours later, he took me to the dentist to get them repaired because he couldn't stand looking at me like that.

Sick and Tired of Being Sick and Tired
At one point in my addiction, I just wanted to stop using. I kept saying to myself, "This is not normal. How did I get here?" I had shut the world down around me for a room and a glass pipe. After I had thought about my life and what was left of it, I decided to call the police and tell them Everything. "I'm messed up; I'm reckless; I need help; I need y'all to take me to get some help."

The officer said, "You're on the right road. This is the hardest part for any addict to come to grips with." They gave me a card and wrote the name of a woman on it and told me to give her a call. I called the lady and started going to meetings the next day. She told me to meet her for lunch in Pomona and started telling me about AAA. I told her that I wasn't an alcoholic, but she still insisted that I go to the meetings.

Meetings
After I left the meeting, I called Vincent and told him that I had been to a meeting to get some help. He was very supportive and happy for me.

"Do you want to come home, Rose?"

I told him I did. I went home and stayed there and Vincent nursed me back to health. He showed me where the meetings were in North Hollywood, and I went to a few and could feel myself coming back to normal.

Vincent or Art
After I went back with Vincent, he gave me an ultimatum regarding Art. He told me that Art could not call or come by ever again. "Do you understand?"

"Yes, I just want to be home." However, after being back for a while, I began to battle those familiar memories of the miscarriages. Vincent didn't know it, but I still had drugs hidden and tucked away for a rainy day in my belongings. I don't know why I didn't throw them all away like they told me at the meetings I attended, but I promised myself I would not use them.

Day at Dodgers Stadium

Vincent asked me if I cared to go to a ball game with him at the Dodgers Stadium. I invited my Momma and dad.I think Dad liked Vincent because Vincent seemed to be straight and consistent toward me. He really tried his best to take care of me.

Next Day I Call My Sponsor

I kept in touch with the lady who got me involved with the AAA meetings to let her know I was doing well and still attending the meetings. Eventually my sponsor wanted me to come up with $40 to go on a weekend retreat. At one of the meetings, I entered a large room with about 15 people there, both men and women: They opened with the Serenity Prayer. I start crying when the words came out of my mouth. "God, grant me the serenity to accept the things I cannot change, courage to change the things I can, and the wisdom to know the difference."

Struggling with Her Secrets

I remember experiencing some emotional breakdowns, but I didn't tell Vincent because he was going to flip out and make me a prisoner in his own home because of my mental state. I began to think about Art. I kept a little stash of cocaine and pinched some off once a day when the coast was clear. I would tell myself, "At least I ain't smoking all day and all night anymore like I use to."

I woke up one morning, and I couldn't fight it anymore. I didn't want to do it, but it was hard. I was sweating and aching inside. I needed a hit. I needed it so bad. I knew I was supposed to call my sponsor, but I didn't want to talk to her. I didn't want to hear what she had to say. I thought about that Serenity Prayer. If only I could accept the things I cannot change. Man, I just wanted my Vitamin E!

I got dressed and called Art to meet me around the corner. Half an hour later, he drove up to the 7-Eleven. He gave me an ounce and told me to go to my favorite chair and have myself a good ole' time. I stayed in the chair about a week before I took my first break. I showered, ate, and started the process over. Eventually I ended up staying back at Art's place. He started wanting to have sex more than in times past. I didn't want to anymore, but I knew I had to in order to keep getting what I really wanted.

Vincent Comes to Get Me

One day there was a knock on the door. It was Vincent. He came to Art's door and wanted me out of there. I could feel the love and pain in Vincent's eyes for me. He looked sorry for me. I put the pipe down and went with him back to his house, promising that I would never do it again. Vincent laid down the law one more time. He said he was not getting emotionally attached to me anymore and that he could not trust me with his heart. Since I didn't want anything more out of life, we could just be roommates if I wanted until I got on my feet, but he wasn't going to just watch me destroy my life.

Meeting Don

After I had been at Vincent's a couple of days, my brother Peter came by. When I opened the door for him, there he stood, and a friend. I invited them in and noticed his friend.

"Hey, sis, meet Don. Don, this is my baby sister, Rose."

Vincent was still in the back room. I began to flirt with Don. My brother brought him over so they could talk music and bass information. He was a bass player. Vincent came out and talked to them. I went to the kitchen so they could talk music and watched TV. Eventually I fell asleep, but I woke up as they were leaving. I needed to talk to my brother. I also took the opportunity to speak with Don and said, "Do you have a girlfriend?"

He said "No".
"Do you want one?"

He laughed. I told him I was just playing. Then I went back upstairs and felt the emptiness building up inside of me. The next day I went to see Peter. I learned that Don lived right across the street. I noticed Don working on his car, a red Corvette, so I walked over there wearing my tight pants and cowboy boots.

"Hi, remember me?"

He just grinned. "Let me go clean myself up. Stay right here."

He returned. "Are you hungry?" he asked me.

"Yeah, I could eat a little bit."

We came back to his house, and he walked me to a room in the back, telling me that he has two roommates in case I heard some noises. Present were his boy, Buster, and his girl and her kids.

"Oh, OK, that's cool," I told him.

He closed his bedroom door, then watched me eat my tacos. He said he loved the way I licked my lips. Then he moved closer to me on his bed. He was taller than me and even when he sat next to me, he was taller than I was. Next, he started kissing my neck and, boy, did that feel good. He put my food down and we fell back on the bed. Don had such a soft touch. He didn't want me to leave, and I didn't want to leave either. I stayed every day for the next week.

Rest Stop

I went to my mom's and I began sleeping a lot. Momma and Daddy didn't like that. They never knew how long I would be there. By the seventh day at their home, I started feeling an urge for Art. I told myself I really missed him and loved him. Or was it really an urge for the Vitamin E? Momma said Art had been calling every day. Before I could pick up the phone and call him, the phone rang. It was Art. Something leaped up in me when I heard his voice. It seemed like whenever I get to this point, Art would either call me or flood my mind with thoughts about him. This morning he called me and said, "I'm coming to get you."

I went back to Art, and this time, I couldn't wait to get into the house because I knew what would be waiting for me. I assumed my place and my favorite chair in the living room. A few weeks later I started getting sick. I told Art I had to go to a doctor. He said there was a clinic up the street.

"Do you think that you are pregnant?" the doctor asked.

"Oh, no. What did you ask?"

"Ma'am, can you understand English?"

The test results came back. I was pregnant. I could not believe it. It had to be Don. I didn't care, I was just so happy. I left the doctor's office and started planning my future. I needed to leave Art because I didn't want my baby to be a drug baby and I sure didn't want to lose another baby.

What about Vincent?

I didn't really talk to Vincent these weeks after I disappeared, I hated that.

More Lies

I come downstairs one night at Don's house. His roommates were there with him and I couldn't believe my eyes. They were getting high. I yelled at him, "I thought we weren't going to get high."

He said, "That's not for me, it's for you."

I got my things and left. I was so pissed I went to Art's house.

More Beatings by Art
My mind is wondering to more beatings by Art. I noticed him changing from day to day, growing more violent toward me and anyone else that would get in his way. All during this time, Art would threaten me and tell me that I better not leave him, and he would hit me, beat me, or do whatever else he wanted to do. I really think he was trying to make me lose the baby.

New Addition
Saturday, August 4, 1984, my contractions were shouting: IT'S TIME! I had a couple false alarms. But they hooked me up to the monitor, and after about 75 minutes, they told me that they were going to release me. I was crying, protesting. I went to the restroom and some gunk came out, slimy stuff with blood. Quickly, I called the nurse, who said that it was a bloody show. I asked, "Can I please stay?" but she told me that she would give me an enema and see how that goes. That helped me. About ten minutes later, I had to go to the restroom again. Again, I called for the nurse, but she didn't come at first. A few moments later she walked in. When she arrived, I apologized, saying, "I'm sorry, I couldn't hold it." She lifted the sheet and started to scream.

"What's wrong?" medics asked.

"The baby is coming out!"

There was no time to get me to the delivery room. My son was born a few minutes later. Then they took him away. By now, the doctor arrived—just in time to take me to the delivery room to deliver the afterbirth.

Vincent My Champion
Vincent comes to the hospital and was there much of the time. The hospital offered a free candlelight dinner on Sunday, the next day, so I invited Vincent (I couldn't reach Don). It was really strange. My son's blood type was "O" and so are Don's and Vincent's. But I knew, unfortunately, Vincent and I would never have a child together. He really loved that boy and wanted it to be his, but the truth of the matter is we had not slept together during that time.

Depression
A few months later after Don left to go down South, I started getting so depressed and I didn't want the baby around me. I asked my Momma to take the baby for a while. She knew I needed help.

To Chicago to Find Don
After about twelve months, I couldn't take it anymore. I needed to see Don, and I wanted to take my baby with me. So I told Art that I was going to visit my aunt in Chicago. He bought me a first-class ticket. I flew to Chicago and went to stay a week with Don's Mom in Gary, Indiana. This was November 1985. After that, I took the bus to Savannah. Don and I had a great time together with our son that week. It was the ideal Thanksgiving Holiday vacation. I decided I didn't want to write any more about my past because I knew the rest of it was all about Art pistol-whipping me whenever he wanted to. I couldn't relive what my boys saw him do to me. I hope Ms. Jackson won't pressure me to write anymore.

When I finally finished my assignment for Breaking Barriers, I felt so many different emotions. I cried a lot while reliving my past. I experienced getting angry at people, including myself. I could see some things that I did that I hated. I saw myself talking to the pages as I read it back to myself, saying, "Rose, why couldn't you see where this was heading?" I hurt inside because I was so naïve, cocky, and self-centered. After Ms. Jackson viewed our stories, she gave us feedback in writing. I was so blessed by her comments when we met privately together. I thought she would have a different opinion about me once she read everything, but instead, she said she wanted to especially talk to me about mine.

After the other ladies left, Ms. Jackson and I sat at the table together. "I know you read my story and learned about all the no-good men in my life," I said, putting my head down in shame.
"Yes, I read about each of them, but I beg to differ about one them." I looked up. Ms. Jackson continued, "Now, who is that Vincent? He sounds like some kind of man."

I laughed to myself and blushed. "Well, Vincent was a pretty good guy, if I have to say so myself."

"What I want to talk about, Rose, is something I think you really need to pay attention to." She wrote questions down on my tablet for me to answer later.

The first question was "How do you define 'neediness'?" She said some people's addiction is really a "need to be needed." I didn't quite understand what she meant. She saw the puzzled look on my face and asked me to explore this theme by looking back through my life and see what I could come up with. Then she warned me that if I didn't work on this particular character defect, I would continue to attract relationships throughout my life that were not balanced or healthy. Then she said this was one of the barriers that I needed to break. Next, she talked about how we hide our neediness in seemingly positive activities.

She asked, "Why do you think you fill your entire day from sunup to sundown, Rose?"

"I want the time to go by so fast that I don't feel incarcerated," I answered.

"Are you sure that's the only reason?" she continued to press me.

"Of course, that's the only reason why. Why else?" I asked her.

"So there is absolutely no payoff for you doing these things?"

"Payoff?" I questioned. "Most of what I do is free and volunteer work."

"Yes, payoff. Meaning, what does Rose get out of it? How do these things, events, and involvements make you feel?"

She continued asking rhetorical questions.

"What impact do they have on your perception of yourself? What do they mean to you? Is there a need they fill?"

I was getting frustrated, so I interrupted. "No, I just like doing what I do!" "Okay, let's see if you do what you like to do. Would you do a little exercise with me?"

"Sure, okay," I responded.

"Now tell me all the things you do in one week."

It took me about two minutes to complete my list of tasks that I do in a seven-day week. She had a strange smile on her face once I finished, as if to say, "gotcha."

"Now let me reiterate your tasks from memory if I can, saying why you said you do them: I like to go to chapel three times a week, I like volunteering at RC four times a week, I like going to prison fellowship and to every self-help group, I like being in charge of the Annual Walk-a-Thon and fundraisers, I like directing the choir, I like being in school and earning every degree I can, I like reading the Bible for two hours a day, I like praying two hours a day, I like making staff look good, I like helping people, I like writing other people that I don't even know just to help them, I like teaching weekly Bible study, and I do all this just because I like it."

She finished and looked exhausted by the time she was through. "Now, I'm going to switch a few words around and replace them with another possibility: I have a need to go to chapel three times a week, I have a need to volunteer for the annual Walk-a-Thon and fundraisers, I have a need to pray two hours a day, I have a need to take care of the choir, I have a need to attend every group on the prison campus, I have a need to help people even if I don't know them, I have a need to write other people because they need me, I have a need to keep going to school and acquiring degrees, I have a need to do all of these things."

She stopped there. "Rose, that sounds different, doesn't it?"

I told her, "Well, they are important, and they are good things that I do. At least I'm not hanging out smoking weed or crack," I defended myself.

"Rose, you are missing me. I am not coming down on you. I'm trying to show you an example about neediness. Neediness is not an all-bad thing; it just has to be a balanced thing. We all have needs, but to what extend do we fill them, and how do we fill them is our daily challenge in life. Some people's needs are so deep they end up behind bars. Do you understand?"

"I don't know exactly what you mean, but around here, that's just who I am."

"Is it, Rose, or is it what you have become around here?"

Whoa, that hit me in the pit of my stomach like a bowling ball. "Hmm, I think I see what you're saying. So you're suggesting I do all these things because I have a need to do them?" I questioned.

She said, "Okay, now take it a little further and add to it by saying why you have a need to do them."

"Well, I guess there's a little need to want to shine in this place as much as I can."

She nodded yes.

"And I guess there's a need to show folk that I'm important and have something to offer even up in here, to show folks that I'm really innocent and better than they treat me. I feel the need to be complimented and preferred. I have a need to help others and show them that I can be useful."

"Now that's really good. Notice, I didn't say what you are doing is wrong. But if we don't have a clear perspective on why we are doing what we are doing in life, we can lose sight of our authentic purpose and be on a superficial extreme.

"Let me ask you, how do you keep track of where you're supposed to be from day to day with your many involvements? I get tired just hearing what you do."

"Actually, I know exactly where I'm supposed to be on a daily basis, because an angel once told me when I was in County Jail to journal daily, and keep a quarterly schedule. I have been doing that for the past five years, ever since I arrived here at CIW. Would you like to see a copy of my record keeping?"

"Sure, when you get a chance. Maybe one day you can keep my calendar and come work with me because I was actually very impressed with your recall abilities and your chronology. But Rose, try to get some silence and solitude in your life. I know you are a praying person and you believe in God. I think that's wonderful. I, too, need to get closer to Him. However, I have to ask the question, how well can you actually hear Him if you are constantly busy doing things all day?"

She gave me so much to think about, and she ain't even saved. I had a lot to sort out. My brain was hurting after I left her so I took a walk around the track. A few weeks passed by and I just wanted to be still and be by myself. I challenged myself to invite more solitude and silence in my life as Ms. Jackson alluded to. I knew my prison life had become a full-time career move, which caused me to be busy sunup to sundown. I thought perhaps I was using all of my groups—volunteer work and chapel work, to fill my neediness void.

Calling Vincent
After speaking with Ms. Jackson about Vincent, I wanted to hear his voice. I took a chance and called him. He wasn't home. I tried later before it was time to go to bed, and he accepted the charges.

"Hi, Vincent."

"Hi, Rose, how are you doing?" he asked.

"I'm doing pretty good."

"Oh, yeah?"

"Yeah, for real. I know that sounds weird being in prison, but God has really been working with me."

"Well, it's good to hear your voice."

"Yours too, Vincent."

"You still work for the law firm, Vincent?"

"Yep, I wish I could retire." We both laugh lightly at that.

"Rose, do you need something?"

"Well, I'm about to start a letter campaign and I may need some copies and stamps to mail these letters out."

"Anything I can help you with, I'm here."

"Vincent, I'll call you tomorrow. They're announcing the last 60 seconds on the phone."

"Take care of yourself, Rose."

I went to my room. The whole time I walked back, I thought about Vincent and how he was always there in my life. He still had that calm voice and way about himself. I think that's why I loved coming out of the storm into his peace whenever life got too crazy. After completing the Breaking Barriers assignment, I found myself reflective and contemplative about the rest of the year. I continued going to group, maintaining my volunteer services, and the other things I did, but with an awareness that made me feel uncomfortable at times. Throughout the week, I would read back on my story like Ms. Jackson suggested I do in order to locate the reoccurring themes of neediness in my life.

My psychotherapy sessions started a couple of weeks after Breaking Barriers ended. I didn't know the mind could be so sick. There were so many things that blew my mind about this group. It was hard at times, just like Breaking Barriers, but I could feel the new Rose emerging from one group to the next. Each time I revisited my past, something else defective dropped off of me. I was viewing my past with clear lenses. I was glad for my psychotherapy and Breaking Barriers group because both allowed me to make sense out of my behavior patterns, my neediness and my compulsive behaviors.

I also realized the fact that even though I was saved and I had come to God, it did not automatically erase my negative behavioral patterns. Those were things that I had to be very deliberate and intentional to put away. Ms. Jackson told me that everything I ever did or had a propensity to do was actually suppressed and I may have hidden it under my religion. She said, "I don't mean that you are not serious or real with serving God. I'm just saying there are certain behavior traits that are in you and will remain in you if you don't expose them and work on transforming them instead of covering them up."

"Well, the blood of Jesus covers everything," I said.

"Rose, I am not a religious person per se, but I have studied behavioral habits, addictions, and compulsions that can be exchanged for other habits."

I didn't like what she was saying because it was easier for me to simply say, I am not that person anymore and I'm brand-new. But then I remembered the time when the judge let me go home to have my baby when I was in County, and the night I went to the crack house. That thought and craving came out of nowhere. I remembered needing something so bad to make me feel good.

I didn't know why I weakened to that same crap that caused me to be in the place I'm in now. Ms. Jackson had a point. If I didn't work on it, it could resurface and destroy me.

New Assignment: I learned that there was a position on the Women's Advisory Council (WAC) for a secretary. I was elected and won. Five months later I was elected to Chairperson, I won that. It was a paid position as well. I stayed in that position for five months until God moved

Chapter 19: A New Year

Family Visit

I was so surprised when they told me that I could have a family visit from the Christmas holiday through New Year's Day. It felt like a week vacation. It was exactly that. This year, I was able to be with my entire family at the unit and each of us planned our New Year's resolutions together. Mom and Dad came by in the afternoon on New Year's Day. They brought us some soul food. My boys were playing outside with their brand-new Angel Tree gifts that they received. They hugged me, kissed me, and thanked me over and over again for getting them exactly what they wanted.

A Blast from the Past, Skip Davis

I was shocked to receive mail from Skip Davis. He was an old friend that liked me. In his letter, he asked me to call him at his office. He said that he had been looking for me for 12 years and when he finally caught up with my brothers, they told him I was incarcerated at CIW.

He then went on to tell me about a situation that was happening at CIW and was concerned for my life and safety. As soon as I finished reading his letter, I jumped up and went to call him. He told me that on national television they had been showing my prison on the news regarding mysterious deaths and disappearances involving guards and inmates. I was shocked. He went on to say that he hoped that I was fine and wasn't in any danger. He said the report was entitled, "Unsolved Mysteries at CIW." He said these incidents started when one staff member started reporting the bad behavior of another staff member and then people start disappearing.

After our telephone conversation, I started asking around to different people secretly and each one already knew about it. My head had really been in the sand, working sunup to sundown. I didn't know why I didn't get wind of this. I created my own isolation within isolation. I had become so isolated I just didn't know what was going on around me. The way the inmates told it was very scary, even more horrific then what Skip described. Then shortly after his letter and our phone calls, I finally saw the report on the evening news about inmates dying and staff coming up missing.

The next thing I heard was about was an inmate found dead and the lieutenant and medical staff tried to change the time of death because the inmate asked for help. I wondered if it had anything to do with the same officer that gave me psyche medicine instead of an aspirin when I first got to CIW. This opened a whole can of worms for unattended sick inmates being denied medical care. As a result, I learned that it became a big issue in every prison in California. All the inmates now had to sho-nuff wake-up and stand-up to be counted. The last scandal concerned people being caught altering records. That's when the officer in charge came up missing. "Mail Call." The guard waved a bunch of letters at me. I got many letters this day. I saw one from Desmond and smiled. Here is this mystery Romeo again. What could he possibly say this time? He always amazed me with having so much conversation and never having seen me. The other letters were from other pen pals that I said I would read later.

LTO'S Good News

I was practically running to the LTO meeting. I had seen Officer Carla earlier, and she told me that I had to be at this meeting because it spoke directly to my case. Many of the group leaders had told all the lifers to make sure they attended this meeting because there were new laws concerning our crimes. I could hear Felicia talking. I walked in very slowly, trying not to distract attention from the meeting.

Felicia stood at the podium when I walked in. She was excited about whatever she was speaking about.

"Now, it's called 'The Battered Women Syndrome (BWS)' (1991 Law) and the definition of battered women is another term for getting you're a-ss kicked all the time." Everybody laughed. This is good news for those of you working on your appeals and those still fighting your self-defense claims.

Attorney's Help, but Not Me
After the new law passed on the BWS, lawyers started visiting the prison to help the formerly battered women who were unjustly imprisoned. I kept trying to get my name on the list to see them and be a part of the mass "Executive Clemency Petition" that they were pushing to be sent to the governor's office. For some reason, they never contacted me. They never included me in the group. Each week I found myself running to the group when I got wind that they were on campus, but I could never get with them.

Some Things Need Prayer
In my visit with Pastor Gardner, he told me that it sounded like politics and someone in the prison may not want me to be part of this group, Executive Clemency Petition. He said I would have to pray and fast because it seemed like something was clearly blocking me from getting to a place that is rightfully mine. He assured me that I would get out in during the time designated. I treasured his weekly visits, especially during this time, because was feeling so helpless and hindered by man's powers. But I knew there was a greater power available for me. He said we had to go over men's heads. I took his advice and vowed that I would fast and pray for two days out of the week until my release. I would fast the day prior to the legal team coming out and throughout the day until they left the campus. I prayed for those two days everywhere I was, whether I was at work, chapel, or school. I began to thank God for being included in the Mass Executive Clemency, even though my name was not yet submitted. I thanked Him by faith that it would happen in the time of completion.

Happy Mother's Day Surprise

I had a family visit scheduled with my mom and two sisters, Diane and Carol, for Mother's Day. It was great. I don't ever recall us bonding as a family of women quite like we did this weekday. God blessed us to grow closer to one another. I was glad they came. Mom told me that the men decided to give the girls in the family a day off so they could come and have girl time with me. We talked about what was going on in Diane's and Carol's life. I was glad to hear the children were growing and how they were doing in school. Mom wasn't feeling too well, but she said she pushed herself. She said it was a virus bug she couldn't quite get rid of. I could tell she was slightly under the weather, but I was so glad she pressed on. I began to sing to Momma some of her favorite songs, like "Blessed Assurance," "His Eyes are on the Sparrow," "Glory, Glory," "This Little Light of Mine," and "Amazing Grace." Carol and Diane joined me. Then Momma started singing with us. Her whole face changed and brightened. We clapped and she sang from one song to the next. Those in the visiting room also joined in and everyone was blessed. I will never forget that Mother's Day. We created a memory of a lifetime. Before they left, we took pictures together. I felt so good all day from that special visit.

Letter to Atujuan Christmas

Honey,

Mommy misses you so much. I was so glad to finally reach you. I prayed and asked God where you were. Where's my son? The Lord showed me. Last I knew, you and Darian were staying at Auntie Diane's. I'm so glad I found you and I hate you are so far away. Your brothers and I miss you so much. I will send you some envelopes so you can write me, ok. I love you a lot, but God loves you the most. MOM

Chapter 20: Divine Assignments

Happy New Year, Darian,

Hi sweetheart. We are going to have Atujuan back soon, so don't you worry, OK? God has been really good to Darian, so you just hold on to all that I share with you. He is able to do more than the Hulk & the Barbarian together. Yes, Jesus is much, much stronger, remember that. We love you and I will keep this short since you probably have to get a little help with some of the words. I'll see you this weekend. I love you.

Mom

Mom Letter to Emzie

Happy New Year Honey,

Momma really hopes you liked the gifts that the Angel Tree people sent me. I am well and so are your brothers. How are Mo-mo and Papa doing? I heard she was really sick, and God may be calling her home. Did anybody really talk to you about your grandma's illness? If your dad doesn't say anything to you, than ask your grandpa Emzie Jr. Then I will call you in a couple of days to check on you. Your brothers miss you terribly. It's funny that Atujuan misses you and Darian misses Atujuan. Our family will always be victorious. Remember that!!! You are a winner. You are special!!

Love,
Mom

Telephone Call to Momma

Later that afternoon when I thought Mom and Dad were home from church, I called.

"Happy New Year, Momma."

"Happy New Year, Rose."

"How's everybody, Mom?"

"Everyone seems to be doing well. The kids are over at Peter's."

"Tell everyone I said hi, Mom."

"This could be the year, Rose, that God opens that door for you."

"I know, Momma. I really think so. How's daddy?"

"He's taking a nap right now, baby, but I'll tell him you called."

"I start my new job tomorrow, Momma, with Breaking Barriers."

"That's good, Rose. You are very smart."

"Thank you, Momma. I love you."

I could tell Momma was tired by the tone in her voice and her heavy breathing.

"Momma, you still have that nasty virus bug?"

"Yeah, baby, it seems that way. Now it done moved in my chest and back. The doctors don't know what it is, but they gave me a lot of medicine that I'm tired of taking."

I didn't keep her long. It hurt to hear Momma in pain. I told her I would keep her in my prayers and up-to-date with the new laws as they continued to come out.

Breaking Barriers
When I was hired by Ms. Jackson in April 1993, I was so happy. I had taken Breaking Barriers as group therapy. Ms. Jackson helped me in so many ways in my group experience. I could never repay her other than to be the best employee she has ever had.

She told me she reviewed my records from the prison and discovered that they were quite impressive. She said the greatest attribute that she noticed each employer I worked with consistently say was that confidentiality was my highest strength.

I went in as a "runner," got promoted to "administrative assistant, and was over all the facilitators. I ran the office.

African-American Women Prisoners Association (AAWPA)
Inmate Lynn invited me to the meeting that would change my perspective about myself and my race forever.

"Girl, it's the most exciting thing going in this prison to me. I never knew anything about my black heritage before I became involved. I had a self-hatred going all of my life. Where I'm from we never saw that many black people owning businesses or any area of community leadership for that matter. I love this group.

Christian Tracks
Working with Ms. Jackson was so much fun. I found myself growing closer to her over these five months. I thought about a great idea after hearing the chaplain's message on witnessing. A church group had come in and left Christian tracks for the inmates. I took some of those tracks back to my unit to hand out and mail to friends, but also I wanted to give Ms. Jackson one. I didn't want to offend her, so I would put them in her work folder between the memos.
I knew she probably figured out that they came from my hands into her folder. I didn't mind that. The preacher said all of us should want people

that we care about saved. And that should push us to see them saved. I wanted my boss saved because she was so special. I felt God sent her my way for a special time.

Sad News
"Dad, hi.

How are you doing?" "I have some sad news." Dad said. "We don't know what all's going on. The doctors tell us that your momma only has six months to live." I talked to dad for a little while, tears rolling down my eyes.

"Rose, everything is going to be alright. God knows what He's doing."

"Daddy, please let Momma know I called. Tell her I love her.

Letter to Dad, June 1993
Dear Daddy,

I just want you to know that for my birthday I'm just asking God to help us, especially YOU through this difficult time. It's been such a long time since I saw Momma, longer than in my whole life. Daddy, you've always gotten through everything, and I've never seen you sweat, but it's OK if you do this time because of your wife of 56 years. The prison told me I have to choose if I want to see her on her deathbed or go to the funeral. I chose the funeral. Also, I'm also able to have a special visit where they will let everyone in to see me all at one time.

Juan still won't go get Atujuan, but I'm not going to let it tear me apart. Anyway, I just wanted you to have this surprise letter.

I love you Daddy,

Rose Ann

Santa Ana Winds

It was January 9, 1994, and I wanted to speak to my mom. I called, it was about 11:14 P.M. we spoke till 12:30 A.M. When I woke up the winds were blowing, and I knew my mom went home to be with the Lord, it was about 1:30 A.M. and I thank God I had the chance to speak to her.

Chapter 21: First Parole Hearing

Dear God,

You saw what happened at my parole hearing. This Board keeps making mistakes with my life and that is not OK with me. I want to go home to my children, Lord. I'm tired of being here!

I'm going to write them a letter, and I don't want to sound angry. Please give me the words to say because right now, I don't have them.

I can't believe after ten years of serving time that they find me unsuitable and denied me parole for three more years. I'm going to fight it. This was my parole suitability hearing. How can they say a three-year denial is OK and it could have been a five-year one, so I should be grateful?! Lord, help me—help me to make it, to appeal all of this. Give me the words to fight and endure for the truth. I just want the next three years to fly by. I'm going to fast and pray and watch You work, God. I know you are working already.

Father, help me complete this form. Give me Your blessings. Let the Board see that I am not attacking them, but I want things corrected and my records to reflect the truth. I tell the truth; how come they can't?

BOARD OF PRISON TERMS (BPT) —STATE OF CALIFORNIA APPEAL

(1) To grant a new hearing at which correct case information and factors are considered.
(2) Correction of the record to reflect accurate information.
(3) The grant of a parole date.
(4) Submission of my case for commutation consideration.
PLEASE STATE (TYPE OR PRINT) AND SEPARATELY
NUMBER EACH BASIS FOR YOUR APPEAL (P.C.S9771)
(1) The denial of parole was base on incomplete and inaccurate information even though the appellate decision clearly sets forth the correct facts of my case. During the hearing, Commissioner Giaquinto repeatedly challenged my statement that the victim had threatened to kill me. At one point, Mr. Giaquinto stated, "No place in any of these documents does it say that he threatened to kill you that day" (RT page 11, lines 21, 22, 23). Later, Mr. Giaquinto said, "There's nothing in the record except what you're telling us right now that he said that he was going to kill you that day" (RT page 16, lines 15, 16, 17). In these and several other instances, Mr. Ganito insisted that I had never previously stated that the victim threatened to kill me, yet the appellate opinion in my case clearly states that I told various police officers that the victim threatened to kill me that day. "On the day of the shooting, they had been arguing and he told her he would kill her," Court of Appeal Opinion, Page 5, lines 2, 3, 4. Although Mr. Ganito said, "Well, you know I've read through this case extensively and that's not the way it reads, and you're here to tell the truth today so we can measure your degree of insight and remorse" (RT page 11, lines 1, 2, 3, 4). Mr. Ganito incorrectly analyzed and misquoted the facts set forth in the appellate opinion, thus, the finding of unsuitability for parole was based on incorrect information, which, in turn, constitutes a denial of due process of law. The use of incorrect information also violates BPT rule 9999 (b), which provides that all relevant, reliable information shall be considered in making a determination of suitability for parole. A decision based on incorrect information is inherently unreliable and cannot stand. Therefore, I am entitled to a new hearing. **(2)** Additional erroneous information was introduced into the record by Mr. Ganito when he stated that there was nothing in the records that established that my brother was engaged in a physical altercation with the victim at the time of the shooting (RT page 16, lines 13, 14, 15). The correct information is again set forth in the appellate opinion which states (page 5) that my brother, Peter January, grabbed the victim and hit him after which the two men continued fighting. This error, coupled with the misinformation set forth in paragraph (1), undermined my credibility to such a degree that I appeared to be evasive, untruthful, and lacking in insight, even though I was telling the complete truth. The errors in the record are substantive and the effect so prejudicial that a new hearing must be granted.

(3) During the hearing, Mr. Ganito referred to Battered Woman Syndrome (BWS), stating that the Board was very sensitive to that issue, but then he went on to state that often women would try to mitigate or justify their crimes by "making stuff up" about the victims. After conceding that I had been battered by the victim, Mr. Ganito said he was exploring the facts to determine if the victim "wasn't either set up or you just got fed up or you were so high on cocaine that you didn't know what you were doing" (RT pages 22, 35). These remarks and the attitude displayed by Mr. Ganito is a flagrant violation of the Penal Code 9999, which requires the BPT to consider BWS and the effect of long-term abuse on the woman who has killed her abuser. The BPT completely disregarded the report submitted by Gail Pincus, a psychologist and expert on BWS, who stated that I was suffering from BWS and acted in fear for my own life when I killed the victim.

(4) CIW Board Report contained incorrect information (1) Aggravating Circumstances and (2) Mitigating Circumstances. This information came from my Probation Officer's Report (PCR), and those issues were overturned by Court of Appeal. **(5)** The POR is inaccurate. There is no record of an addendum or supplemental POR taken following the Appellate Court's Decision May 1988. This incorrect POR reflects my Board Report, Psychiatric Report, and Closing Statements by District Attorney (RT page 58, lines 24, 25, 26, 27, and page 59, lines 1–9). **(6)** The decision refers to a prior petty theft arrest in my past. However, I have never been arrested for petty theft, and there are no documents to support that erroneous allegation. **(7)** The denial of suitability for parole was partially based on the claim that the offense was committed in a cruel and callous manner with disregard for the life of another, which, again, contradicts the appellate opinion. The Court of Appeal described the crime as "spontaneous" (Appellate Opinion page 11), stating that I "shot wildly," grazing my own brother with the first shot and missing the victim with the second shot. The court also stated that the manner of the killing was more of an "explosion of violence" rather than a "preconceived design." It should also be noted that at the beginning of the hearing, Mr. Ganito specifically stated that the panel does accept as true the court findings (RT page 4, lines 20, 21). Since the panel is following the court findings, it is inappropriate to reach a decision that contradicts those very findings. **(8)** The decision which finds me unsuitable for parole violates 3041 of the California Penal Code which specifically provides that the Board of Prison shall "normally" set a parole release date at a prisoner's initial hearing. The Board of Prison Terms grant less than 5% of all prisoners a parole date, and in my particular case, the decision to deny parole is unreasonable. I have no previous criminal history, and I pose no risk to the community. Prior to my trial, I was released on my own recognizance, and I led a stable, law-abiding life. I have strong family ties, excellent community support, and current job offers and opportunities. The failure to find me suitable for parole constitutes an abuse discretion and violates statutory law.

BOARD OF PRISON TERMS | **APPEAL** | STATE OF CALIFORNIA
(TITLE 15, CCR §§ 2050-2056)

	CDC STAFF USE ONLY
NAME: Rose AnnParker	
CDC NUMBER: W#-25811	LOG NUMBER:
INSTITUTION: California Institution for Women	DATE RECEIVED:
DATE SUBMITTED: 12/3/96	

DECISION BEING APPEALED	BASIS FOR APPEAL
	DATE OF DECISION/HEARING BEING APPEALED (SPECIFY):
☐ PAROLE REVOCATION	May 21, 1996, (transcript received 10-11-96)
☐ REVOCATION EXTENSION	☒ THE DECISION WAS BASED ON INCOMPLETE OR INCORRECT INFORMATION.
☐ RETAIN ON PAROLE	☒ THE DECISION IS UNREASONABLE IN VIEW OF THE FACTS.
☐ SCREENING DECISION	
☒☒ LIFE PRISONER	☐ THE DECISION IS ILLEGAL.
☐ MENTALLY DISORDERED OFFENDER	☒ THE DECISION VIOLATES THE FOLLOWING BOARD REGULATIONS OR RULES. (SPECIFY):
☐ OTHER (SPECIFY):	BPT Rules Title 15 § 2402 et seq

WHAT ACTION ARE YOU REQUESTING THE BOARD TO TAKE? (1) To grant a new hearing at which correct cas information and factors are considered (2) Correction of the record to reflect accurate inform ation (3) The grant of a parole date (4) Submission of my case for commutation consideration per P.C. §4801

PLEASE STATE (TYPE OR PRINT) AND SEPARATELY NUMBER EACH BASIS FOR YOUR APPEAL.

(1) The denial of parole was based on incomplete and inaccurate information even though the appellate decision clearly sets forth the correct facts of my case. During the hearing, Commissioner Giaquinto repeatedly challenged my statement that the victim had threatened to kill me. At one point, Mr. Giaquinto stated, "No place in any of these documents does it say that he threatened to kill you that day" (RT page 11, lines 21,22;23). Later Mr. Giaquinto said, "there's nothing in the record except what you're telling us right now that he said that he was going to kill you that day." (RT page 16, lines 15,16;17). In these and several other instance Mr. Giaquinto insisted that I had never previously stated that the victim threatened to kill me yet the appellate opinion in my case clearly states that I told various police officers that the victim threatened to kill me that day. "On the day of the shooting, they had been arguing and he told her he would kill her" Court of Appeal Opinion, Page 5 lines 2,3;4. Although Mr. Giaquinto says, "Well, you know I've read through this case extensively and that's not the

SIGNATURE (All appeals must be signed.)	CDC NUMBER	INSTITUTION/REGION

BPT 1040 (rev. 9/88)

Attach more pages if necessary.
See other side for instructions.

PERMANENT ADDENDA

PARKER APPEAL, PAGE 2

way it reads, And you're here to tell the truth today because were trying to measure your degree of insight and remorse (RT page 11, lines 1,2,3;4). Mr. Giaquinto incorrectly analyze and misquoted the facts set forth in the appellate opinion, thus the finding of unsuitability for parole was based on incorrect information which in turn constitutes a denial of due proce: of law. The use of incorrect information also violates BPT rule §2401(b) which provides that all relevant, reliable information shall be considered in making a determination of suitability for parole. A decision based on incorrect information is inherently unreliable and canno stand, therefore I am entitled to a new hearing.

(2) Additional erroneous information was introduced into the record by Mr. Giaquinto when he stated that there was nothing in the records that established that my brother was engaged in a physical altercation with the victim at the time of the shooting. (RT page 16, lines 13, 14;15). The correct information is again set forth in the appellate opinion which states (pag 5) that my brother, Peter January, grabbed the victim and hit him after which the two men continued fighting. This error coupled with the misinformation set forth in paragraph (1) undermined my credibility to such a degree that I appeared to be evasive, untruthful, and lacking in insight even though I was telling the complete truth. The errors in the record are substan tive and the effect so prejudicial that a new hearing must be granted.

(3) During the hearing Mr. Giaquinto referred to Battered Woman Syndrome (BWS) stating that the Board was very sensitive to that issue, but then he went on to state that often women woul try to mitigate or justify their crimes by "making stuff up" about the victims. After conceeding that I had been battered by the victim, Mr. Giaquinto said he was exploring the facts to determine if the victim "wasn't either set up or you just got fed up or you were so high on cocaine that you didn't know what you were doing." (RT pages 20,21) These remarks and the attitude displayed by Mr. Giaquinto is a flagrant violation of the Penal Code §4801 which requires the BPT to consider BWS and the effect of long term abuse on the woman who has killed her abuser. The BPT completely disregarded the report submitted by Gail Pincus, a psychologis and expert on BWS who stated that I was suffering from BWS and acted in fear for my own life when I killed the victim.

(4) CIW Board Report contained incorrect information (1) Aggravating Circumstances and (2) Mitigating Circumstances. This information came from my Probation Officers Report (POR) which those issues were overturned by Court of Appeal.

(5) The POR is inaccurate. There is no record of an addendum or supplemental POR taken following the Appellate Courts Decision May 1988. This incorrect POR reflects my Board Report, Psychiatric Report and Closing Statements by District Attorney (RT page 58 lines 24, 25, 26, 27 and page 59 lines 1-9.

PARKER APPEAL, PAGE 3

(6) The decision refers to a prior petty theft arrest in my past, however, I have never been arrested for petty theft and there are no documents to support that erroneous allegation.

(7) The denial of suitability for parole was partially based on the claim that the offense was committed in a cruel and callous manner with disregard for the life of another, which agai contradicts the appellate opinion. The Court of Appeal described the crime as "spontaneous" (Appellate Opinion page 11) stating that I "shot wildly" grazing my own brother with the firs shot and missing the victim with the second shot. The court also stated that the manner of the killing was more of an "explosion of violence" rather than a "preconceived design". It should also be noted that at the beginning of the hearing Mr. Giaquinto specifically stated that the panel, "does accept as true the court findings" (RT page 4 lines 20,21). Since the panel is following the court findings, it is inappropriate to reach a decision that contradict those very findings.

(8) The decision which finds me unsuitable for parole violates §3041 of the California Penal Code which specifically provides that the Board of Prison shall "normally" set a parole release date at a prisoner's initial hearing. The Board of Prison Terms grants less that 5% of all prisoners a parole date, and in my particular case the decision to deny parole is unreasonable I have no previous criminal history and I pose no risk to the community. Prior to my trial I was released on my own recognizance and I led a stable law abiding life. I have strong family ties, excellent community support and current job offers and opportunities. The failur to find me suitable for parole constituties an abuse of discretion and violates statutory law.

ENCLOSED ITEMS: BPT 1005 Parole Denial
CIW Board Report
Domestic Abuse Report
Probation Officer's Report
Court of Appeal Opinion
Psychiatric Evaluation
Superior Court SBDNO Jail Order

Prayer

After I typed the document, I prayed to God to bless my corrections and let it arrive safely in the hands of the authorities with compassion and integrity.

Dear God,

I really don't feel like journaling tonight. All I want to do is get in bed and pull the covers over my head. But I remember that You told me that I would not have to be in here forever. You promised to vindicate me, and I am holding You to Your word. Please help me to get right to sleep. I don't want to think about it anymore. The next morning, the Lord let me know I needed to put together all my paperwork and be prepared for when the opportunity availed itself to prove my innocence. He told me that I would be given that opportunity soon.

Letter to the Governor
On December 17, 1996, the Lord spoke to my spirit again and said it's time to write to the governor. He showed me how to put the package together to present in my defense for a Parole Date. He instructed me on how to point out that the Board of Prison Termers had made too many mistakes over and over again.

Letter back from the Governor

January 31, 1997, I received a letter back from the governor that stated:

This will acknowledge receipt of your December 17, 1996, letter, which included copies of your December 3, 1996, Appeal to Board of Prison Terms Initial Parole Consideration hearing (May 21, 1996), as well as a
portion of your trial transcript.

We appreciate your providing us with a copy of these materials and will make them a part of your pending application for Executive Clemency.

I jumped up for joy in my room as I finished reading that letter. Then I thanked God, I praised God, and I adored Him. He had their attention now. I knew something good was going to come out of it.

Chapter 22: It's A New Year

Blind-sided Attack

Just when I really gained some footing on my letter campaign, I receive the worst letter in the world. Out of the blue, my sons' father served me with custody papers. During the process, I was glad the court ordered DNA testing for Darian. I was devastated to learn that Art was Darian's real father. But I thank God for my baby and something wonderful and precious did come from my involvement with Art.

Letter from Classification and Parole Representative

Attn: Appeals Coordinator
BOARD OF PRISON TERMS
428 J. Street
Sacramento, CA

From: CIW

Subject APPEAL OF INMATE Rose Ann Parker (W-25811)

Please note the attached BPT 1040. Ms. Parker was interviewed on December 28, 1996, and she is requesting a new hearing based on incomplete and Inaccurate information because the panel questioned her on information that had been deleted by a prior appellate decision.

Ms. Parker indicates that the Probation Officer's Report (POR) was never changed. The Court of Appeal's overturned the circumstances describing the crime, and lowered/reduced the degree of the crime. She admits to shooting the victim, but she is contesting premeditation and the latter was supported in the Court of Appeal's opinion, by reducing her sentence from First-Degree Murder to Second-Degree Murder. She is also requesting a modification and, as indicated above, a rehearing. A BPT investigation request may also be appropriate.

For your review note:
1) BPT Form 1040 dated 12/3/96 (3 pages)
A. Inmate's submission of evidence for appeal.
1) Copy of BPT 1001 dated 5/21/96
2) Copy of May 21, 1996, Hearing Decision, pages 74–78 If you have any questions or concerns, feel free to contact me.

Sincerely,

Classification and Parole Representative

After receiving a copy of this memorandum, it was confirmed that God was leading me all the way with putting together my defense and my knowledge. God kept me learning and examining documents and forms.

Mail Call

I received a copy of a letter from my Probation Officer, Mr. LaCues. After I read it, my heart was filled with so many emotions because Mr. LaCues was the first person that would determine that I was not guilty and that I was suitable for release. He was appalled that I was still in prison, especially after the O.J. matter in 1995. It was this letter that gave me the strength I needed to put together a better letter campaign than I ever did before. OK, devil, it's on.

Letter from Probation Officer

April 8, 1997
To Whom It May Concern:
From Supervising Probation Officer

The purpose of this memo is to relate the impressions that I had after interviewing the defendant on two occasions in 1986. I had been assigned the pre-sentence investigations involving the offense that resulted in the imprisonment of Ms. Parker. In 1986, I was a Probation Officer III, assigned to the Rancho Cucamonga Probation Office.

Ms. Parker did not impress this officer as being criminally sophisticated or as being a threat to others, generally. While there is no excuse for her crime, this officer believes, after talking to Ms. Parker's numerous family members and reviewing the police reports describing the murder, that there were mitigating factors that make the crime understandable.

This officer believes that Ms. Parker truly feared for her life on the evening of the offense, and her victim appeared to have the capacity to do her harm.

At the time I interviewed Ms. Parker, I did not believe that she was in need of imprisonment. She had three children, including a newborn, and she appeared to be profoundly impacted by the offense. Her remorse appeared genuine, and I believe that she intended to change the course for her life.

The Penal Code did not allow for the grant of probation, so there was no alternative but to recommend that Ms. Parker be sentenced to prison.
The statutory prohibition in Ms. Parker's case was frustrating to me because I did not, and still do not, believe that Ms. Parker, or society, benefited from her imprisonment.

This officer, in the course of almost twenty-four years of employment by the California Youth Authority and the San Bernardino County Probation Department, has interviewed numerous convicted murderers and Ms. Parker is the only one for whom I would endorse a release from prison.

Prophetic Ministry
T.D. Jakes Ministry wanted to set up a satellite visitation at CIW. I was so excited. Outside guest ministers came to our facility to participate in this powerful presentation of Woman Thou Art Loosed. I was never the same.

Missing Dad
This morning I couldn't wait for dad to arrive so I could tell him about the presentation from Bishop T.D. Jakes last night. 1 P.M. came and went, and then 2 P.M. Where was Dad? He had never missed a Friday since he started visiting me. I thought to myself, Something's wrong Then I could feel it. After two hours, I had to call home.

"Yes, I will accept the call," a calm, male voice said. It was David.

"Where's Dad?" I quickly asked.

"Rose, Dad had a heart attack Wednesday. He's still in the hospital."

I screamed, "What?!"

"Rose, he's better, a lot better, and the doctors say he can come home this week."

Then I asked him about my sons and the rest of the family. Everybody seemed to be fine. I prayed all the way back to my cell. I couldn't take losing another parent while in this place. I couldn't stand losing anyone else, for that matter. I cried to the Lord to keep my daddy and to let healing enter his body.

Sound the Horn of Victory

That night I walked into the chapel. The first thing I said is, "Does anybody want to give God an 'In spite of' praise? In spite of your circumstances, praise Him; in spite of your prison sentence, praise Him! In spite of your cellie, praise Him." Praise Him in everything.

God must have given me twenty in spite of's for us to praise Him over, and by the time I got to the end, the women were all on their feet, shouting as each one identified with the one that touched them! Once the crowd came under control, I shared with them about my afternoon.

I told them my dad just had a heart attack this week, but God wants me to press on and trust Him. I decided to not be down and out! God can be everywhere I can't, and He can do more than I ever could. The women were encouraged. I was still hurting inside and broken over it, but I chose to show up for God. God is all-powerful. I must have sung myself happy that night. I was drained by the time I got back to my cell.

Letter to Daddy

Hi, Daddy,

I hope you are feeling better. I knew something was wrong when you weren't here at 11 A.M. I gave a testimony at church that gave the devil a black eye. I had to do the praise and worship after they told me you had a heart attack. I praised God so hard that I know that God is healing your body now. Oh, Daddy, I sent a copy of the letter that Mr. LaCues, the probation officer, wrote to the DA, the governor, and everybody else that I could think of. I still can't believe that he said that he was frustrated all these years 'cause he did not believe that I was in need of incarceration. Look at GOD. Daddy, get well and know that you have raised up a soldier. Oh, Daddy, one more thing. The bishop that comes on TV was here the other night. I'll tell you about it when you come to see me.

I love you,

Rose Ann

The following day, I told my supervisor about my daddy. She encouraged me and told me about a special board meeting later and asked me to go with her to it. I went to the meeting that afternoon. Many high-powered officials were there. The Lord told me to take my sons' and other family pictures with me. I put them in my purse and told Ms. Jackson I was ready. Then I grabbed my pen and pad.

I was listening and writing every word down. After the meeting was over, I broke out my pictures. One of the officials said, "I know this man, Rev. January. Many years ago, I attended his church."

I said, "That's my father."

He looked surprised and said, "Is that right?" He continued, "Then, I know your entire family."

Joy lit up in my heart. I asked his name and he told me Ted Rich. I couldn't wait to tell Daddy I met someone he knew. That night, I remembered when Momma used to tell me that there were people watching over me in this place. I never knew what she meant. Could she have meant people like Ted Rich, who is on a deciding Board?

Miracle Visit

God blessed me with a visit from my dad the following week after his heart attack. It was a miracle. I knew God was up to something. That's why I gave Him an "in spite of" praise and He gave me a miracle.

Journal Entry

Lord Jesus,

This has been some kind of year, but I made it! And I know that it was only by your grace and Your mercy that I did. It seemed that every time I turned around, the enemy was coming up with something new. But no matter what came my way, You, Father, made the difference. Thank you for the family visits that You gave me with my sons this year. Thank you, God, for protecting them.

Thank you for what my sons shared with me when they visited early July about the gangs trying to jump them. Darian can get another bike, but he can't get another life. Lord, thank you for giving them running ability and speed in their youthful feet to get to that garage. But the real praise report is that those same boys came to the house and apologized to both of them. Lord, you know that was my prayer.
Lord, when Daddy had that mild stroke and heart attack, You were my victory. Thank you. Then two weeks later, when my brother, Joseph, was killed witnessing for Jesus on the streets, You were my peace! But, Lord, You know I really struggled through that period. And God, You are really

going to have to heal my broken heart over his death. I know Your Word says there is an appointed time to every man and woman to die, but it just feels like he died at the wrong time. God, he had just given his life back to You and was starting to do street witnessing to drug addicts. To be shot down while trying to give a tract to a dealer is way more than I can handle right now. Then my other brother Paul nearly died from brain surgery and had to learn to speak and walk all over again. This was more than Daddy could take. That's probably why he had a heart attack.

Lord, You surely trusted me more than I did myself. Thank you. I didn't think I could stand this year with still being heartbroken over Momma. I guess that place of missing and more missing will always be there. When I learned that I had lumps in my breast late this summer, I could not bring myself to tell my family with all the sickness and death that was going on. You know I decided to stand on Your Word for my healing. You did not fail me, and so I want to thank you again for this year being a year of peculiar healing. I know that there is nothing You wouldn't do for little ole Rose January Parker. Lord God, thank you for delivering me from Tia and the strongholds of my flesh. Thank you, Jesus, for Your wonderful grace, love, and mercy!

Lord, we are depending on You to see us through. I know our lives are in Your hands. Please keep us. And thank you again for seeing us through this tumultuous year. And finally, Lord, thank you for Mr. LaCues' letter saying that I should be set free. I believe I can see a light at the end of my tunnel. You are a good God!

I love You, Father,

Rose Parker

Chapter 23: Another Year

Journal Entry
My letter to the Lord

This is another year You allowed me to see. What a blessing You have given me. Thank you for how You kept me and my boys and family. Father, I lay before You my quarterly agenda that I wrote up last night.

I walked around the track that morning with praise on my lips and sang to the glory of God. At times, I ran to feel the wind blow upon my face like the breath of God's Spirit. Then I started my workday with a smile on my face.

Special Events
The year so far was not so bad with all the letters of support coming in and the district attorney as well as the public defender investigating my case. It just hurt that the governor had not made a move to release me yet.

In May 1998, Pastor Ron Gibson visited the prison. He came with a ministry called "On the Way." I did not know he was Pastor Ron until I really listened to him speak. I told him, "I recognize your voice. You're Pastor Ron. I have your tapes. They really bless me in here." He smiled and thanked me.

It was my tradition to walk the volunteers all the way to Control at the Administration Building. This particular night I stopped at the corner instead of going all the way.

Pastor Ron and I had been talking. He loved the praise & worship that I led and the choir that I directed, but what he did not know was that I was an inmate. When he found out, he went berserk.

"What!? You're an inmate?"

I smiled and nodded my head yes. He then looked at the volunteers that accompanied him and said, "She's an inmate!" He asked me again several times and just shook his head in disbelief. About a month later, I was blessed to hear another one of his tapes. This time, he was talking and preaching about me, the inmate who was so beautiful, and dressed so well and believed God that she was coming home.

The Potter's House
A team came in from the ministry that hosted a conference via satellite last year. It was awesome to know that they had a powerful ministry that focused on prisons and care. I will never forget that experience.

July 1998
Hi, Daddy,

I tried to call you to tell you I won my appeal to the BPT. Just in case something happens, I want to make sure I get this letter to you in the mail. They have to give me a new parole date and they have to put me on the next calendar, so they may have to take someone off or make more time when they come. Look at God, Daddy.

I love you,

Rose Ann

Finally in August 1998, the investigators contacted the district attorney, public defender, and others to discuss the matter and wrote on my behalf. I could not believe how they all said that I was not supposed to be in prison. After reading each of their letters, I found myself becoming more and more emotional as I saw the hand of God upon these people's hearts toward me.

September 1, 1998

To: Board of Prison Terms
From: Office of the District Attorney
Re: Rose Ann Parker

Dear Ms. Axelrod:

This is in response to your letter of August 27, 1998, soliciting my views as the prosecutor of the above person in order to determine if executive clemency would be appropriate pursuant to claims of Battered Woman Syndrome.

This case was tried before a jury before the label "Battered Woman's Syndrome" had been created. Nevertheless, the defense presented evidence, acknowledged by the prosecution to be true and accurate, that the victim had previously physically abused Ms. Parker prior to the killing. My recollection is that the police investigators themselves acknowledged to me that Mr. Boga was a narcotic-trafficking, heavy-handed boor who had previously been involved in violent altercations, some involving Rose Ann Parker. The answer to your question, then, is that evidence of domestic abuse was introduced at trial. Moreover, the prosecution argued to the jury that the motive for the killing was Ms. Parker's (illegal) preemptive strike against Mr. Boga in anticipation of future abuse. To put it in other words, we utilized the defendant's abuse to point out to the jury that his killing was not merely happenstance, but based upon a thought-out deliberation. I have always accepted and believed that Ms. Parker was, in fact, abused by Mr. Boga.

At the time of the offense, Ms. Parker readily cooperated with the police and explained not only that she had intentionally shot Mr.Boga, but also described the reason for her behavior. Her testimony on the witness stand was, in my view, candid and forthright, and she made no attempt to minimize or evade responsibility for her actions. She was courteous, polite, and respectful of the judicial proceedings and those persons, such as myself, who were involved therewith.

Much to the surprise of the judge and the courtroom staff, the jury concurred with my view that the defense argument of imperfect self-defense was not reasonable. Later, the Court of Appeals reduced the offense from first-degree (willful, deliberated, and premeditated) murder. I concur with that action by the appellate court.

To give you some idea of how the trial court viewed this case, it should be noted that Ms. Parker was allowed to remain out of custody on her own recognizance during her murder trial, based upon her lack of prior criminal record and the facts of the case.

I must confess that as a career prosecutor, I am philosophically skeptical (to say the least) about various newfound syndromes which seek to free criminal defendants from accountability and legal responsibility for their actions. That notwithstanding, I am now, and always have been, of the opinion that Ms. Parker truly believed that she needed to use force and violence as a result of her prior abuse at Mr. Boga's hands. Apart from that abuse, I doubt that the killing would have occurred.

And while it would be foolish to act as a guarantor of a person's future behavior, I, nevertheless, would be quite surprised if Ms. Parker has any future contacts with the criminal justice system. I, thus, would look
favorably upon an exercise of discretion pursuant to Penal Code sections 4800 and 4801.

Please feel free to contact me if I may be of further assistance.

Deputy District Attorney

COUNTY OF SAN BERNARDINO

Office of the District Attorney

DENNIS L. STOUT
DISTRICT ATTORNEY

September 1, 1998

Board of Prison Terms
ATTN: Senior Investigator Connie Axelrod
428 J Street, 6th Floor
Sacramento, CA 95814

RE: Parker, Rose Ann
Your case No.: BPT 92-0025

Dear Ms. Axelrod:

This is in response to your letter of August 27, 1998 soliciting my views as the prosecutor of the above person in order to determine if executive clemency would be appropriate pursuant to claims of battered women syndrome.

This case was tried before a jury before the label "battered women's syndrome" had been created. Nevertheless, the defense presented evidence, acknowledged by the prosecution to be true and accurate, that the victim had previously physically abused Ms. Parker prior to the killing. My recollection is that the police investigators themselves acknowledged to me that Mr. Boga was a narcotic-trafficking, heavy handed boor who had previously been involved in violent altercations, some involving Rose Ann Parker. The answer to your question, then, is that evidence of domestic abuse was introduced at trial. Moreover, the Prosecution argued to the jury that the motive for the killing was Ms. Parker's (illegal) pre-emptive strike against Mr. Boga in anticipation of future abuse. To put it in other words, we utilized the defendant's abuse to point out to the jury that the killing was not merely happenstance, but based upon a thought-out deliberation. I have always accepted and believed that Ms. Parker was in fact abused by Mr. Boga.

At the time of the offense Ms. Parker readily cooperated with the police and explained not only that she had intentionally shot Mr. Boga, but also described the

606 East Mill Street, San Bernardino, California 92415-0615   (909) 891-3899   Fax (909) 891-3890

reason therefore. Her testimony on the witness stand was, in my view, candid and forthright and she made no attempt to minimize or evade responsibility for her actions. She was courteous, polite and respectful of the judicial proceedings and those persons such as myself who were involved therewith.

Much to the surprise of the judge and the courtroom staff, the jury concurred with my view that the defense argument of imperfect self-defense was not reasonable. The Court of Appeals later on the courts own motion, reduced the offense from first degree (willful, deliberated and premeditated) murder to second degree murder. I concur with that action by the appellate court.

To give you some idea of how the trial court viewed this case, it should be noted that Ms. Parker was allowed to remain out of custody on her own recognizance during her murder trial, based upon her lack of prior criminal record and the facts of the case.

I must confess that as a career prosecutor I am philosophically skeptical (to say the least) about various new-found syndrome's which seek to free criminal defendant's from accountability and legal responsibility for their actions. That notwithstanding, I am now, and always have been, of the opinion that Ms. Parker truly believed that she needed to use force and violence as a result of her prior abuse at Mr. Boga's hands. Absent that abuse I doubt that the killing would have occurred.

And while it would be foolish to act as a guarantor of a person's future behavior, I nevertheless would be quite surprised if Ms. Parker has any future contacts with the criminal justice system. I thus would look favorably upon an exercise of discretion pursuant to Penal Code sections 4800 and 4801.

Please feel free to contact me at (909) 891-3898 if I may be of further assistance.

CLYDE A. BOYD
Deputy District Attorney

cc: Rich Maxwell, Chief DDA
    David Negus, Chief DPD

CAB/pdh

Dear God,

Sometimes I'm up and sometimes I'm down, almost leveled to the ground, just like the song.)? I'm depending on You. Thank you for the letters that are coming in that You showed me. There is so much to say, but I'm going to stop now. Watch over my family, please. Amen.

Letters from Sons

September 1998

To Whom It May Concern
Subject: Let My Mom Out

My mom has helped a lot of people and has given them better lives. Now it should be her turn to be helped and no longer be locked up. She probably could help you and your life, too.

She is very close to God. You should be too, and then you would understand and agree that she needs to be with her family, or what family she might have left. Our family would probably be a lot closer and stronger if she could be out so she could help us like she helps the people locked up.

If I were to take one of your family members and lock that person up, you would probably try to hurt me or lock me up, so I should feel the same toward you, but I have a mother named Rose Parker, and she would not allow me to do that anyway. All I can do is pray for her and for you and hope for the best.

Also, she needs her father, and he needs her. You need to let her out so she can be with us while the world is still turning. It's your choice.

Sincerely,
Atujuan J.J. Douroux
High School Student

Younger Son

My mom is a very good person. Her name is Rose Parker. She loves God more than most people do. If I were you, I would let her go. I can't make you, but I can ask you. She is important to me. She is a good business person. You believe in the policies to keep her; I don't. It's just "make-believe" rules to me. All they want is your money. I'm a nice guy if you're a nice guy. We are both businessmen, am I correct? Let Mom go or I won't pay taxes when I get older.

I miss the way she cooks. I'm sure you have somebody that cooks for you and how would you feel if she was taken from you? Not very good, huh? Think about it.

I hope you make the right choice.

Sincerely,
Master Darian J.J. Douroux
Middle School Student

Letter from Public Defender

Date: September 10, 1998
To: Senior Investigator
From: Public Defender

On August 26, 1998, you solicited my views as defense counsel on the case of Rose Ann Parker. She has applied for executive clemency. I sincerely hope the governor acts favorably on her application.

I believe Ms. Parker has been the victim of bad choices I made when I represented her. Had I been wiser and more experienced, I believe she would have long ago successfully completed her parole.

At the preliminary hearing, the magistrate held her to answer only for manslaughter, not for murder. As was his right, the prosecutor refiled the murder charges in Superior Court. Nonetheless, the prosecutor offered a plea bargain of six years on a manslaughter charge. Unfortunately, Ms. Parker felt that the decision on her future was in the hands of God and did not want to plead guilty. I was too young and foolish to attempt to convince her to take the offer.

At the trial, no evidence concerning the Battered Woman's Syndrome was presented. At the time, I was not aware of the literature on that issue. Instead, I relied on a theory of self-defense. Ms. Parker testified.

She told of her fear. As in all cases of Battered Woman's Syndrome, it was difficult for the woman to explain why she felt the threat of death was so immediate. I relied on an expert in cocaine addition to explain the seemingly irrational parts of her behavior. This testimony met with little sympathy from the jury. Had there been an expert in Battered Woman's Syndrome, these issues could have been explained in terms more likely to have been understood by the jury.

Sincerely,

David W. Negus
Chief Deputy Public Defender
Complete Letter Attached; Adapted Above

Journal

Dear Lord,

Now I sho'nuff know that you are doing something. You touched my attorney's heart to pour out his support for me to the Board. It takes a great man to admit some of the things that he admitted concerning his lack of knowledge and him wishing he had more wisdom during the time of my case. I can only pray for him and hope the best for him because he did the best he knew at that time. Thank you for touching his heart. I will treasure his letter forever. I read it three times that day and found myself praying for him out loud.

Law Offices of the Public Defender

COUNTY OF SAN BERNARDINO

DAVID L. McKENNA
Public Defender

WEST VALLEY DIVISION
DAVID W. NEGUS
Chief Deputy Public Defender
RENAE D. CARPENTER
Supervising Deputy for Superior Court

Deputy Public Defenders
JEFFREY A. AARON
LISA R. BAKER
JOSEPH O. CANTY
DAVID CIANCHETTI
JAMES M. CLOYD
C. CHRISTIAN CRUZ
PATRICIA D. DIAMOND
DAVID DURDINES
DONNA K. FERNANDEZ
SUSAN GILES
KATHERINE R. LARA
VICTOR C. MARSHALL
CAROLLE LE MONNIER
DANIEL J. MANGAN
TERESA SNODGRASS
SUSAN M. STARBUCK
DAVID R. VIRDEN
SANDRA L. WAITE
HERBERT E. WILLIAMSON III

PLEASE REPLY TO:
8303 Haven Avenue
Rancho Cucamonga, CA 91730
(909) 945-4100
Fax (909) 945-4285

13260 Central Avenue
Chino, CA 91710
(909) 465-5212
Fax (909) 465-5338

September 10, 1998

Ms. Connie Axelrod, Senior Investigator
Board of Prison Terms
428 J Street, 6th Floor
Sacramento, CA 95814

Dear Ms. Axelrod:

On August 26, 1998, you solicited my views as defense counsel on the case of Rose Ann Parker. She has applied for executive clemency. I sincerely hope the governor acts favorably on her application.

I believe Ms. Parker has been the victim of bad choices I made when I represented her. Had I been wiser and more experienced I believe she would have long ago successfully completed her parole.

At the preliminary hearing, the magistrate held her to answer only for manslaughter, not for murder. As was his right, the prosecutor refiled the murder charges in Superior Court. Nonetheless, the prosecutor offered a plea bargain of 6 years on a manslaughter charge. Unfortunately, Ms. Parker felt that the decision on her future was in the hands of God, and did not want to plead guilty. I was too young and foolish to attempt to convince her to take the offer.

At the trial, no evidence concerning the Battered Woman's Syndrome was presented. At the time I was not aware of the literature on that issue. Instead, I relied on a theory of self defense. Ms. Parker testified. She told of her fear. As in all cases of battered woman's syndrome, it was difficult for the woman to explain why she felt the threat of death was so immediate. I relied on an expert in cocaine addiction to explain the seemingly irrational parts of her behavior. This testimony met with little sympathy from the jury. Had there been an expert in the Battered Woman's Syndrome these issues could have been explained in terms more likely to have been understood by the jury.

Ms. Parker's background:

Ms. Parker was one of several children of Rev. Emmanuel January, a prominent local minister. She was an attractive and talented young woman who went off to Hollywood to make her fortune. There she met Art Boga, a gambler and drug dealer. Ms. Parker showed bad judgment, becoming involved with Mr.

Boga, and becoming addicted to cocaine. Mr. Boga was a source of cocaine for her for several years. She became his mistress and lived with him in Woodland Hills.

Mr. Boga's history:

Mr. Boga was an imposing man in his fifties. He had a long police record, primarily for gambling and drugs. He also had an arrest for carrying a concealed weapon. When he arrested a second time for a weapons violation in 1982, a search warrant was obtained for his home in Woodland Hills. Three pounds of cocaine were seized.

During the time Ms. Parker lived with Mr. Boga he was a controlling personality. The nature of the man can be seen from his automobile, an Excaliber sports car. The car does not have a front license plate. Instead, there is a plaque which reads: "Remember the Golden Rule: whoever has the gold makes the rules."

Mr. Boga ruled Ms. Parker primarily through fear and drugs. He frequently would threaten to kill her if she disobeyed him. He would humiliate her in front of his friends. He would not allow her to leave him. On occasion he used physical violence against her. In one incident which we documented at trial, he pistol whipped her on Christmas day in 1985. She did not seek medical attention until some time later. At one time I had the medical reports, but no longer do so. They were not in the court file. As I remember, the records documented the head injury, but did not mention Mr. Boga as the person who inflicted the injury.

Mr. Boga traveled in entertainment circles, and was known a's a supplier of cocaine. When my investigator and I searched the Excaliber at the impound lot, we found in the glove box an envelope with the return address of a well known singer. At the preliminary hearing, the bailiff noticed that a member of the audience, a well-dressed middle-aged black person named Dr. Lowell Augustine, to make a gesture toward Ms. Parker of cutting a throat. To Ms. Parker, Mr. Boga appeared powerful, well connected, influential, and frightening.

The offense:

On March 27, 1986, Ms. Parker had gone to her father's house to try to escape from Mr. Boga. Mr. Boga followed her. Ms. Parker told Mr. Boga she was pregnant by another man. (In fact, years later, paternity testing revealed that Mr. Boga was the father.) Mr. Boga threatened to kill her. Fearing he would, she got one of his guns and shot him once, then again.

Corroboration came from a neighbor who testified that there was loud arguing coming from the residence A male voice, which circumstances identified as Mr. Boga, yelled, "Rose Ann, how could you do this? You're dead." A shot followed, and then shortly after there was another shot.

After the shooting Ms. Parker's brothers hid Mr. Boga's body in a closet.

The police responded to the location of the shooting. They had received reports of shots fired. The police ordered everyone out of the house. Then Sergeant, now Chief of Police, Lloyd Scharf, approached Ms. Parker. Ms. Parker told him she had shot Mr. Boga. Ms. Parker also told Sergeant Scharf that the body was in a closet.

Taken into custody Ms. Parker waived her rights, gave a taped statement to Officer Tejas. She admitted she had killed Mr. Boga. She said she did so because she feared he would kill her. A transcript of that interview is enclosed.

As I told you on the phone, my file was lost by the USC post-conviction project, so all of the investigation which I did which could not be introduced at trial is lost. I believe we had discovered other assaultive conduct toward women by Mr. Boga, but for some reason, did not have the witnesses to introduce at trial. Ms. Parker was not the only woman which Mr. Boga kept as a mistress.

I have located some documentation about the case. The District Attorney had a copy of a petition for writ of habeas corpus prepared with the help of the USC group. It has some exhibits which I think will be helpful. These include portions of the testimony of Rose Ann Parker, Bonita Money, Emzee Parker, Iris De Large, and William Covert. The transcripts are incomplete. I believe the Attorney General will still have the complete trial transcript. In addition I have included a copy of the transcript of a statement made by Ms. Parker once she was taken to the police station.

I know that the DA sent to you a summary of Mr. Boga's criminal history. I also located in the Superior Court exhibits room, some documents which were not marked at trial. These include the police reports concerning Mr. Boga which I subpoenaed from the LAPD, the autopsy protocol and the death certificate. I am sending all of this material to you. Finally, in case you do not have it, I have submitted a report from Gail Pincus diagnosing Ms. Parker as having the Battered Woman's Syndrome, which was submitted to the Board at Ms. Parker's lifer hearing in 1996.

I have kept in touch with Ms. Parker since her conviction, through phone calls and legal visits. She has matured over the years. I do not believe there

Page 4

is any chance of her returning to drugs, or putting herself in a situation where she poses a threat to anyone. Her son by Mr. Boga is being raised by her aging father. She loves her sons. It would be wonderful if she could be released while her father is still alive.

If there is any other information I can give you, please do not hesitate to call me.

Sincerely,

David W. Negus
Chief Deputy Public Defender

DWN/sf

Passing the Choir Director Baton

I told Mary Thompson, my assistant choir director, that I was stepping down and appointing her as the new official choir director. She smiled and said, "What's going on, Rose?"

I replied, "Girl, I'm passing the baton because I'm going home.

I've I put my heart in the choir, so take care of it for me and lean on God."

Journal Entry

Dear God,

Lord, I was happy to receive a letter today from Cheryl Brown from the Black Voice Newspaper. She attended our group AAWPA last night and thanked me for sharing my story. You sure got people thinking about me.

My new hearing finally came. I knew the first one was wrong.

It's been three years. I can't believe they denied me for another year. I'm going to appeal this one too. God, help me.

Chapter 24: Happy New Year, 1999

In Feb. 1999, I received my transcript of my December 1998 hearing after sixty days from the hearing of December 1998. I couldn't wait to read it to make sure the corrections had been made and that the record was finally straight. I just hated that they denied my parole. More errors, Can't they get anything right? I pulled out a BPT Decision Review Corrective Sheet and began to complete it.

BPT DECISION REVIEW CORRECTIVE SHEET

INMATE: Parker, Rose
TYPE OF HEARING
CDC NUMBER W-25811
DATE OF HEARING Initial Parole Consideration 12/30/99

1. Page 1, Line 9: After "enhancement," add Penal Code Sections violated 187 and 120225.
2. Page 1, line 10: change "15" to "17."
3. Page 13, line 6: after "crime," add, "The Panel recommends that the prisoner remain disciplinary free, participate in self-help and therapy as available, get current letters regarding job offers." (Taken from decision fact sheet.) I put it in an envelope and placed it in the outgoing mail for the day. Then I started on my assignments that Barbara had lined up for me. I was so grateful that she supported me and gave me freedom with love to handle my legal stuff.

BPT Response to Rose Parker

Less than a month later, I received a response from the BPT Board. They made a recommendation that gave me a glimpse of hope again. It read:

Recommendation: To correct the error(s) set forth above in the hearing transcript and read the following language into the record at the next scheduled parole consideration hearing:

Adopted above.

After I read the BPT response, I had to write them back immediately. I prayed before I sent it.

Date: March 13, 1999To: Chief Executive Officer, BPT From: Rose Parker

I received the BPT 1135 (a) with your signature dated 2/23/99 on 3/3/99. This is my response to that letter:

I requested (in my appeal) that a new hearing be held to correct the errors from my initial hearing of 5/96. I also requested that the record reflect correct information. Neither of those requests were met. The BPT gave me another "Initial Hearing" and I was not permitted to discuss, or recount any of the issues I had raised on appeal.

You want the record to "reflect" that the prisoner's 12/30/98 hearing was her first subsequent, when, in fact, it was held as an INITIAL. I would also like to add that in the "denial" of parole, references were made to that being my Initial in the decision. This recommendation/decision is not correcting that error, or any of my initial requests on appeal.

The record has reflected that this Board has made errors in every hearing, paperwork, and decision beginning with the circumstances of my case, the hearing transcript from my Initial hearing (partially granted on appeal), hearing transcript from the new Initial hearing of 12/30/98(see BPT Decision Review Corrective Sheet), then this letter that paperwork erroneously stated that the 1998 hearing was a rehearing, terming the hearing an initial hearing. The comments in the hearing decision made by Deputy Commissioner Griffith (pg. 74, line 3 & 4) referred to the BWS as an aggravation fact instead of mitigating fact (which the police department, prosecutor, probation department, and defense council all elaborated on and gave recommendations).

I have taken responsibility for this crime since day one. I also know that my victim would have killed me, my unborn child, and family members and that "fact" will not change. I did put myself in the position of being involved with that person. However, don't forget—I left, and he came to find me. I have made tremendous growth since my arrival to CIW, which is documented in my 12/98 Psych Report.

This Board keeps making errors and mistakes with my life and it's like, "It's OK." Well, it's not. It is my request that an immediate hearing be scheduled for an actual "first subsequent" (my first subsequent was initially schedule for 5/99). This way, we

---

can address and go over the issues that were raised on appeal. Then, my next hearing (if necessary) would be a second subsequent. I also request that the Board refer me to Governor Davis for an Executive Clemency ASAP. I do believe that GOD will move mightily on my behalf with HIS favor. Thank you for your time and concern.

Sincerely and respectfully submitted, Rose Parker W25811 CIW

Gray Davis Declares No Support for Lifers- Prophetic Signs

On April 29, 1999, and October 3, 1999, Governor Gray Davis declared that "I will never let a lifer out of prison under NO circumstances! Forget it!"

Prophetic Signs

In April of 1999, I start posting signs to encourage the lifers. They read, "Do not put your trust in man; only God can help us." The lifers started tearing the signs down wherever they appeared. I didn't understand this. It felt like they just wanted to wallow in the discouraging words of the governor that he would not help a convicted murderer while he was in office. I was convinced if God wanted to change his mind that He could and I was a prime candidate for the exception.

Chapter 25: It Is Finished!

Dear God,

Thank you so much. Today, Father, I received a copy of a letter from the judge that tried my case. He remembers everything clearly and it has been fourteen years since I was in his courtroom, but You caused him to remember little ole' me. My God! The king's heart is in Your hands. Thanks so much for being on my side. I love You, love You, love You.

Letter from Judge to Senior Investigator

January 21, 2000
Senior Investigator, BPT
Sacramento, CA 95814

Re: Rose Ann Parker, DOB 6/3/59, OR 11536

Dear Ms. Axelrod:

Thank you for your inquiry of January 20, 2000. My memory of this case is hazy after fourteen years. The file is in archives, but I could get it out if you need more specific information.

My recollection is that I always thought Rose Ann should have been acquitted, or, at most, found guilty of voluntary manslaughter. Had it been a court trial, I would have found her not guilty. However, the jury felt otherwise, and I did not feel I could upset their verdict.

As for the victim, Arthur Boga, my recollection is he was a worthless piece of humanity, and it is likely he would have ended up killing Rose Ann had she not done him in.

At that time, I don't recall there being any Battered Woman syndrome defense available. I don't recall any expert testifying regarding same. I can't recall if Rose herself testified. It sticks in my mind that even through the prosecution witnesses, the evidence of past abuse and her statements to the police regarding fear of Boga came into evidence.

Finally, it is my recollection that I had no options insofar as the sentence went. I either had to grant a new trial—which I didn't feel would have proper—or follow the law regarding sentencing.

I would certainly recommend either clemency or parole. In my mind, Rose was never a threat to society. She has paid a considerable price for what may well have been a non-criminal act.

If I may be of any further assistance, please do not hesitate to call on me. I would even be willing to testify, if the law permits it.

Sincerely,

Judge William P. Hyde

Superior Court Judge Retired

My Last Attorney Visit

I had a couple of attorney visits preparing for my Parole Hearing. Every time I brought up God, one of my attorneys would say "The governor is not letting anyone out, Rose. He made that clear." But I remained positive.

Here We Go Again: Parole Suitability Hearing 9 A.M.

William Pitt Hyde
Superior Court Judge, Retired

OO FEB 10 PM 12: 15

Upland, CA 91784

Fax: ~~909-946-1402~~

January 21, 2000

INMATE COPY

Connie Axelrod
Senior Investigator
Board of Prison Terms
428 J St., 6th Floor
Sacramento, Ca 95814

Re: Rose Ann Parker, DOB 6/3/59, OCR 11536

Dear Ms. Axelrod:

Thank you for your inquiry of January 20, 2000. My memory of this case is hazy after 14 years. The file is in archives, but I could get it out if you need more specific information.

My recollection is that I always thought Rose Ann should have been acquitted, or, at most, found guilty of voluntary manslaughter. Had it been a court trial, I would have found her not guilty. However, the jury felt otherwise, and I did not feel I could upset their verdict.

As for the victim, Arthur Boga, my recollection is he was a worthless piece of humanity, and it is likely he would have ended up killing Rose Ann had she not done him in.

At that time, I don't recall there being any Battered Woman Syndrome defense available. If it was, I don't recall any expert testifying regarding same. I can't recall if Rose herself testified. It sticks in my mind that even through the prosecution witnesses, the evidence of past abuse and her statements to the police regarding fear of Boga came into evidence.

Finally, it is my recollection that I had no options insofar as the sentence went. I either had to grant a new trial - which I didn't feel would have proper - or follow the law regarding sentencing.

I would certainly recommend either executive clemency or parole. In my mind, Rose was never a threat to society. She has paid a considerable price for what may well have been a non criminal act.

If I may be of any further assistance, please do not hesitate to call on me. I would even be willing to testify, if the law permits it.

Sincerely,

William Pitt Hyde

~ 329 ~

The day of my hearing finally arrived. The USC law team was there and presented the following Parole Suitability Submission.

I. Introduction

Rose Parker has come a long way since arriving at CIW in March of 1987. During years of incarceration, she has transformed herself into a productive, independent, and fully rehabilitated person who has come to terms with both the crime that she committed, as well as the lifestyle of drug dependency and tolerance to abuse which facilitated the crime itself. Today, Ms. Parker is a remorseful, educated, and insightful young woman with a strong network of supportive friends and family, marketable job skills, and clear plans for the future.

Meeting Legal Requirements

Ms. Parker clearly meets all the legal requirements for suitability. She has accepted full responsibility for her action that led to Mr. Boga's death, and is filled with sorrow and remorse. Furthermore, she has also come to accept responsibility for allowing her life to get out of control, and has taken steps to regain full control of her life. Immediately upon her arrival at CIW, Ms. Parker took affirmative steps through active involvement in therapy and self-help programs.

Support Base

Ms. Parker is now forty years of age, and although she realizes nothing will ever undo her actions of that night, she is asking for a second chance in order to do something positive in the remaining time she has left in this world.

Family

Ms. Parker has tried her best to be a responsible mother to her three young boys, and is now anxious to raise them on her own and instill in them these same values and life lessons that she has learned while incarcerated. She has been able to maintain a close relationship with her father during her incarceration. He has supported her these thirteen years, and she hopes to care for him in his declining years.

Initial Hearing: (See Hyde 2000 Letter, Exhibit A. Page 1.)

In her initial hearing, the Board expressed concern over two circumstances indicating unsuitability for parole. However, Ms. Parker's sentencing judge, the Honorable William Pitt Hyde, asserts that "Rose was never a threat to society. She has paid a considerable price for what may have been a non-criminal act."

II. Ms. Parker Meets All Criteria for Suitability The materials attached and submitted to the Board, including her parole packet, illustrate the depth of Ms. Parker's rehabilitation and her present suitability for parole, exceeding the criteria established and set forth in California Code of Regulations Title 15, Section 2403. Specifically, her parole suitability is supported by her psychiatric report by Dr. McDaniel; her sentencing judge, William Pitt Hyde; the district attorney who prosecuted her; her supervising probation officer; and by the remarkable outside support she has continued to receive from friends and family. However, Ms. Parker's suitability for parole is most evident by her own renewed sense of self-worth, positive attitude, and her unabashed enthusiasm and courage in helping others who are facing the same demons she fought thirteen years ago.

Judge Hyde has stated that "had it been a court trial, I would have found her not guilty. I would certainly recommend either executive clemency or parole. In my mind, Rose was never a threat to society."
See Hyde 2000 Letter, Exhibit A, Page 1.

Similarly, Richard LaCues, her Supervising Probation Officer, has noted, "This officer, in the course of almost twenty-four years of employment by the California Youth Authority and the San Bernardino Probation Department, has interviewed numerous convicted murderers and Ms. Parker is the only one for whom I would endorse a release from prison." See LaCues 1997 Letter, Exhibit B, Page I. Finally, Clyde A. Boyd, the Deputy District Attorney who prosecuted Ms. Parker, is also of the opinion that she is suitable for parole, stating that "I would nevertheless be quite surprised if Ms. Parker has any future contacts with the criminal justice system."
See Boyd 1998 Letter, Exhibit C, Page 2.

In short, everyone involved with this case, and every individual who has witnessed Ms. Parker's remarkable positive transformation in prison, now agrees that she should be granted a parole date.

A. No Juvenile Record
Ms. Parker has no record of juvenile crimes. See 2000 Parole Hearing Packet.

B. Ms. Parker's many long-term relationships reflect a stable social history. During her thirteen years of incarceration, Ms. Parker has been successful in developing several long-term, meaningful, and healthy relationships. Because Ms. Parker acknowledges that her previous drug addiction and the crime itself resulted in part from her inability to sustain such healthy relationships, she has been active in trying to build deep and lasting friendships with the outside world even while incarcerated. In the course of re-establishing her own self-confidence, Ms. Parker has reached out to her family, therapy leaders, religious leaders, and others on the outside who share her interests in religion and victims awareness, and to other inmates working through their own painful rehabilitation process. The true value of these relationships is apparent in the tremendous network of support eagerly awaiting Ms. Parker's release. See Letters of Support, Exhibit B.

Ever since her childhood and to this very day, Ms. Parker's family has been the most integral aspect of her life. They constitute a fundamental part of her being, as she is theirs. Ms. Parker has three young boys, ages thirteen, fifteen, and twenty-three, whom she has tried to the best of her abilities to raise while incarcerated. Under these circumstances, Ms. Parker remains remarkably close to her children, who eagerly anticipate the return of their mother. I must mention Ms. Parker has been consistently involved in LTO, CWAA, AA/NA and other self-help groups.

III. Leads JTS (Janitorial Training Services) (2/91 to 2/92)
Supervisor work evaluations rated Ms. Parker as exceptional.

IV. Recoding Secretary and Chairperson for WAC (Elected Position 1/91 to 2/92) In this position, as in all her other jobs, Ms. Parker was consistently commended for her excellent work. She was elected chairperson of WAC. In her position as chairperson, she was described as "very professional in her interactions with staff and inmates alike," and as "devoted to promoting a positive environment at the institution." (See Exhibit 17.)

V. Clerk to Protestant Chaplain (2/88 to 1/90) In this position, Ms. Parker was commended many times for her dependability, skill, cooperative attitude, and pleasant personality, and for being "a great asset to the religious program."

VI. Volunteer Charitable Work and Other Activities 1. Training Facilitator
After completing the "New Beginnings" Victim Awareness Program herself, Ms. Parker volunteered to work as a training facilitator in the program, which she has done consistently since January 1995. As part of the program, Ms. Parker regularly leads two-hour presentations with other inmates to help them understand the impact of their criminal behavior on others and learn constructive interpersonal skills. She has been commended for her good work and ethics in the program, and for her numerous volunteer hours. (See Exhibit 19.)

2. African-American Prisoner's Association (AAWPA) Ms. Parker has been involved with AAWPA since 1993, serving as a volunteer public relations officer for the group and then secretary for the last two years. She has been commended for displaying "exceptional teamwork" and "outstanding participation."

3. Women's Advisory Counsel (WAC) Prior to serving as executive secretary of WAC and later, as chairperson of the group (a full-time position), Ms. Parker was a member from 1988. She received a "Certificate of Appreciation" for her many contributions to the organization. (See Exhibit 21.)

4. Support Care Unit (SCU) Volunteer Work Since 1990, Ms. Parker has led several activities on a volunteer basis. She teaches Bible study groups and aerobics classes weekly in SCU, as well as serving as volunteer dance and choir director for their special events.

5. Reception Center Volunteer Work Since Ms. Parker's arrival at CIW in 1987, she has actively participated in the In-House Ministries Program with the Inter-Faith Chapel.

6. Children-at-Risk Walk-a-Thon

Ms. Parker has been actively involved with the Children-at-Risk Walk-a-Thon since the inception of the program in 1989. She has been commended for her "conscientiousness and willingness to always go above and beyond the call of duty."

7. Volunteer Aerobics Instructor
In addition to teaching aerobics to inmates in the Psychiatric Ward at Frontera (SCU), Ms. Parker also taught weekly aerobics classes to inmates in the general population on a volunteer basis from approximately 1988–1992.

8. Volunteer Bible Study Leader
Ms. Parker led volunteer Bible study groups in the closed custody housing unit.

9. Ministry to AIDS Patients
Since 1991, Ms. Parker has done volunteer work, ministering to inmates who have HIV/AIDS.

10. Choir Director and Special Events Music Coordinator
Ms. Parker has been actively involved with the choir group sponsored by the Interfaith Chapel, and served as choir director for several years. She has also worked as special coordinator for the musical component of inmate plays, talent shows, and inspirational singing programs. (Se Exhibit 22.)

11. Other Volunteer Activities
As is apparent above, Ms. Parker shows exceptional energy involving herself in volunteer work to help other inmates. Additional chronos tell of assistance she has rendered to other special events and other activities too extensive to mention. For example, just five months ago, Ms. Parker was commended for assisting with a special project to provide materials for self-help programs at CIW-Alaska. (See Exhibit 24.)

VII. Disciplinaries
As her long list of positive accomplishments and extensive positive evaluations demonstrate, Ms. Parker has been a model prisoner. Although she has been exceptionally active in the institution, interacting constantly with other inmates and staff, she has received almost no Disciplinaries.

VIII. RELEASE PLANS
Before the current offense, Ms. Parker had no criminal history, and the life she would be released to–unlike that which sadly confronts many other inmates–is a healthy, middle class, and stable one. Ms. Parker's family is loving and close-knit with many links to the community, particularly in Christian ministries. They are eager to welcome her back to the outside and provide her with a caring home and stabilizing environment. When Ms. Parker is released on parole, she plans to live in San Bernardino with her father, Reverend Emanuel January, a retired business owner and pastor, and care for him and her two children, Atujuan, 12 years old, and Darian, 10 years.

Ms. Parker has received numerous job offers to begin upon her release that would utilize the vocational skills she has developed during her incarceration in word processing and computer programming. Her brother, Peter January, now married with children and completely recovered from his own drug problem, owns a computer business, and has offered her a job in his business. (See Exhibit 27.) This is ideal for Ms. Parker, as it not only dovetails perfectly with her vocational training, but will also place her in a uniquely supportive and loving environment. She plans to begin first with this position during her "transition period."

Throughout her life, Ms. Parker has been devoted to helping others, as she has demonstrated in her extensive volunteer and charitable activities while in prison. She has shown special leadership skills and dedication in this area. This commitment has been an outgrowth, in part, of the strong religious values with which she was raised. Spirituality has always been a major source of strength in Ms. Parker's life and a transformative force during her incarceration as she has worked to understand the mistakes leading up to her offense.

Ms. Parker has received several job offers to work with Christian outreach organizations upon release, assisting Christian leaders she knew before incarceration, and with who she has remained in contact during her time at Frontera. (See Exhibit30.) Additionally, Ms. Parker has sent several letters to alcohol and drug rehabilitation centers with a Christian focus, seeking a position, as well as contacting numerous other places to explore positions of employment. (See exhibit 31.) Her long-term goal upon release is to make a career helping others within these types of organizations. In the short run, as well as working first with her brother, she plans to do volunteer work with the elderly in nursing homes, because, as she says, she "can't sit still" when she knows others need her.

IX. CONCLUSION

At Ms. Parker's last appearance before the BPT for a Documentation Hearing in November, 1993, the Board specifically noted that Ms. Parker "looks like a good candidate for parole release," noting her "limited criminal history and excellent prison adjustment." (See Exhibit 28.) She has
continued to make even further positive strides since that time.

Ms. Parker has been a model prisoner at Frontera, receiving almost no disciplinaries in the last ten years. She has used her time at CIW in distinctively constructive ways, engaging in self-help and therapy, completing her education, developing her vocational skills, and devoting herself to numerous charitable activities. She has shown herself to be an unusually energetic and cheerful person and a positive influence on those around her. Since the moment she arrived at Frontera, Ms. Parker has freely devoted herself in giving to others, as well as in developing herself. She has worked hard to understand and change the destructive patterns that led to her offense and is now ready and eager to return to her children and family to devote herself to contributing to society in a positive way.

Respectfully submitted,

Authorized Representative of
Rose Ann Parker

The BPT Hearing Panel asked if there were any additional submissions. Pedram, the law student working on my case, said no. But I stood and said, "Yes, I have my own documents on my behalf." I was very adamant about the actual facts of the case. We went back and forth. I clearly stated that I never meant to be disrespectful at any time. All of a sudden, the commissioner said, "Ms. Parker, can you step out for a moment. We are going to deliberate."

I thought, Oh-oh. A very neutral, somber-looking panel eyed me as I returned. The commissioner stood and made the statement, "Ms. Parker, we find you suitable," trying to hold back the excitement that suddenly erupted in that room.

"Thank you, Jesus," I said, full of smiles. "Is this for real? I'm going home, huh?"

"Ms. Parker, you're going home."

I looked at each person's face and everybody was happy. I couldn't wait to get out of there to sing my song, "I'm Free," by Yolanda Adams.

Back in the yard, the word traveled fast. "Rose Parker was found suitable for parole and she has a date."

Unbeliever's Report
For the next few months, it was uphill. On Mother's Day, my heart was puzzled. Inmates and staff kept telling me that the governor was not going to sign my release. Afterwards, while in my cell, God whispered verses from Revelations 3:7–8 to me which read,

He hath the key of David and opened and no man close and close and no man open. See, I have given you and have set before you an open door that no man can close.

After I read this, my heart was pounding and then I heard these words, I know you have little strength and you have kept my word and not denied my name.

Tears started rolling down my face. God knew and He actually cares. He is still helping me with my case. "He said he would open a door for me," I said out loud. I went to sleep in peace that night.

In July 2000, Mr. B said I was not going home. I said, "Yes, I am."

"You don't have it in writing," he teased.

"Yes, I do." I grabbed my Bible and said I have it in black and white and red! I showed him where God said, "He will open a door that no man can close."

"So, Mr. B, you decide. Am I going home?" I smiled.

In August 2000, there was still no word back from the governor. There was supposed to be a rule that if the Full Board does not make a timely decision, that I was to be released, but now they are saying that is not for murder cases.

I still walked about, trying to share every little piece of knowledge that I was learning with other lifers, but they only resented me, especially because I had a parole date.

One Saturday night, I remember being in church and at a particular moment, I blurted out, "I feel the governor is thinking about me right now." You should have seen the faces on everyone. But God always has a tiny remnant that will praise with you and will hope with you and believe with you.

The next morning, there were more problems at the church. That night, I went to my cell and fell to my knees before the Lord. "Father, I am ready. I am ready to go home. It's time now, Lord." I was crying even harder. "Help me make it through, Lord." I fell asleep praying and crying.

That next morning, September 25, 2000, my door popped open. I jumped up and ran out the door, startled, noticing everyone was still locked in. "Rose Parker, you are going home." Lt. Mabry was walking down the short hall toward me. He had a newspaper in his hand, which he handed to me and told me to read. The headline of the newspaper read, "Ontario Killer to be Released, Battered Woman Obtains Freedom."

I read the story over and over again, not realizing it was me. I read it because it said she would be released on December 8, 2000. Then I said, "Wait a minute, this is me, this is me. I'm going home."

I sat in amazement, then in anger. Why are they still making me wait? My family and kids will be disappointed again. I was to be released technically August 8, 2000, and here it is almost six weeks later and I receive this information.

When my door popped open again at 6 A.M., I called home and told my family everything that I had just found out. After that, I went to work and then I was summoned to administration.

I received a fax from the governor's office. The date on it said, Saturday, September 24. That was the day when I sat in church, proclaiming that the governor was thinking about me.

I looked at the fax from the governor's office that I just received.

It read:

September 23, 2000
To: Ms Rose Ann Parker W25811
From: The Office Of The Governor Gray Davis

Dear Ms. Parker:

Penal Code section 3041.2 authorizes the Governor to review parole decisions of the Board of Prison Terms concerning persons sentenced to an indeterminate term upon conviction of murder.

After considering the same factors considered by the Board, the Governor has invoked his authority to modify the Board's decision to grant parole in your case. The Governor's statement of the reasons for his decision is attached.

A copy of this letter is being provided to you via facsimile, and the signed original (along with a statement of the reasons for his decision) is being sent by mail. Additionally, we are transmitting a copy of this letter and the attached decision to the Chairman of the Board of Prison Terms.

Sincerely,
Secretary of Legal Affairs and
Counsel to the Governor

INDETERMINATE SENTENCE PAROLE RELEASE REVIEW

(Penal Code Section 3041.2)
ROSE ANN PARKER, W-25811
SECOND-DEGREE MURDER WITH THE USE OF A
FIREARM

NO ACTION: _____
MODIFY: X

REVERSE: _____

ADDITIONAL GOVERNOR'S COMMENTS:

On rare occasions, a case arises in which we must give weight not only to extraordinary and compelling circumstances, but to legal defenses adopted in law since the original jury verdict. This is such a case.

There is no question that Rose Ann Parker believed she was in imminent danger of losing her life, as well as that of her two-year-old son and her unborn child, when she shot and killed Arthur Boga, with whom she had a four-year relationship marked by violence and abuse.

On the day of the murder, March 27, 1986, Boga learned that Ms. Parker was pregnant by a former boyfriend. Boga arrived at their apartment armed with a .38-caliber revolver. He took Ms. Parker and her two-year-old son into a bedroom and demanded she have an abortion. When she refused, he threatened to kill her, the father of her unborn child, and members of her family.

Ms. Parker begged him to put the gun down, and when he did, she picked it up and shot him in the back. Boga died of the gunshot wound.

A neighbor who heard the shots summoned police officers. An officer using a loudspeaker requested that the occupants of the house come out. Approximately twenty minutes later, Ms. Parker and her family emerged. She told authorities that she had shot her boyfriend because she was afraid he was going to kill her.

Ms. Parker was convicted by a jury of first-degree murder and was sentenced to fifteen years to life, with a two-year enhancement for the use of a firearm.

Ms. Parker committed a grave crime. However, this case has all the characteristics of Battered Women's syndrome, a now-legally recognized defense but which was not available at the time of her trial.

As the San Bernardino County Deputy District Attorney Clyde A. Boyd said, Ms. Parker "believed that she needed to use force and violence as a result of her prior abuse" at Boga's hands, and "absent that abuse, I doubt that the killing would have occurred."

I also note that Retired Judge William Pitt Hyde of the Superior Court of San Bernardino County, who sentenced Ms. Parker, said that he always thought she "should have been acquitted, or, at most, found guilty of voluntary manslaughter."

The Board of Prison Terms imposed the following special conditions of parole: That Ms. Parker submit to anti-narcotic testing, attend Narcotics Anonymous, and participate weekly in a local domestic violence program for a minimum of six months.

However, due to the gravity of her crime, I have decided to impose additional parole conditions: that Ms. Parker submit to periodic THC (marijuana) testing based on her history of drug use; and that she successfully complete a recognized course in parenting skills.

According to the Board of Prison Terms, Ms. Parker, at the time of her proposed parole release date, will have spent approximately fourteen years and eight months in prison. I am further extending her parole release date to December 8, 2000, at which time she will have fully served a fifteen-year term, the minimum for which she was sentenced.

Accordingly, I MODIFY the Board of Prison Terms' decision to parole Ms. Parker to include the special conditions of THC (marijuana) testing, the successful completion of a recognized course in parenting skills, and the extension of her parole release date to December 8, 2000.
Decision Date: Sept. 23, 2000
Gray Davis, Governor

Dear God,

Thank you that it is over. Help me with these last few weeks to be a blessing and to think about others and use my time wisely. Amen.

Thanksgiving

I coordinated my last Victim Impact class. My guest speaker was the chief of police of Ontario, who was the former detective in my case. He said he was impressed with what I had done. He educated the women and told them that if someone tells you that they are going to kill you, it's now called a terrorist threat. Many laws have changed. That was an exciting tie-in for me, plus he was able to see all that I had accomplished and the warden was impressed too.

Jubilee Month

My final week in prison had really arrived! In seven days, I will be going home! Praise be to God, MY Father! He has been good to me! Oh, man! I will be able to touch and hold my sons as often and as long as I want to. I can go to the bathroom in private and lock the door. I can eat what I want, whenever I want it. I will be able to cook the food or I can go to a restaurant. I can go to the drive-through at Taco Bell and McDonald's. I will be able to watch TV in every room of my house. I can go shopping. I can visit my neighbors. I can drive a car. It's been fifteen whole years, people—fifteen years. Father, how can I thank you enough for getting me through this?

The rest of the week was amazing. God opened the door that no man could close. I'm free! I'm free! When I walked out of CIW, news cameras and reporters will be there to witness the release of Rose Parker.

TO GOD BE THE GLORY!

Photo by Gabriel Acosta

A Special Message from Dr. Rose

If you scream uncontrollably at your mate, push, shove, kick, slap, withhold finances or sex; fail to communicate or respond to his or her needs – You Are an Abuser and need help. YOU ARE NOT ALONE. Some of you are acting from learned behavior or hurt. There are other reasons, for this behavior, but YOU can control this destructive behavior. The first year in CIW Prison, I found myself attempting to control the circumstances with inmates and hollering at my children for no reason. I realized I was doing what was done to me. There was no reason for me to raise my voice to get attention or a better response, all I was doing was making another individual uncomfortable, or fearful. When this was brought to my attention, I immediately took measures to note MY BEHAVIOR and adjust it. YOU CAN TOO. Please release your anger, hurt and unforgiveness and be free.

If you have suffered hurt from someone that says they love you. Remember You Are Loved, You Are Special and You WILL Survive!!! Make it a point to be in a safe place . Find support groups. Remember, You Are Not Alone. I felt so bad, and I was told that I was stupid, no good, no one would want me and everything was my fault. I did make mistakes, but no one had a right to slap, punch, kick or beat me. No one had a right to scream at me. Now, I make choices and refuse to discuss things with an individual if that individual raises their voice, or cannot control their anger. You can too. It should not hurt to go or be home. You are Somebody.

If you have read this book, and you want what it took, to give me strength and faith to persevere and believe the impossible, then you have to do what I did. I simply asked God, if he could really protect me and give me peace to please take my life, and my heart and help me. You can too. The Lord gave me peace and strength, mercy was renewed for me each morning and great was and is HIS faithfulness.

I asked God if He would come into my heart and live, life I've heard ministers and people say, He said yes He could, He did and guided each day for 15 years at the prison, and He helped me to walk in love and forgiveness. He released me from a LIFE SENTENCE, and he continually helps me to live one day at a time. If you did what I did (or pretty close to it) tell someone. Find a place to worship and fellowship. IF you are in prison, military or the hospital ask for the Chaplain. Also, please write to me and let me know. You will get a response for sure, as quickly as we possibly can.

Dr. Rose Parker

P.O. Box 756 Rialto, CA 92377 ALL PROCEEDS FROM THIS BOOK WILL GO TO:
THE VICTIMS & DOMESTIC VIOLENCE